WHAT HAPPENED TO CARRIE LOVE?

Kelley Eberle identified herself as Carrie Love's former roommate. Trooper Brown was careful not to alarm her, despite the circumstances and the unsavory contents of the sleeping bag. He simply told her that Love's purse had been found and asked if she knew where he might reach Carrie Love.

She told him Carrie left for California the day before with Jesse Pratt, Carrie's employer. She volunteered the opinion that "Jesse is shady," and she was clearly uncomfortable with her friend having agreed to make the journey with him. It was her understanding that Carrie and Jesse were driving to California in a company truck to start a new business down there. Carrie had said she was going to stay with her father in Cerritos.

William Eckhart was Carrie Love's father, and he was worried about her. He had expected Carrie by 4:00 P.M., but she hadn't arrived, nor had she called. He told Brown he had no idea what her job was at Northern Star Trucking.

Cory Kupferer said that he was Carrie's boyfriend and Kelley had called him. He knew something was wrong because he hadn't heard from Carrie. He emphasized that Carrie had wanted to fly to Los Angeles, rather than drive down there with Jesse, but Jesse had insisted. Carrie really didn't want to go at all, Kupferer added. Jesse, he thought, "just wanted to get into Carrie's pants."

BOOK YOUR PLACE ON OUR WEBSITE AND MAKE THE READING CONNECTION!

We've created a customized website just for our very special readers, where you can get the inside scoop on everything that's going on with Zebra, Pinnacle and Kensington books.

When you come online, you'll have the exciting opportunity to:

- View covers of upcoming books
- Read sample chapters
- Learn about our future publishing schedule (listed by publication month *and author*)
- Find out when your favorite authors will be visiting a city near you
- Search for and order backlist books from our online catalog
- Check out author bios and background information
- Send e-mail to your favorite authors
- Meet the Kensington staff online
- Join us in weekly chats with authors, readers and other guests
- Get writing guidelines
- AND MUCH MORE!

**Visit our website at
http://www.kensingtonbooks.com**

FATAL JOURNEY

JACK GIECK

PINNACLE BOOKS
Kensington Publishing Corp.
http://www.kensingtonbooks.com

Some names have been changed to protect the privacy of individuals connected to this story.

DEDICATION

To my collaborator, Pete McDonald—architect, artist, designer, forensic scientist, friend.

Preceding page: A painting by artist/forensic scientist Peter McDonald, inspired by this case; part of his traveling art show, *Tracking Them Down*.

Mysteries are irresistible to me, and a trail is something that must be followed until it gives up its secrets or puts me onto the trail of something that is even more amazing. The first track is the end of a string. At the far end, a being is moving: a mystery dropping a hint about itself every so many feet, telling more about itself. The mystery reveals itself slowly, track by track. . . .

—Naturalist Tom Brown Jr., *The Tracker*

PREFACE

There was a rumor going around Klamath Falls. People said there was this guy in town who was writing a book about Jesse Pratt. The way people said his name it sounded like an epithet. They didn't want to talk to the guy or even meet him—especially if Pratt was going to get any money out of it.

A rapist-murderer twice convicted of the same crime, Jesse Clarence Pratt was residing on death row in the Oregon State Penitentiary in Salem at the time. Yet many people remained terrified of him—former wives, girlfriends, his sisters—even his own mother! Some witnesses, scared to death, had agreed to testify only if the towns where they lived were kept secret. The courtroom had been filled to capacity every day as the trials ground on. Publishing detailed daily accounts of them, the *Klamath Falls Herald and News* had kept tempers hot throughout the community, yet the young women in Klamath County Courthouse who came in contact with Jesse—judicial assistants, court reporters, bailiffs—all found him charming.

I managed to make it clear that the book was not to be about Jesse Pratt, and that he certainly wasn't going to get any money out of it. Rather, the book was to be about the outstanding investigatory and forensic science work and the dogged prosecutorial efforts that had brought Carrie Love's killer to justice, and how tenuous his conviction would become under the rules of justice designed to protect the innocent.

People warmed up—especially the Oregon State Police detectives, criminal investigators, prosecutors, defense counsels, forensic scientists, one of Pratt's former girlfriends, Carrie Love's mother, and other witnesses who had been a part of the case. While in Oregon (and in Seattle and Spokane, Washington), I photographed the crime scene, some of the murderer's haunts, and the courthouse where he was brought to justice twice.

In the eerie silence of Klamath County's long-deserted "Old Jail," with my handheld Nikon, I made photocopies of evidentiary material, police reports, witnesses' statements, and trial transcripts, illuminated only by the muted glow of daylight filtering through the barred window of the dusty cell in which these records were stored—since the facility no longer had any electric power. Next door, in the adjacent county courthouse, court personnel permitted me to relive the entire second trial, listening to some two hundred hours of tape.

These were lucky breaks since, not long after I returned to Ohio, the entire complex would be destroyed in an earthquake.

I had first heard a shorter version of this story over lunch with my friend Peter McDonald, who retired as Firestone's director of tire design. In his second career, Pete has become an internationally known forensic scientist. His knowledge of *Tire Imprint Evidence* (the title of his book—a standard reference) has resulted in the conviction of more than a dozen felons who made the mistake of leaving tire tracks at the scenes of their crimes—and he has exonerated several innocent suspects.

Pete had just returned from Klamath Falls, where he had testified in Jesse Pratt's second trial. Our lunch lasted more than two hours. Within weeks, my wife and I were on our way to the Pacific Northwest.

Jack Gieck
Akron, Ohio

PART ONE

ONE

Curiosity is the lifeblood of real civilization.
                    —G. M. Trevelyan, 1876–1962
                    English Social History, 1942

Recoiling from the contents, Bruce McDonald zipped up the sleeping bag and threw it back into the bed of the pickup. Because the bed roll had a red-plaid lining, he hadn't noticed the blood when he picked it up by the side of the road.

His adrenaline pumping, Bruce opened the lid of the plywood chest he had built behind the cab of his Toyota compact and pulled out the stuffed pillowcase he had also found in the roadside ditch. Although he hadn't noticed them earlier, those reddish-brown blotches on the blue-and-white fabric looked like they, too, could be bloodstains.

As he later told the Oregon State Police, "Putting the two together at the time, I just grabbed the pillowcase and dumped it out. And there was this woman's purse in there—and her billfold—all her ID and everything. There wasn't any money or anything in it, though. And there was a pair of tennis shoes. And those hair curlers."

Bruce and Dorothy McDonald had left their

home in Crescent Lake early that morning, on Tuesday, June 17, 1986. They had stopped for breakfast at the Chalet, a restaurant in Chemult, east of the Cascade Range in the Pacific Northwest—a region that had once been a volcanic ash desert downwind from Crater Lake. The land has long since been reclaimed by lush green conifers and is now part of the Fremont National Forest.

Bruce had taken the day off from managing the tackle shop at Crescent Lake Lodge so he and Dottie could visit his seventy-eight-year-old mother, Frances, in Klamath Falls. Traffic was heavier than usual on Oregon 97, separated into stringy clots by an occasional slow-moving tractor-trailer rig. The jack pines lining the two-lane highway cast long westward-pointing shadows across the road before them as the sun began to break through the morning haze.

Headed south, cruising along at about fifty miles an hour, they had just passed Military Crossing near Milepost 220. McDonald was scanning the wooded area on both sides of the road—alert for deer, which had caused more than one accident in the area by darting out onto the highway. To the west, the snow-covered peak of Mount Scott glowed warmly in the morning light.

Suddenly Bruce hit the brakes.

In the ditch just beyond the right shoulder was a rumpled gray-green *something*, which appeared at first glance to be a body. He made a U-turn across the highway and pulled off onto the opposite shoulder. As he walked across the road, Bruce was relieved to discover what it was.

"It's a sleeping bag," he called back to Dorothy.

"Looks like it's in pretty good shape. Must have blown off somebody's camper. And there's a pillow-case with stuff in it."

He picked up both, tossing the sleeping bag into the truck bed and securing the blue-striped pillow-case and its contents in the wooden chest. He had forgotten all about the items until he and Dottie and his mother left the old lady's mobile home to drive to the Chuck Wagon for dinner.

"Where'd you get the sleeping bag at?" Frances asked, spotting the bedroll as Bruce helped her up into the truck. She adjusted her hearing aid.

"Found it on the side of the road," he explained, pulling it out of the bed to show it off. "Looks like it's a nice one."

That's when he opened it up and changed his mind. Bruce got back into the truck cab, his appetite having evaporated.

"If you ladies don't mind," he managed to say, "I'd like to make a stop before we go to the Chuck Wagon."

Trooper Eric Brown had just come on duty after shift change when the tan Toyota pickup pulled into the parking lot of the Oregon State Police Klamath Falls Post. As later documented in his report, it was 6:15 P.M.

On the way to their cars, Sergeant Phillips and another officer had stopped to speak with the middle-aged couple when Trooper Brown came out of the building. A product of his training, Brown noted that the man had steel-gray hair and heavy white sideburns. He also had the look of an outdoorsman whose wife was a good cook. The driver was showing the officers something in the back of the truck as Brown approached.

A seasoned trooper working on his fifth year, Brown invited the McDonalds inside, helping Bruce carry one of the two bundles he had taken out of the truck. The officer led them into the cramped office of his sergeant and sat down behind his boss's desk. Pulling a ballpoint pen out of the scalloped shirt pocket beneath the silver star on his blue summer uniform, he intended to record the substance of the interview. His full mustache made him look a little older than he was; it helped when making arrests.

Bruce was sorry he couldn't remember the mile marker where he had found the sleeping bag and pillowcase, but he thought it was near Sand Creek, a combination filling station, country store, and diner south of Military Crossing. Eric Brown's report indicates that he relieved McDonald of the items he brought in at 6:50 P.M. and he thanked him for getting involved before he left.

Trooper Brown's supervisor, Sergeant Toddy, helped him inventory the materials McDonald had left behind. Brown took the assorted items to the evidence room, together with the detailed list the two of them had prepared:

1. *Green sleeping bag with red and black checked interior. Brand name not observed. Bag appeared worn.*
2. *Gray purse with zipper on top. Approximately 12 inches long. Purse contained the following:*
   A. *Washington driver's license issued to CARRIE*

LYNETTE LOVE, DOB/03-03-66, WA #LOVE*CL341DC.

B. Military I.D. issued to AMN CARRIE LOVE, SSAN [deleted]. Red colored I.D. Card.

C. AT&T "Call Me" card issued to CARRIE LOVE, [deleted].

D. Pink nylon wallet with black stripes. Item was empty.

F. Pink nylon checkbook. Item was empty.

G. Blue checkbook with checks to CARRIE L. LOVE, PO Box 142, Easton, WA, [phone number deleted]. Contained Tacoma Credit Union blank check #800.

H. Blue savings deposit book to CARRIE L. LOVE, 12057 Roseburg Ave. S, Seattle, WA, [phone number deleted]. Savings book is from Ranier Bank.

I. 2 quarters, 5 pennies.

J. Yellow paper with following information in it: Ph: [deleted]. Ph: [deleted]. 12057 Roseburg Ave. S, Seattle, WA. Northern Star Trucking, SSN# [deleted]. DOB/03-03-66. Mother's maiden name, Vandenberg. Dated 5-01-86.

K. Prescription bottle with several pink pills.

L. Also contained miscellaneous papers and cards.

3. One pillowcase, white with light blue and dark blue stripes. Item was dirty and had what appeared to be bloodstains on the case. Item contained the following:

A. Green paper towel wrapped with gray tape.

B. Yellow paper towel.

C. White paper towel.

D. *2 Eye bolts.*

E. *1 Piece of wire.*

F. *1 Bolt.*

G. *1 Hex wrench.*

H. *Cigarette Lighter to a vehicle.*

I. *1 Pair shoes, Pro Wings tennis shoes, white in color.*

J. *1 Carbon gas receipt #032052.*

The pillowcase, item 3, enclosed a pillow, which Brown put into the evidence locker together with all of the items inventoried.

Sitting back down at his sergeant's desk, Trooper Brown brushed back his wavy brown hair as he pulled the telephone in front of him. His first responsibility would be to try to return the items in the inventory to their owner.

Brown called the first telephone number listed in item 2J. He got an answering machine telling him that he had reached Northern Star Trucking. The machine went on to announce the company's business hours and hung up. Brown tried the second number.

The voice was that of a young woman. Kelley Eberle identified herself as Carrie Love's former roommate. Brown was careful not to alarm her, despite the circumstances and the unsavory contents of the sleeping bag. He simply told her that Love's purse had been found and asked if she knew where he might reach Carrie Love.

Eberle told him that Carrie had left for California the day before, on Monday, June 16, with Jesse—Carrie's employer at Northern Star Trucking. She volunteered the opinion that "Jesse is shady," and she was clearly uncomfortable with her friend having agreed to make the journey with him. Eberle added that Jesse also owned a business called Double Jack. It was her understanding that Carrie and Jesse were driving to California in a company truck to start a new business down there. Carrie had said she was going to stay with her father in Cerritos.

Kelley told the officer she didn't have Carrie's father's phone number handy, but she would call back. Brown's phone rang minutes later and Kelley gave him the number. Brown immediately punched it up.

William Eckhart answered. Yes, he was Carrie Love's father and he was worried about her. He had expected Carrie by 4:00 P.M., but she hadn't arrived, nor had she called. He told Brown he had no idea what her job was at Northern Star Trucking, and he knew nothing about the business. But he'd have Carrie call about her purse when she got in.

Trooper Brown had finished documenting the substance of his two telephone conversations; he was about to conclude his longhand report when his phone rang again. It was 9:45 P.M.

Cody Kupferer said that he was Carrie's boyfriend and Kelley had called him. He was worried, he said, and knew something was wrong because he hadn't heard from Carrie.

Yesterday morning, Kupferer said, he had dropped Carrie off at Northern Star Trucking about 11:20 A.M. She was a secretary at the company, he explained, and had been scheduled to leave at 4:00 P.M. with her boss to open a new office in Los Angeles. She was going to stay with her father in L.A. until Thursday, then fly back to Seattle. He emphasized that Carrie had wanted to fly to Los Angeles rather than drive down there with Jesse, but Jesse had insisted and said he would only pay for Love's return flight.

Carrie really didn't want to go at all, Kupferer added as his stream-of-consciousness monologue ran on. Jesse, he thought, "just wanted to get into Carrie's pants. He's made advances to her in the past." He was worried, he repeated, because Carrie was to call him that afternoon to tell him her arrival time so he could pick her up at the airport; she was going to fly back so she wouldn't miss her National Guard drill. She hadn't called.

Brown asked Cody if he could describe the truck they were riding in, but the young man said he had never seen it. He did know it was a big tractor-trailer rig, that it had a sleeper, and he believed the trailer was a "reefer"—a refrigerated unit. They were driving empty as far as he knew, and he didn't know what route they might have taken.

As Brown continued his questioning, Kupferer remembered that his girlfriend was carrying a suitcase, and he knew she had a pair of Pro Wings tennis shoes in it and one of his football jerseys. The pink pills, he thought, might have something to do with her period, which he knew had started that past Sunday.

Half an hour later, Brown's phone rang again. It was Kelley Eberle offering some additional background after thinking things over. Carrie, she said, had gone to work for Northern Star Trucking just six weeks ago. In May, she said, she and Carrie were having lunch at Flynn's Café on Airport Way when this bushy-haired man in the next booth apparently overheard Carrie talking about her job hunting. "He came over and invited her to join him at his table. Within minutes, he offered Carrie a job as a secretary/dispatcher at his trucking company." Impulsively, Carrie had accepted Pratt's offer. Since she'd been at Northern Star, Kelley added, Carrie had learned that Jesse had another business called Double Jack Escort Service, in which "people would call up for an escort for the evening." When Carrie hired on as a secretary, bookkeeper, and dispatcher, she had moved out of Kelley's apartment to move into one that Jesse was now paying for—since her salary wasn't much.

"Carrie lives alone and pays her own bills, though," Kelley was quick to add. But about a month ago, only two weeks after she had gone to work for him, Jesse had asked Carrie to work for his escort service. Jesse told her that his clients included two gay men and all she would have to do is stand nude in front of them while they did their thing. Carrie had refused.

Kelley then told Brown that something "mysterious" had happened between Carrie and Jesse. Only last week, she said, Carrie had called her and said she needed to talk because she was in trouble. But the next time Kelley saw her, she said, Carrie wouldn't talk about it. Worried, Kelley had spoken to Cody Kupferer's mother, who said that Cody had told her "he couldn't say what happened, because if he did, Jesse would kill both Carrie and him."

Trooper Brown's report concludes:

TWO

Every time we get called, it's like walking up to a table on which there are the scattered fragments of a thousand-piece jigsaw puzzle—and it's all white. It's your job to put that puzzle together, and you have only so much time to put it together. Finally, when it's all together, then you get to turn it over and see the picture.

—Detective Ken Cooper

On Wednesday morning, sitting under the stuffed deer head in the Sand Creek store and drinking his second cup of coffee, Bruce McDonald told Sergeant Richard Hein two things he'd forgotten to mention to Trooper Brown: There'd been a small piece of white paper crumpled up in the barrow pit near the sleeping bag, and he'd noticed a blue IHC Scout sport utility truck parked on the east shoulder of the road south of where he had found the articles. The vehicle had California license plates, he said.

Sergeant Hein dispatched Trooper Barker to go have a look and to radio Klamath Falls with the license number if the Scout vehicle was still there.

* * *

Earlier that morning, Detective Kenneth D. Cooper, a twenty-year veteran of the Oregon State Police, had received a phone call from Sergeant Hein asking him to come in early. Hein wanted Cooper, an experienced homicide investigator, to examine the sleeping bag and other items left by Bruce McDonald the night before and then join him at Sand Creek to interview McDonald and check out the area.

Arriving at the police post fifteen minutes later, Cooper picked up Trooper Brown's report from the officer in charge, Sergeant Dennis O'Donnell. "Take the evidence into the back room and do your thing" was all O'Donnell said. It was an order that would launch Ken Cooper into becoming the case agent and lead investigator in a criminal case that would occupy his attention for the next several years.

A sandy-haired, slightly built, hyperactive bundle of energy, then in his midforties, Cooper prided himself on his intuitive ability to project himself into the minds of the people he pursued, seeing things through their perspective, anticipating what they were likely to do—what he calls "playing dangerous mind games."

It is a talent that nearly cost him his life in 1976, when he apprehended a "gun nut," as Cooper described him, armed with a 44-40 rifle, a twelve-gauge sawed-off shotgun, and a stolen AR-16 assault rifle. "The man was fleeing a bar at the east end of Sixth Street in Klamath Falls, where he had just killed six people, including a pregnant woman. The victims' names were on a hit list of *nine* the psycho had prepared at another bar earlier in the evening."

During the ensuing chase, Cooper correctly guessed the gunman's probable escape route, doubled back and crashed his cruiser head-on into the suspect's car. In the gunfight that followed, Cooper was wounded by a bullet that entered his chest between the panels on his bulletproof vest.

Returning a fusillade of shots in a pattern no bigger than a football on the suspect's windshield, the officer wounded and captured the assailant, who is now serving six consecutive life terms. After he recovered from his own wound, Ken Cooper's heroism was rewarded with a citation, a substantial raise in pay, and a promotion that took him out of the prowl car and led to his present assignment as a detective–criminal investigator.

Laying out the evidence on the floor of the long, narrow room he shared with three other officers, Detective Cooper began matching the assorted items against Trooper Brown's inventory. The stained sleeping bag got his immediate attention.

"We're going to be looking for a *body*," he told O'Donnell. "It isn't unusual to find blood where a rape struggle has occurred—especially if the victim is menstruating at the time. But involuntary excretion is a strong indication of a violent killing. We've got *both* blood and feculence here."

Sticking to the bottom of the pillowcase was a small mass that wasn't on Trooper Brown's list.

"It looked like a handful of crumpled paper towels," Cooper later explained. "It was semihard and crusty, as if it had been wet and then dried. And there was other stuff stuck to it.

"The minute I picked up that ball of green paper towels and duct tape and stuff, I thought it had to be something important. As I'm rolling this thing around, just feeling it, I got to a point where some of the tape had come undone. And when it came undone, the ball just kind of opened up.

"You could feel it was *layered*: towel-tape, tape-towel. And when I opened it up a little more, as I'm looking at this thing, holding it in front of my face, suddenly it was like looking at a *hologram*. I could see protrusions—indentations where my nose and chin could go. Reversed in the bottom of this bowl was a *face*.

"I could see a little blood around the mouth. And I could see the excretion of nose stuff encrusted there by the two nostril holes. I wondered if the woman—I assumed it was a woman—might have been *suffocating*.

"And then I saw this yellow tissue. When I opened it a little, I could see this solid black hexagonal earring inside. It had been shoved into her face and taped over!"

As he relived the experience, Cooper got so visibly angry that he began to hyperventilate.

"I take homicides very personally," he declared.

THREE

*I do not much wish well to discoveries, for I am
always afraid how they will end. . . .*
— Samuel Johnson (1709–84),
Letter to W. S. Johnson, 1773

By the time Ken Cooper got to Milepost 230, south
of Sand Creek, it was almost noon. Several police
cruisers were parked beside the road next to an
abandoned IHC Scout with California license plates.
The jeeplike vehicle was on the east shoulder of the
road facing north. It was to be picked up by Jay's
Towing of Klamath Falls and taken to the company's
impound lot, since California State Police in Eureka
had advised that an IHC Scout with license number
879 MVL had been reported stolen.

A homicide team had already been assembled,
consisting of local, county, and state police. Bruce
McDonald was there, too. Sergeant Hein introduced
him to Detective Cooper.

"Bruce," Cooper said, "I don't know how much
they've told you about this case, but we're looking
for a body. I want you to come with me and pick out
any likely spots that you think *might* be the place
where you found this stuff."

McDonald did his best.

"It all looks the same to me," he finally admitted. "Gray asphalt and deep ditches on both sides." Bruce McDonald was excused.

Splitting up into groups, the police team began walking the shoulder on the west side of the road, leapfrogging ahead with their cars. They looked for anything that might be helpful—footprints, tire tracks, debris, whatever.

At 1:20 P.M., at Milepost 221.4, Ken Cooper spotted a wadding of light green paper towels that appeared to have the same embossed pattern as the towels he had found that morning in the pillowcase. He also picked up a Merit cigarette butt.

Detective Cooper and Sergeant Hein marked the spot with silver spray paint on the adjacent asphalt pavement. They also drove a stake into the ground where the towels were found, and they marked an adjacent pine tree "KDC 6-18-86." Each took out a 35mm camera, and they both photographed the scene. That done, Cooper suggested they go back north, in the direction from which the vehicle had probably come before the sleeping bag was discarded.

Cooper knew the area well from his days as a trooper. Playing his trademark "mind game," striving to project himself into the consciousness of the perpetrator, Cooper suggested there were two likely spots in the area where a rapist might plan to do his thing. Both Military Crossing and the truckers' "Loop Road" turnout, just south of Chemult, were farther north, in the direction from which the vehicle would have come. And both were secluded areas. The Oregon State Highway Department stored piles of gravel and cinders at these locations, using the aggregate to provide traction on Highway 97 during the area's heavy winter snowstorms.

The Military Crossing intersection on the east side of the road was only a mile and a half north of the spot where they had found the towels. Cooper, Hein, and two other officers began searching the ground between the cinder piles, also scrounging into the surrounding sagebrush and juniper trees. Their results were negative. Nothing in the area had been disturbed. The group then headed for Milepost 206.

The officers left their cars at the turnoff entrance to the Loop Road and walked down the short bypass road. Behind the trees lining the highway, two commercial-hauler semitrailers were parked.

"Truckers often park here to take a nap," Cooper told the others. "The area is scheduled to become a rest stop when the state gets around to it."

By now, it was late afternoon. West of the trucks was a clay bank that had been cut into the hillside when the Loop Road was graded. Cooper clambered to the top of it to survey the area. Between the bank and the bypass road were the remains of a large pile of gravel. Cooper had a plan, and he asked his fellow officers for help. Spacing themselves five to ten yards apart, the officers formed a fan with Ken Cooper as the pivot on top of the cut bank.

It was when they began their swing through the area that Cooper saw it. Eerily, a woman's hand—thin, pale, long fingers curled slightly—protruded from the aggregate.

"Part of a thigh, half a breast, rib cage . . . two sets

of toes sticking out," Cooper recalled. "At that point we locked everything up."

The two truckers were awakened, interviewed briefly, and sent on their way. The area was cordoned off. The record reveals that the body was found in the gravel pile at 3:47 P.M.

The police team went into standard homicide procedure. They called both the medical examiner's office and the district attorney's office in Klamath Falls, as well as the State Police Crime Laboratory in Bend. There, Lieutenant Michael Howard and fellow criminalist Larry Dickenson left at once to join the officers assembled south of Chemult.

Detective Cooper began photographing what they had found, shooting several rolls of 35mm Ektachrome color slides. With his own camera, Sergeant Hein duplicated the photo survey in black and white. Ken Cooper documented what they had found. His notes include: ". . . a bloody, 'pounded out' area east of the body on the gravel shoulder. The area contained what appeared to be blood, hair, tissue, and brain matter. From the bloody spot, a long, continuous, arching *drag mark* was observed, leading west over the north end of the gravel pile."

To fix these locations, Cooper drove stakes into the ground while the group sprayed the bases of two pine trees with silver paint, labeling them "A" and "B" for triangulation. Cooper began drawing a series of geometric diagrams that would later become court exhibits.

Other homicide personnel began converging on the crime scene. Lieutenant Edward Hanson, Sergeant Dennis O'Donnell, and Sergeant Richard Stroup arrived from Klamath Falls at 4:38 P.M. At

5:45 P.M., District Attorney Ed Caleb drove in with two of his deputies. The medical examiner Dr. Robert Jamison, a pathologist, arrived about fifteen minutes later, as did Lieutenant Howard and criminalist Dickenson from the State Crime Laboratory.

Dickenson took the temperature of the body, then stuck his thermometer into the adjacent gravel to see how its temperature compared. Detective Cooper assisted Dr. Jamison, slowly clearing gravel from the body. Soon he had completely uncovered the nude body of a slim young woman with brown hair. Her head had been crushed.

There were other obvious injuries. Dr. Jamison recorded "small puncture wounds in the center and left chest area." After the body was turned over, more were discovered on the back and side of the neck. And there were still more along the woman's spine. The medical examiner noted that it looked like she had been stabbed with an "ice pick–like instrument."

Criminalist Howard pointed out what he later testified to as "faint lines on both wrists and on the neck area where it appeared that tape had been used to bind the victim." Cooper was already convinced that she had been bound and had said so that morning—having found long strands of sticky gray masking tape attached to what he characterized as the "mask."

After dust was carefully washed from the woman's skin, a large bruise appeared on her left arm. To the investigators, it looked like a tire imprint. Cooper went so far as to identify it in his notes as a "burnt-in pattern made by the *side of a tire tread.*" It had been produced, he wrote, as "the victim was run over from

FOUR

*Innocence is thought charming because it offers
delightful possibilities for exploitation.*
　　　　　　—Mason Cooley, *City Aphorisms*

Born on March 3, 1966, Carrie Lynette Eckhart
didn't know her father very well. Her parents had
divorced when she was five years old, not long after
Carrie's sister, Kelly, was born. Later the same year,
her mother, a nurse, married James Love.

"When I married Jim," Connie Love explained,
"Carrie thought she had married Jim Love, too. Besides, she thought it was kind of a unique name and
started using it—although she never had it formally
changed. Even when she was five years old, she had
a mind of her own.

"When she was in high school, Carrie Love particularly liked mathematics," Connie continued, "and
considered becoming a CPA." Her daughter was active in DECA (a West Coast equivalent of Junior
Achievement) and Future Homemakers of America—as was her mother before her. Although she was
very sports conscious, Carrie's five-foot-two-inch
stature mitigated against her becoming a star athlete,
so she became a batgirl, a scorekeeper, and a

"Guardian Angel," a girls' club organized as a morale builder for the school's teams. The Angels attended all the football games and individually "adopted" selected athletes and cheered them on.

Connie described her daughter as outgoing, full of energy, willing to try anything, and a very caring person.

"One of Carrie's first jobs after graduating from high school in 1984 was working in a nursing home, and she really enjoyed taking care of the elderly patients there. When she baby-sat, her clients were often amazed when they came home to find their kitchen floor scrubbed or sometimes their whole house cleaned—although I had to break her arm to get her to clean her room at home." Connie smiled as she said it, but her eyes filled with tears.

After high school, Carrie joined the Oregon National Guard. She took her basic training in San Antonio and was later trained as a weather observer at an air force base in Illinois. This led to a civilian job as a weather observer for High Life Helicopter Service at Stampede Pass, from which she soon moved to an assignment on Sexton Summit in Washington's Cascade Mountains.

As her mother pointed out, for a girl with Carrie's gregarious personality, this lonely seven-day-a-week job on a mountaintop with a dog and a cat, making charts and calling in data gleaned from her weather instruments, was not a good fit. She took to visiting friends in Seattle whenever she could, and by early spring in 1986, she had moved in with her friend Kelley Eberle while looking for a job in that city.

After going to work for Northern Star, Carrie moved to Air Vista Apartments on Military Road.

Because her salary wasn't much, her employer paid her rent. There she sometimes received gifts from a secret admirer who called himself "Spider."

Carrie didn't think Spider was either of her recent boyfriends. Jim Hancock, a biker who sometimes spent the night at her place before she met Cody Kupferer, didn't have that kind of sensitivity. Besides, Cody was still in high school and didn't have the money. When he took her to his high-school prom, Cody borrowed Jesse Pratt's gold-speckled Cadillac for the occasion. At work the next day, Jesse twitted her about it.

"When you want a real man and not a kid, come and see *me*."

Young Cody had become upset when he heard that Jesse also told Carrie the names of each of the places the two of them had been on prom night. Pratt obviously had been spying on them.

That was one of the reasons Cody hated the idea of Carrie's traveling to Los Angeles with Pratt—and he told her so, getting her to promise (as he later explained to the police) that "if Pratt 'tried anything,' she would get out of the truck and would call me, and I could come and get her, wherever she was at."

FIVE

He's very charismatic. . . . He's got something.
    —Former girlfriend of Jesse Clarence Pratt

Jesse Clarence Pratt, named after his father, claimed to have been born on the Fourth of July. But as his birth certificate shows, he was actually born on July 3, 1944, in Tyler, Texas. Pratt's mother always thought his father was killed in action in Germany, having received a starred telegram and a visit from an army sergeant during World War II, but there were elements of the sergeant's story that didn't quite ring true.

Jesse had a number of stepfathers, some of whom, he later claimed, had sexually abused him. He also claimed his mother was a drunk. Despite whatever hardships, he obviously developed a personality sufficiently charming to have persuaded at least four women to marry him, and several more to live with him without going through any ceremonial motions. And he also seemed to have developed a knack for talking people out of substantial sums of money.

A high-school dropout, Pratt drove a gravel truck for a local company during construction of the Alaskan pipeline. Jesse dreamed of being a big-time trucker. He had the reputation of constantly trying to cultivate a macho image—of sporting gold neck chains and bragging about his female conquests. It didn't matter to him that most men considered his girlfriends overweight, sloppy, and unskilled at personal grooming, some with garish makeup and outdated hairdos. His flattering attention played to their insecurities and destructive self-images, and it usually made points with them.

Many of his "girlfriends" were physically abused by Pratt, and he actually persuaded some of them to work for him as prostitutes. Even after they fled from the physical and emotional damage he had inflicted on them, Jesse was somehow able to talk them into coming back—to convince them that they needed him, enjoyed him.

"He's very charismatic," one of them explained for the record. "He's got something. He really knows how to suck you in—how to manipulate you."

Another former girlfriend, a pretty young black woman born into the squalor of Seattle's inner city, remembered Jesse's car from her drug-hazy days with him: "It was a classic 'pimpmobile' we rode around in—an aging, gold-speckled Cadillac with fur on the dash!"

By the time he met her, Pratt had acquired a lengthy police record. He had served time in Alaska for stealing and cashing a U.S. government check. When he was tried for kidnapping and rape in Washington State in 1980, he beat the rape charge because the kidnapping had occurred in Washington, while the rape happened in Oregon. Although he had been sentenced to ten years in Washington State Penitentiary, he was released after serving less than four years at Walla Walla. No one seems to have paid attention to the warning issued by the prison psychologist when Pratt was being considered for parole: "Whoever releases this man must bear the responsibility for his actions."

In pursuit of his ambition of becoming a big-time trucker, Jesse Pratt borrowed money from a girlfriend in Alaska so he could shop for a truck in the Pacific Northwest. Once in Oregon, he looked up Cecilia, his half sister, and her husband, Gary Gunn, and persuaded them to lend him their truck—keeping his girlfriend's money. When the couple tried to get their truck back, he deliberately wrecked it.

Consistent with his wishful macho image, Pratt eventually bought a racy green 1976 Kenworth with white pinstripes, stainless-steel fuel tanks, and chrome stacks. A high-powered truck tractor made in Seattle, Kenworth has a reputation in the industry as the "Rolls-Royce of trucks." Except Pratt never paid for it.

In June of 1986, this aging used vehicle was the total fleet of Northern Star, Inc., which was also known to suppliers as Double Jack Trucking, since many of Northern Star's debts were paid by checks written on the Double Jack bank account—Pratt's escort service. Neither name was registered as a business with the state of Washington.

The company rented space in a building occupied by several other businesses on the edge of Boeing Field in Seattle. The firm's trailers were all rented, and Northern Star had earned a reputation among trailer rental companies as a dead-beat outfit—which is why Double Jack checks were sometimes substituted when the ones issued by Northern Star were refused.

In recent months, several truckers who drove their own rigs had briefly joined the firm but had quit after only a few weeks when they found their association with Pratt was costing them more money than they were making.

By the time Carrie Love disappeared in June 1986, Jesse Pratt's dream of big-time trucking had been reduced to almost nothing. He had one truck, which he didn't own, the rent on his building had gone unpaid for months, and his credit was so bad that he had the telephone listed in another name—curiously, that of one of his former stepfathers. His "expansion" into the Los Angeles area smacked more of skipping town than it did of sound business judgment.

SIX

My boss is a very volatile person. Pratt has the feeling that sex is always readily available, whether it be by pay or for free.
—Northern Star driver Mel McClintock

By 10:00 A.M. on Thursday, June 19, Sergeant Rich Hein had already landed at the Seattle-Tacoma Airport. It had been a short night. About 8:30 on Wednesday evening, his investigating officers having missed both lunch and dinner, District Attorney Ed Caleb suggested they drive up the road to The Wheel Cafe in Chemult when their work was complete. Here they held an impromptu strategy conference, which broke up around 10:30 P.M. It was midnight by the time Hein got home.

During the meeting, Sergeant Rich Stroup reported a couple of things he had learned earlier in the day before he drove up to join the group. Bruce McDonald's wife, Dorothy, had remembered seeing a green Kenworth truck parked at Manley's Tavern on Highway 58 in Crescent Lake on the evening of June 16. Manley's was just west of Highway 97, so Stroup had asked Trooper James Rector at the

Gilchrist State Police Post to interview local residents in the area to inquire about a man and a woman seen in the tavern by one of the waitresses that night.

Stroup also told the group that he had called Northern Star Trucking Wednesday morning, using the number in the purse McDonald had found—after determining that the company was not listed in the Seattle telephone directory. Stroup's call was answered by a woman who said she was "Mona Bennett." The officer identified himself and said he was attempting to locate Carrie Love. He asked whether she worked there.

Bennett tried to be helpful. She said that Carrie, another secretary at the firm, had left on Monday afternoon with the line's owner, Jesse C. Pratt. Pratt was driving a rig to Los Angeles to open a subsidiary office there, she said, and to pick up a load of potatoes destined for Arizona. Carrie was hitching a ride to Los Angeles, where she would visit her father, William Eckhart. Since her boss would be going on to Arizona, Carrie would fly back for weekend drill with her 123rd Air National Guard Weather Flight Unit.

Stroup said he had asked Bennett whether she had heard from her boss. Mona said Pratt had called in several times, that he told her he had completed his business in Los Angeles, and that he had picked up a load of potatoes in Fresno and was headed for Arizona, where he was to pick up a load of onions. He had said nothing about Carrie Love.

Detective Richard Krogh of the King County Sheriff's Office was waiting for Sergeant Hein at the Sea-Tac airport on Thursday morning. Together they drove to 8465 Perimeter Road on the east edge of Seattle's Boeing Field, where Northern Star Trucking rented space in a modest two-story gray clapboard structure owned by Frontier Aviation Resources. There appeared to be no garage or other maintenance facilities for trucks.

The officers found the Northern Star office and introduced themselves to Mona Bennett. Bennett said she had gone to work for Jesse Pratt only ten days ago, and that the office was usually occupied by Carrie Love and herself, and sometimes by Jesse Pratt as well.

The Los Angeles trip had been planned before Mona had come to work for the company, she said. Pratt had discussed it with them on June 12 and wanted one of them to accompany him. Which one would go along, he left up to them. Since Carrie was more familiar with office operations (she had been employed at Northern Star more than five weeks, compared to Mona's two days at the time), they decided that Mona should go. Mona, however, couldn't find a baby-sitter, so Carrie went instead.

Bennett spoke enthusiastically about how the Los Angeles operation would improve the business. Pratt, she said, was going to set up an arrangement in which he would haul Seattle seafood to L.A., then pick up California produce for the return trip. So she could understand why her boss was upset when the company's other driver, Mel McClintock, was late bringing the truck back on Monday. Pratt had planned to leave early that morning, and Mc-Clintock didn't arrive with the Kenworth until three o'clock in the afternoon. If they went to a truck stop and filled the tanks, it would get even later. After complaining loudly and bawling out Mc-

Clintock, Jesse decided that since they would be running with no load, there should be enough fuel to get into Oregon, where fuel was cheaper. Accordingly, he elected to skip the fuel stop.

Carrie had brought in her suitcase when she arrived with her boyfriend, Cody Kupferer. She was excited about the opportunity to see her father and was eager to get going, Mona said, adding that Carrie had told Cody, as well as her former boyfriend, Jim Hancock, that she would call each of them, since she "was afraid that Pratt would make a pass at her."

Asked whether she had received any more calls from Pratt, Bennett said that she had heard from Jesse on Tuesday morning, June 17, at about 10:30. He was wondering how things were going at the office.

Because of what she had learned from the state police in Klamath Falls, Mona had asked to speak to Carrie.

Pratt told her he was alone, that after they had left on Monday, Carrie had decided she wanted to fly to Los Angeles and he had dropped her off near the Sea-Tac Airport.

Mona got another call from Pratt later the same day, asking what had been received in the mail. He asked her to make several phone calls to get some loads scheduled. He had called again on Wednesday morning, and this time he asked if she had heard from Carrie.

The officers asked Bennett if she could get in touch with Pratt. She promptly sent a radio message requesting that he call. As they were completing their interview, the telephone rang.

Mona answered. It was Jesse Pratt.

Hiding his surprise, Sergeant Hein sat back in his chair, excusing the interruption with a wave of his hand. He could hear half the conversation. Mona told Pratt that Carrie was missing and that her purse had been found in Oregon, along with some of her personal belongings.

Unasked, Jesse Pratt began adding detail to his earlier statements to Mona. He said he had dropped Carrie off at My Place Tavern, a local strip joint he frequented near the Sea-Tac terminal, since he couldn't drive his rig into the airport. He figured Carrie could get a taxi from there, but Carrie might have gone with "Bill," an old friend of Carrie's, he said. Pratt said he was calling from Dunnigan, California.

Mona told him she had a call about Carrie that morning from Detective Krogh of the King County Sheriff's Office. Pratt told her to be "cooperative," adding that, "because of what was going on with Carrie," he had decided he would not go on to Los Angeles but would try to get a return load where he was.

Hein and Krogh exchanged glances. Pratt's last comment was obviously at variance with his earlier statement that he had completed his business in Los Angeles and had picked up a load of potatoes in Fresno. Mona seemed not to have noticed.

Instead of leaving, the officers now continued their interview with Bennett, ostensibly filling in details about the business.

Two hours later, Pratt called back. To the surprise of the officers, as Rich Hein's report reflects, "Mona's conversation with Pratt became very emotional, calling him 'baby,' 'sugar,' 'sweets,' and so on." She now told Pratt that she was being interviewed by the two police officers.

Suddenly Mona held out the telephone at arm's length.

"Jesse wants to talk to you."

Hein accepted the telephone and introduced himself.

Pratt wanted to know what the officer knew about Carrie's whereabouts.

Hein told him she was dead.

Pratt wanted to know how she died and where she was found.

He couldn't discuss these matters over the phone, Hein said, but he would talk to Pratt when he returned to Seattle.

Without prompting, Pratt suddenly launched into a detailed personal itinerary, telling Hein that he had traveled down I-5 to Eugene and had stayed overnight at a truck stop—the T & R. Here he had taken a nap in the sleeper and then left, going southbound on I-5 on Tuesday morning, at eight o'clock. He went down to Eugene and across Highway 58 to Highway 97, he said, continuing southbound on 97 to the 18-Wheeler Truck Stop at Klamath Falls, Oregon, arriving there about noon. "The old man at the Eighteen-Wheeler Truck Stop knows me as 'the man from Alaska,'" Pratt added.

It sounded to Hein like Pratt was building an alibi.

Sergeant Hein's report notes that, in a seeming non sequitur interrupting his lengthy recitation, "Pratt also advised he had lost a cap from his fuel tank, that he had proceeded south on I-5 and crossed the scales below Weed at about 5:00 P.M., 6-17-86."

Pratt told Hein that he could stop in Klamath Falls to see him on his way back if the officer wished.

Hein told him Seattle would be fine.

Pratt then asked if he should be "looking over [his] shoulder."

Surprised but noncommittal, Hein told him that was up to him. He asked Pratt about his truck.

Pratt told him it was "a long-nose Kenworth conventional, green in color, with the company name, 'Northern Star,' on the doors, and a commercial vehicle registration that he thought was PUC number 84-4225." Pratt then asked to speak to Mona.

After a few minutes on the phone, Mona handed the instrument back.

"He wants to speak to you again."

This time Pratt wanted to know "where the body would be sent—if it would be sent to Seattle."

"Those arrangements were unknown," Hein replied, "the next of kin will make those determinations." Pratt had a final few minutes with Mona before hanging up.

Hein and Krogh concluded their interview with Mona Bennett. Quite open about her private life, Mona had volunteered the information that she didn't date Pratt, that she was not married but was living with someone. She described her boss as having "an Afro hairstyle that was balding in back, a full beard, wears glasses, has long, skinny arms, is six feet two inches tall, and has a potbelly." She said that when he left on Monday, Pratt was wearing blue jeans, a T-shirt, and cowboy boots, as best she could recall.

Sergeant Hein also recorded Mona's statement that neither she, Jesse, nor Carrie smoked. The officer's question had prompted her to ask whether cigarettes were found at the scene. Hein didn't say.

Leaving the Northern Star office, Sergeant Hein and Detective Krogh drove to the Goldblatt Tool Company to meet Kelley Eberle. Willingly taking time from her job, Kelley repeated the information she had given to Trooper Brown, adding that Carrie's ex-boyfriend, Jim Hancock, lived in Redmond, Washington. She also told Hein that Carrie's doctor in Grant's Pass had been a Dr. Jones and the pink pills in her purse had probably been tetracycline, which Carrie was taking for chlamydia. Kelley couldn't shed any additional light on the "trouble" between Carrie and Jesse Pratt.

The following morning, Friday, June 20, Krogh and Hein met Mel McClintock in the parking lot of the Omni Restaurant in Seattle. The Northern Star driver told the investigators why he was late returning the truck in which Carrie and Jessie Pratt finally left on Monday afternoon. When he called his wife, Connie, on his way back to Seattle, he said, he had learned that she had car trouble, so he had stopped by their house, taking her with him to the Northern Star parking lot so she could get his personal pickup, which he had left there.

But that didn't seem to account for several hours' delay. McClintock then admitted he had gotten a traffic citation at the Everett, Washington, weigh scales because his vehicle was improperly registered and its Washington license plate had expired in 1985. He had given the ticket to Pratt, he said.

McClintock was able to provide a detailed inventory of the items that had been in the truck cab and sleeper when he left it. One of these items was Jesse Pratt's sleeping bag, "green in color, having an inner lining of checkerboard plaid design," Hein recorded. McClintock had left the extra bedroll in the truck's sleeper while he was on his Canadian trip so he could put it under his own for additional cushioning, he explained.

Other articles in the truck had included a toolbox, a five-cell flashlight, two portable television sets (one his, one Pratt's), an AM/FM radio, a CB radio, several blue beach towels, and two pillows, which he'd brought from his home: one was a silver "living-room pillow" and the other a down-filled bed pillow in a floral design pillowcase. The down pillow, he thought, was half of a set that had a mate at his residence.

Finally, McClintock told the officers, the sleeper contained two new rolls of green paper towels. Jesse Pratt had bought these the week before and had given them to him to put in the sleeper.

When he turned over the truck to Pratt, he remembered his boss had asked Carrie "if she had gotten the money." He said the two of them had left for Los Angeles about 4:00 P.M. that day.

Mel volunteered that Pratt preferred traveling Highway 97 to California instead of I-5 because the route used less fuel. He didn't mention that it could also be a way of avoiding I-5 weigh scales on the California border if the ones on the less-traveled two-lane highway were closed.

He knew Jesse well, McClintock said. They first met in 1978 when both worked for the Burlington

Northern Transport Company. Sex had always been pretty high on Jesse's priority list, he said. At one truck stop, when girls knocked on the door of his truck, Mel figured Pratt had sent them. He assumed, but didn't know, that Pratt and Carrie Love had been intimate. McClintock did not mention the darker bonds that had developed over the years between Pratt and himself.

When Detective Krogh and Sergeant Hein interviewed McClintock's wife, Connie, at their home, she remembered seeing several of the items in the truck that Mel had mentioned, including the blue beach towels and "two new rolls of Scott paper towels still in the plastic wrapper and a roll of white toilet paper." She also remembered a roll of duct tape on the floor of the passenger side of the cab because she had kicked it several times.

Connie vividly recalled Pratt's "commenting" on their being late, adding that "Pratt is boisterous and his temper goes up and down." By contrast, she said, "Carrie was excited about going, and her attitude was very bubbly that day."

She had seen Pratt put a "three-in-one fold-over suitcase" into the truck, and Carrie had "a suitcase and a brown attaché case." Hearing that Carrie was going on a working vacation, Connie said she warned her that the rig had a rough ride when the trailer was empty.

Hein asked whether she had seen the pillows in the sleeper and did she have mates to them. Mrs. McClintock got up and left the room, returning with two pillows, one of which, Hein wrote down, was "white in color with blue striping and a light floral design on the pillowcase." Connie consented to the officer's request to "borrow them for a while." Thanking her and putting his initials on the pillows, Hein gave her a receipt and carried them out to the car.

Leaving the McClintocks' home, Krogh and Hein now drove to Cody Kupferer's residence. Kupferer told them he had first met Carrie in July 1985, and they had "become closer friends since January 1986," when he had become her boyfriend. Cody was several years younger than Carrie, he said. He was, in fact, still in high school and seemed a little embarrassed about it.

Cody said Carrie had told him that Pratt's business was a front for other things. At first, she had not been specific. But "Pratt requested her to pose in front of two naked guys while they were making love for four hundred dollars, and that she could get one thousand dollars for watching a guy masturbate, as well as an act being performed."

Cody repeated his earlier statement that he had told Carrie that he didn't like her traveling with Pratt. She had responded that "if Pratt 'tried anything,' she would get out of the truck and would call me, and I could come and get her, wherever she was at." They had discussed this strategy several times on the weekend before her departure.

On Monday morning (having spent the night with her former boyfriend, Jim Hancock), Carrie had phoned Cody to say they needed to talk. Late that morning, Carrie picked up Cody at Foster High School and the two of them drove back to her apartment to pick up her bag and attaché case. On the way, they had a serious talk about their age difference. To Cody's chagrin, when they got to her place, her former boyfriend, Jim Hancock, was still there.

On the way to Northern Star, the couple stopped at a bank, where Carrie had transacted some business. When they arrived at the trucking company, Cody took Carrie's bags into the office and left for his job at a local theater. She later called him there, about four o'clock, just before they left. When he last saw Carrie, Cody said, she was wearing blue jeans, Pro Wings tennis shoes, blue and white in color. He didn't remember what kind of top she had on, but he knew she had a yellow gold ring on her right hand. On that day, she had carried a gray purse with a zipper top. He didn't remember whether she was wearing earrings, but she sometimes did and he knew she had pierced ears. And she wore contact lenses.

Getting back to Pratt's activities, Cody thought of a conversation that took place between Kelley and Carrie at a restaurant to which the three of them had gone one day. During the exchange, Carrie mentioned Pratt's escort service, and Kelley got pretty loud about it. Carrie told her "if she didn't knock it off, she would end up dead!"

Carrie had also confided to Cody that in recovering answering-machine messages at Northern Star, "one morning there was a message requesting the 'candy man,' but she didn't know what this had reference to. So Carrie asked Pratt who the candy man was, and Pratt told her what it was all about—and that it's cocaine. Pratt told her he was running cocaine from Mexico to California, and to Tacoma, Washington, and Vancouver, and British Columbia."

The cocaine, Kupferer thought, was hidden under the truck in some way, and the run Mel McClintock had just returned from had "probably been to service a B.C. dealer, which is why Pratt had been so upset when the truck was late."

Cody told Hein he had a key to Carrie's apartment because he had agreed to take care of her pets while she was gone. He offered to take the officers to her place and used the key to admit them to Air Vista Apartment #158. While there, Sergeant Hein asked Cody whether he had had sexual intercourse with Carrie during their relationship. Cody said he had. The last time had been on Sunday afternoon, June 15. Carrie was just beginning her menstrual cycle, he added.

At the officers' request, Jim Hancock came over to Carrie's apartment for an interview. Although he was no longer Carrie's boyfriend, he said, he had remained her friend. He had known her for about a year and had come to see her on Sunday evening because he was worried about her. When he had last talked to her on the phone, he "felt there was something bothering her," but she never would tell him what it was.

Because he had arrived on his motorcycle, and since it had started to rain, he had spent the night. And yes, they had had sex that night—twice actually. Asked about his blood type, Hancock said it was Type O Positive.

In light of Carrie's call to Cody the next morning, it seemed probable to Hein that Cody's days as Carrie's boyfriend may have been numbered.

SEVEN

*When I first met Ken Cooper, I told him, "I don't
want you to think this isn't an important case."
He really bristled at that, and I'll never forget what
he said:*

*"When I found this girl's body, she became my
little girl. I have her picture on my wall, and it will
stay there until the case is resolved to my satisfaction.
Carrie no longer has a voice, so I will be her voice."*

—Connie Love

Back in his office in Klamath Falls on Monday
morning, June 23, Sergeant Hein received several
telephone calls. The first one came from Dan Johnson of the 123rd Airborne National Guard Unit of
Portland. Johnson reported that he had last heard
from Carrie on Monday morning, June 16, and she
told him about going to Los Angeles but planned
to be in Portland on Friday night for their weekend
drill. Carrie, he said, had seemed "her normal,
cheerful self."

Hein's next call came from Jerry Kettwig, owner
of the Utility refrigerated trailer that Pratt was rent-
ing. The vehicle had been contracted in February,
but the only payment Kettwig had received was on

a closed checking account. When he called Jesse Pratt about the matter and asked that he return the trailer or give him a valid check, Pratt "became very outraged and made the statement that anyone who came near the trailer would get hurt." That was 2 ½ months ago. Kettwig had since started a civil suit to recover his property.

Rich Hein's last call was from Cody Kupferer, who had prepared a list of the clothing he believed Carrie had packed in her bags. It included two of his own football jerseys, each with the number 67 and the name Kupferer on the back.

In the write-up of his trip, the officer's twenty-eight-page report lists the following items that were placed in the Klamath Falls evidence room:

1. *White pillow with blue striping and light floral design. Writer's initials "RBH" and date 06-20-86 are pen marked on the pillow.*
2. *Silver and gray living room style pillow. Writer's initials "RBH" and date 06-20-86 are inked on the cover.*
3. *Photograph of Carrie Lynette Love received from Cody Kupferer on 06-20-86.*
4. *Three index cards with writings, signed by the name of "Spider," also received from Cody Kupferer on 06-20-86.*

While Hein was in Seattle, Carrie's mother, Connie Love, drove down to Klamath Falls from her home in Spokane, Washington, to identify her daughter. Connie, proud of her role as a nurse, insisted on seeing the body—against the advice of the police and the funeral home's director.

"I had to be sure," Connie explained. Although Carrie's face was badly disfigured, positive identification was easy, she said, because the little finger on her daughter's right hand was one joint short—a small genetic defect that she called her "stubby," Connie said.

It would not be Connie Love's last trip to Klamath Falls.

Ken Cooper had attended Carrie Love's autopsy on Thursday, June 19. The 9½-hour procedure was conducted at the Davenport Funeral Home by Medical Examiner Robert Jamison, M.D. Jackquelyn Hathorn, R.N., deputy nurse of the Klamath County Sheriff's Office, assisted the doctor.

Although Dr. Jamison's death certificate lists the cause of Carrie's death as simply "stab wounds to heart and great vessels," his autopsy protocol details "multiple stab wounds compatible with ice-pick wounds to abdomen, chest, neck, and back," as well as "stab wounds to the left superior pulmonary vein [and] superior vena cava, with extensive bleeding into the pericardial cavity."

Other findings described in the medical report include "stab wounds to the left lung, causing pulmonary edema," and the conclusion that "the victim probably died from a combination of suffocation and loss of blood due to the stab wounds."

Dr. Jamison's protocol also states that the victim suffered a crushed skull, broken cartilage, and broken ribs on the left side, as well as a broken neck; the pathologist, however, believed these injuries had occurred postmortem. He also notes "tape marks on face, neck, hands, and lower back" and that the victim's left arm had been "driven over by a tire." Finally, he reported "numerous well-preserved spermatozoa present on vaginal smear." Nurse Hathorn's three-page write-up details dozens of lesser injuries.

All of the tissue damage was photographed both in color and black and white. Fingernail scrapings were collected. These yielded some "foreign" fibers that would later be subjected to microscopic and ultraviolet examination, to be compared with fabrics in the suspect's clothing and materials found in his truck cab.

While the autopsy was going on, Troopers Ray Rathke and Don Bertram would return to the Loop Road at Milepost 206 with a metal detector, searching "for any object that may have been used in committing the crime." All they found was a collection of "nails, bolts, and other various pieces of metal that had obviously been in the area for some time." Thinking about how the murder weapon might have been hastily disposed of, they even threw several plastic-handled screwdrivers into the woods from the gravel pile, then searched the area where they landed. Their results were all negative.

EIGHT

It was a really *clean truck.*
                    —Patrolman William Conley

When Patrolman William Conley approached Milepost 115, two cruisers were waiting on the right shoulder. They pulled in behind him, matching his speed of seventy-five miles an hour. Minutes later, they spotted the reefer in the right lane up ahead. On Conley's signal, all three cars switched on their flashing red lights.

The team overtook the tractor-trailer rig and effected a stop—one patrol car halfway up the side of the trailer and two immediately behind, beams from their rotating emergency lights stabbing through the gathering dusk. Eastbound traffic on the interstate slowed to a trickle as vehicles crawled by the cruisers in the remaining left lane. It was 8:25 P.M.

At 6:00 A.M. on Friday, June 20, Ken Cooper was awakened by a phone call from Rich Stroup. Jesse Clarence Pratt, Stroup said, was in custody in Phoenix, Arizona. His Kenworth tractor and the reefer van it was towing were in the Department of Public Safety impound lot in Buckeye. Cooper's feet hit the floor.

Within hours, the pair boarded a plane for Phoenix, taking with them Warrant #86-1550FL, signed by Judge Wayne Blair, charging Jesse Clarence Pratt with aggravated murder. They were met at the Phoenix airport by a Maricopa County deputy sheriff, who took them to his headquarters on West Madison. There they met Arizona Highway patrolman William Conley.

Conley had been fueling his cruiser the night before with his CB radio on, he said, when he heard a trucker identify himself as "Northern Star."

"This was the logo that was supposedly on the side of the '76 Kenworth in the 'Attempt to Locate' bulletin we'd received," he told the Oregon officers. "So I broke into conversation like another trucker and asked the Northern Star driver whether he was 'the long-nose Kenworth who'd blown my doors off a few minutes ago.'

"He said he was. So I notified the dispatcher that I thought we'd located the KW, and I was getting onto Interstate ten. I spotted the truck a few minutes later about four miles east of Exit ninety-four."

Stroup and Cooper wanted to know how the arrest went.

"He was cool," Conley said. "And after seeing him, I was glad he was. He appeared to be very calm. It didn't really seem to bother him that we'd stopped him.

"The only driver's license Pratt could furnish was a Washington passenger car license," Conley added. Pratt didn't have a current medical card, which is required of all operators of commercial equipment on the highway, nor could he produce a chauffeur's license. He told Conley he just hadn't had time to get one.

Patrolman Conley ticketed him for both violations and cited him for being an unqualified driver. The officer told Pratt he was wanted for questioning in connection with a homicide. Pratt said he knew it.

Conley called over one of the other officers as a witness while he recited Pratt's Miranda rights before continuing his questioning.

"I asked him what route he had taken getting here," Conley continued, getting out a copy of his arrest record. "He said he left Seattle about six o'clock on Monday, the sixteenth, and had driven to the T and R Truck Stop just off I-5 at Albany. When he left there, he continued to the Trocadero Truck Stop in Weed, California, where he bought fuel, and then proceeded to Dunnigan, California, and spent the remainder of Tuesday [there]. He then drove to Hayward, California, and loaded a load of potatoes to Phoenix. His route from Dunnigan: he said he proceeded on Highway 99 to Highway 58, to 395, to I-15 over to I-215, to Interstate 10 eastbound. Interstate 10 would have brought him into Phoenix."

When he invited Pratt to tell him what happened, Conley got more detail than he expected, he said.

"He told me he'd picked up a girl at the office where he worked, and she was going to ride with him to Los Angeles to set up another office for his company. They went by his place to pick up a suitcase and there 'she said she wanted some love and attention.' So they went from his apartment to a truck stop,

Evergreen Truck Stop, where Mr. Pratt said they engaged in intercourse in the tractor—in the sleeper compartment.

"After that, he said, he took her to a bar called My Place, outside the entrance to the airport, because she had changed her mind and decided to fly. He told me that was about six o'clock. Later on, he told me five o'clock, and then he told me between five and five-thirty.

"I asked Mr. Pratt what airline she was flying on. He didn't know. I asked him if he knew the flight number, and he said he didn't know. I asked if he knew the time she was supposed to be leaving. He said he didn't know. I asked him what time she would arrive in L.A. He didn't know.

"When I told him that this would seem peculiar—that as owner of that company, when he would be paying for those tickets and her transportation, that it was unusual that he didn't know anything about it. At that point, he just shrugged. And he really didn't say anything after that. The other cars took him to the Maricopa County Jail, while I drove the rig to the evidentiary yard on Buckeye Road."

There, Officer Conley said, he had searched the truck.

"The first thing that struck me as being peculiar was the fact that there were no sheets in the sleeper itself—on the mattress. There was a new blanket that was still in the wrapping. It hadn't been removed from the plastic wrapping.

"The truck was *clean*. It was a *really* clean truck. I was surprised at a truck that old being that clean. It was just a *clean truck*."

* * *

While Stroup and Cooper waited in the office of the Maricopa County Sheriff, Jesse Pratt was brought over from the jail facility through an underground tunnel.

The figure that entered the room was a Hell's Angels caricature. Distended by a huge, low-slung belly, the orange jumpsuit was stretched into the shape of a giant gourd, capped by a bulging sphere of unkempt hair, which blended into an equally scraggly beard overflowing the collar of the jail uniform. Jesse Pratt's eyes were hidden behind tinted glasses.

To the surprise of the officers, the prisoner arrived with attorney Mike Sullivan. Mona Bennett, worried about Jesse, had gone to her own attorney in Seattle, and he had contacted a lawyer in Phoenix.

Detective Ken Cooper formally arrested Jesse Clarence Pratt in the presence of his lawyer. Cooper read him his Miranda rights once again.

Lawyer Sullivan intervened. He said his client wouldn't discuss anything relating to the death of Carrie Love. But he agreed to have him sign a "Form 45," permitting the officers to search Pratt's person and his truck. Both also signed an extradition waiver so that Pratt could be taken to Oregon.

After consulting with Sullivan, Pratt agreed to provide blood samples. To have two 10cc vials drawn, the four had to go to the West Valley Emergency Clinic on North Litchfield Road. On the way back to the sheriff's office, according to Cooper's report, "Pratt was fed by officers at the place of his choice: McDonald's." It would be his last meal at a public restaurant.

Pratt was fingerprinted and photographed—full front, with and without glasses, and from both sides. In these pictures, Jesse Pratt presents the spectacle of an overweight (230 pounds) Caucasian with an Afro hairstyle, his light brown bushy hair contiguous with a massive, untended beard. Long, thick strands of his scraggly, overgrown mustache drooped over his mouth in a horseshoe shape. Staring into the camera with pale blue eyes lined with long, dark eyelashes, the face is expressionless and grotesque.

Pratt's clothing, including the red T-shirt he had been wearing when arrested, was seized as evidence. Also taken were saliva samples, fingernail scrapings, and hair samples from his head, mustache, beard, arms, and pubic area. While he was naked, they photographed his body, documenting several long scratches on his rib cage and on his ample paunch. His ribs appeared to be bruised.

Detective Cooper and Maricopa County Homicide detective Darrell Smith returned Pratt to his jail cell by 9:30 P.M. Their prisoner complained of stomach pain. Cooper got him a bottle of Mylanta.

The next morning, at the Department of Public Safety impound lot in Buckeye, Cooper and Stroup met Lieutenant Mike Howard and criminalist Larry Dickenson, whose assistance they had requested before leaving Klamath Falls. Sergeant Loren Laird of the Oregon State Police Fingerprint Identification Bureau had also been summoned. Detective Darrell Smith and Charles LeBlanc, Arizona Department of Public Safety evidence technician, joined the Oregon officers.

Ken Cooper and most of this group would spend the next five days examining the contents of Jesse Pratt's truck, while their prisoner waited for them in the county jail.

Mike Howard began by photographing the exterior of the truck and trailer, including details of the tires. Two of these seemed to have a tread pattern similar to the one on the victim's arm. He cut slices of tire tread from each.

Howard then turned his attention to the truck interior. After carefully removing loose hair and debris, including such tiny items as "what appeared to be a normal fingernail clipping," he vacuumed the entire cab, bagging and labeling the resulting contents of the hand vac.

Having personally examined and photographed the tire mark on the victim's arm during the autopsy, Ken Cooper now photographed all thirty-four tires on the rig, numbering and indexing them on a diagram, noting their position on the vehicle and writing in the exposure number of each picture he shot. One of the two tires Howard had cut tread samples from—the newest-looking tire on the trailer—was the right rear of the eight tires on the trailer's tandem axles. On his diagram, Cooper identified this one as "Axle #5, Tire #1." With the tire still mounted on its steel wheel, he had it unbolted from the axle, crated, and sent to Klamath Falls.

To avoid possibly smearing fingerprints by dusting its interior surfaces, Loren Laird opted to "bag" the truck. With large sheets of brown wrapping paper and tape, he encased the entire cab. After others had left the garage area, he filled the interior with the toxic gas produced by fuming Super Glue, leaving the fumigant in the blimped truck overnight—a process that causes latent fingerprint images to appear. He would photograph them in the morning after ventilating the truck.

NINE

Pratt was always coming on like a big shot, trying to put his arm around one of the female employees in the building. He was known as a very loud person who usually used vulgar, abusive language. I spoke to him about it—told him other tenants had complained about his foul language. I could hear him verbally abusing Carrie, yelling and cussing and calling her a "cunt." I saw Carrie come out of the office crying more than once and I told her she didn't have to take that and she should get out and find another job.

—Rebecca Lehnerz, rental manager,
Frontier Aviation Resources

Their work in Phoenix complete, Sergeant Stroup and Detective Cooper returned to Klamath Falls, changing planes in San Francisco with their manacled prisoner. He wore the orange Maricopa County Jail jumpsuit and the soft slippers issued to him at the jail. The latter are deliberately designed to be less than track shoes for a man in a hurry.

At 1:00 A.M. on June 25, Jesse Clarence Pratt was booked into the Klamath County Jail. His white-walled, twelve-foot-square cell had a small, heavily

barred outside window. Furnishings included a steel
cot, a seatless ceramic toilet, and a small sink bolted
to the wall. Toilet articles and reading matter could
be stored on a recessed shelf above the sink. Pratt,
however, had never learned to read.

On Monday, June 30, three of the witnesses
Sergeant Rich Hein had questioned in Seattle
were brought to Klamath Falls. Sergeant Rich
Stroup and Detective Ken Cooper interviewed
them. The information provided by Mona Bennett proved less than reliable.

"Jesse owns a truck and three trailers," she told
the officers. "Other drivers own their own trucks
and the company provides trailers."

Bennett didn't know why Jesse had two trucking
companies. She thought Double Jack was a new
one that was just getting started. She said she knew
nothing about the escort service.

"It's not illegal," she added, spoiling her denial.
"The police have checked it out. Dan Gates runs it."

She described Gates as "short, chubby, and ugly,
also sleazy. He's about thirty-seven years old," she recalled; she didn't think Jesse was connected with it.

Bennett proved to be very free with office gossip.
She and Carrie didn't fight, she said. But "Carrie was
protective and jealous of Jesse. She liked having all of
his attention. I told Jesse I thought Carrie was in love
with him. Jesse took care of Carrie. He was fatherlike
toward her. He loaned her money. Carrie had a lot
of personal problems and she leaned on Jesse.

"She was dating Cody but wouldn't tell anybody.
She told Jesse that she and Cody were just friends,

nothing more." Mona knew that "Cody was upset about Jim Hancock having spent the night at Carrie's apartment." Carrie had told her about it at lunch on Monday, she said. "There was a big hassle over that."

Bennett went over the telephone calls she'd had with Pratt the previous week. When she told him that Carrie's purse had been found and that she was missing, "he wasn't too worried. He said Carrie was 'flighty.' He said Carrie was talking to two people at the tavern after he dropped her off, and he thought she went with them. He also said that Carrie had walked up to people outside the bar and he assumed they were friends of hers."

During one of his telephone conversations with Mona, Jesse casually volunteered the information that he and Carrie had had sex in the truck before he took her to the airport, and she believed him. Jesse, she said, had told her previously that he'd had sex with Carrie. "Still," she went on, "it could be just locker-room talk."

Sergeant Stroup's report of the interview with Mona Bennett concludes:

"Mona doesn't think Jesse did it. He wouldn't be that sloppy. He's smart, been in the Walla Walla State Pen, been around. If he had done it, they never would have found her."

Stroup and Cooper interviewed the McClintocks the following morning. Asked what he knew about Jesse Pratt's prior arrests, Mel said he was aware that Jesse had been in prison, and he knew most of the details about that case because he had been working with Jesse at the time.

Pratt had been seeing a woman who worked for a truck brokerage firm, he said, and personnel there had tried to come between him and "Thelma." Jesse had become very upset at the time, and insisted on talking with Thelma to get things straightened out between them. On the day of the "incident," Jesse was to have met the McClintocks at the Tukwila Inn. But Jesse never showed. To their surprise, they learned he had been arrested in Eugene, Oregon—for kidnapping.

Mel visited Jesse in jail after he was extradited to Tacoma, Washington. There, Jesse complained about his heart and said that no one would take care of his problem. He asked Mel to find him an attorney. Mel called his own attorney, Terry Watkins.

Both he and his wife, Connie, were afraid of Jesse, McClintock said. After Jesse went to jail, they decided not to let him know their whereabouts. But after he got out, Jesse found him—about a year ago—and offered him a job. Jesse promised Mel that he would become office manager, only occasionally having to make trips in the truck.

When Jesse located the McClintocks, he talked about wanting to meet their stepdaughters. Connie, however, didn't want Pratt around because they had learned he was involved with prostitution. And there was the "incident" that had sent him to prison because he and a partner had been having sex with Thelma during the kidnapping.

Getting back to the case at hand, McClintock recalled that on Monday, June 16, Jesse's sleeping bag was still in the truck when he and Carrie left. He also distinctly remembered that his boss had earlier given him two rolls of paper towels and a bottle of

Windex, which he had wedged into the corners of the sleeper.

Asked about masking tape, McClintock said he bought it by the case from Sea-Land Trucking and he knew he had at least one roll of it in the truck. He'd used it to tape up the CB antenna lead over the door on Sunday night; after which, he remembered, he had left it on the floor. He also remembered that Connie kept kicking it when he picked her up on Monday.

The cassette player in the truck was his but it wasn't working properly and the knobs kept falling off from road vibration. As a result, he'd taken them off and put them either into the glove box or under the passenger seat.

He had last fueled the truck at Biggs Junction, he said. He believed the truck could have traveled about three hundred miles on what was left in the tank.

The officers showed McClintock the sleeping bag that Bruce McDonald had found. He identified it as almost certainly the one belonging to Jesse Pratt, adding that he had taken his own vinyl-covered one out of the sleeper when he turned in the truck on Monday. What made him sure it was Jesse's were the white drawstrings that had been added by punching holes in the bag.

Mel confirmed that Carrie had started working for Northern Star in May. "Within a week, Carrie ran the office, and a week after that, she found additional clients for the company. She was very good at the job. But although she was good, she needed to grow up. She was the all-American Girl—bubbly—and naive."

The company also had a second office in Belle-

vue, Washington, McClintock said. He believed
there was a dating or matchmaking service in
volved. He had met Dan Gates, the man who ran
that business. Mel described him as having a
"craggy face, pudgy build, mustache, black hair
with some gray in it."

McClintock believed Double Jack was just another
business name. He didn't know why Jesse Pratt had
that company. "Donald Hudson" was the name on
the Double Jack phone bill. Mel thought maybe he
owned the company. He had never met Donald Hudson, but Mona told him that she thought Donald
Hudson and Jesse Pratt were the same person.

Like Mona Bennett, Mel McClintock doubted
that Pratt was guilty of the crime. He'd be too smart
to let the police find the body. Sergeant Stroup's report of the interview doesn't mince words:

". . . McClintock didn't want to volunteer any information that would piss Jesse off, since he is
afraid of Jesse. He said that if Jesse had told him to
lie about the pillows he would have done so. If Pratt
knew he was cooperating with the police, McClintock believes his life would be in danger. He thinks
Jesse is capable of killing someone; on the other
hand, he believes that out of the 150 Teamster
Union members that he knows, there are at least 30
guys who could also kill."

Connie McClintock was interviewed separately.
She had told Mona, she volunteered, that she was
worried about Carrie after she and Jesse took off in
the truck that Monday.

"Knowing Jesse, he was going to have a good time."

Connie felt that Carrie was a real asset to the Northern Star office. "But she was *not* available to Jesse. She was the cheerleader type—very outgoing and cheerful, but she was out of Jesse's league. He didn't intimidate her. She just took him in stride."

When Mel told Connie that he believed the Bellevue office was an escort service, she wasn't surprised, he said. "Knowing Jesse, it wouldn't surprise me if it was a front for whores."

She explained why she and her husband got along better with Jesse Pratt than other people did. Shortly after she and Mel got married, she said, when she was trying to get work at Burlington, she would sometimes ride with other Burlington drivers, and they became her friends. She knew them all, she said, and "they used to tease me good naturedly about traveling with different guys all the time.

"Jesse came in and took it seriously. He told me to put up or shut up. He asked me to go to his truck and have sex with him.

"The other drivers were ready to tear him apart. Mel walked in behind Jesse and, making a joke of it, said, 'That's right, and I collect the money.' Mel got Jesse out of a bad situation. A couple of nights later, Mel saved Jesse's hide again. After that, Jesse was like a puppy with us. He was always around. But I've been careful never to be alone with him!"

Some years earlier, Connie added as an afterthought, when her husband had been questioned about possible sexual abuse of one of his stepdaughters, Jesse offered to have the daughter killed.

PART TWO

TEN

Oregon law has five levels of homicide: aggravated murder, intentional murder, manslaughter in the first degree, manslaughter in the second degree, and criminally negligent homicide. Aggravated murder is the only one carrying a potential death penalty upon conviction. Alternatively, a court can sentence the convicted defendant to life in prison, or to life in prison without possibility of release or parole.

Aggravated murder is defined by the circumstances under which the crime is committed. These include murder for hire, murder having been committed after a previous conviction for any homicide, a murder related to the performance of the victim's official duties in the justice system (e.g., killing a police officer, judge, juror, or any officer of the court), murder committed in an effort to conceal the commission of a crime or the identity of the perpetrator of a crime, killing someone while in prison or after having escaped from prison, or killing more than one person in the same criminal episode.

—OURS 163.095

On July 2, 1986, the day before his forty-second birthday, Jesse Clarence Pratt was indicted for aggravated murder. The substatute under which he was indicted [163.095(e)] specifies that "the homicide occurred in the course of, or as a result of, intentional maiming or torture of the victim."

Case Agent Ken Cooper's job would be to help the prosecution gather sufficient evidence to prove to a jury beyond a reasonable doubt that this is what happened to Carrie Love and that Jesse Pratt did it. The fact that there was no eyewitness to the crime would present a formidable challenge. Dr. Jamison's autopsy report would be helpful in establishing the probability of torture and even maiming, but it would take more than the items logged into the evidence room to convict Jesse Pratt. Loren Laird's fingerprint analysis, for example, while technically excellent, proved disappointing. It was no surprise to find fingerprints of Jesse Pratt in his own truck, nor those of Carrie Love, driver Mel McClintock, or Patrolman Conley.

Detective Cooper would travel thousands of miles across the United States, including two trips to Alaska, to interview relatives and associates of both the suspect and the victim. His findings would suggest a strong likelihood that Jesse Pratt could be the murderer. But he would have to do better than that in a trial involving a potential death sentence.

Typical of Ken Cooper's approach, he turned back more than once to the logistics of the crime to see how his puzzle pieces fit. He had suspected from the beginning that the itinerary Pratt had recited to authorities was an effort to build an alibi.

He now compared it against the suspect's Driver's Daily Log.

Although nearly illiterate, Pratt had somehow mastered the ability to write down his travel destinations, dates, and the time of day, including off-duty time. Cooper compared the entries in Pratt's logbook with the receipts found in his briefcase.

Plotting Jesse Pratt's probable route on a Rand McNally map, Cooper calculated the truck's incremental mileages. He then prepared a mileage chart, starting at the Northern Star Office:

Seattle, WA to Woodland, WA (Hwy I-5)	152 *Miles*
Woodland, WA to Albany, OR	89
Albany to Eugene, OR (58-97)	44
Eugene to Chemult, OR	94
Chemult to Klamath Falls, OR (97)	73
Klamath Falls to Weed, CA	83
Weed to Mount Shasta, CA	10
Mount Shasta to Red Bluff, CA	87
Red Bluff to Corning, CA	18
Corning to Dunnigan, CA	77
Dunnigan to Davis, CA	29
Davis to Hayward, CA (I-80)	80
Hayward to Livermore, CA	22
Livermore to Fresno (580-I5-152-99)	138
Fresno to Kramer Junction (4 Corners)	210
Kramer Junction to San Bernardino, CA	69
San Bernardino to Colton, CA (I-215)	5
Colton to Blythe, CA (I-10)	166
Blythe to Ehrenberg, AZ	6
Ehrenberg to Phoenix, AZ	168

With this chart and his marked-up map, Cooper

retraced Pratt's entire route in his own car—partly in search of Carrie Love's missing suitcases.

Many weeks later, having returned from several trips across the country, the investigator was still bothered by the fit of some of the pieces in the puzzle. One evening, as he sorted through the contents of the black Samsonite briefcase yet again, Cooper had a revelation.

"It slapped me right in the face," he later explained. There, among the receipts, was one dated June 16,1986—from Redd's Tires, 608 West Scott Avenue, Woodland, Washington, Mobil Oil gas receipt #K0937775 for $95 worth of diesel fuel at $1.02 per gallon, for which Pratt had paid cash.

When he saw the receipt this time, Cooper had suddenly remembered Pratt's statement that he *never* fuels up in Washington when going down to Oregon because fuel is cheaper in Oregon. And McClintock had said the truck had at least a quarter tank of fuel; that could easily get him to the T & R in Albany, Oregon, and maybe even as far as Eugene. Woodland, Cooper knew, was a small town in southern Washington near the Columbia River Gorge on the Oregon border. If Pratt's story about dropping Carrie Love near the Sea-Tac airport was true, he would be alone when he got there.

Cooper dialed the telephone number printed on the receipt.

Gregg Taylor, manager of Redd's Tires, answered the phone. Cooper's report indicates he made the call at 2:24 P.M. on August 13.

Identifying himself, but being careful not to lead any potential witnesses with too much information, Cooper told Taylor he was trying to get some information on a truck from Seattle that bought fuel there in June. The semi had the name Northern Star on the gas tanks.

Taylor said he didn't have any information on the vehicle, but he asked the officer to hold on.

"This guy half covers up the phone," Cooper later explained, "and calls out, 'Jeff! I've got a cop here that's lookin' for a rig out of Seattle that came through here southbound in June, with the name Northern Star on it.'

"I hear this kid in the background, 'You mean that green KW with the name on the gas tank—or on the door?'

"I couldn't believe it! I asked him to put that kid on the phone. I said, 'What do you mean *green* KW?' I never mentioned the color."

"'No,' the kid said, 'but I remember it was a long-nose green '75 or '76 Kenworth—with a sleeper.'

"I was pretty excited. This guy knows trucks! And I realized I had to handle this kid right. So without saying anything else, I asked, 'Can you tell me anything about the driver?'

"There was a long pause. Finally, he said, 'Yeah. He was an older guy with a pot gut, scrawny arms and a big potbelly. He had a curly, overgrown bushy head of hair, a full beard, and a big pot gut.'

"I'm on a roll! I asked if he could tell me what the driver was wearing.

"'Yeah,' he said. 'Cowboy boots, Levi's. He had on a blue plaid checkered shirt, unbuttoned, with the sleeves rolled up. If you can show me pictures, I'll show you who I'm talking about.'

"I've got to be careful that I don't lead him. So all I said was, 'Anything else you can tell me about him?'

"The kid mentioned 'chrome gas tanks and stacks.' And I asked, 'Anything else?' There was a long pause and he goes, 'Yeah, that little girl that was with him was a lot younger.'

"This kid blew me away! It had been two *months*! Now we've got an eyewitness that puts her as far south as Woodland. So I asked, 'What can you tell me about her?'

"First, he said he hadn't really paid much attention because he was gassing up another truck when she got out and went to the rest room. But then he added, 'She had medium short brown hair. Small. Wore a white or light-colored coat and Levi pants.'

"I asked him if he noticed what she was wearing on her feet.

"'She didn't have shoes on—only those short bootie socks.' And then he threw in, 'She needs braces.'

"I told him I'd bring him a picture."

Cooper had a Polaroid color picture of Pratt, taken at the time of his arrest. He took it to the police lab, where technicians made a copy negative and reproduced it in black and white, matching its size to some black-and-white photos of somewhat similar-looking men—all of the pictures having about the same resolution, looking like they might have come from a common source.

To make a similar lineup for identifying the victim, Ken Cooper got a copy of the Klamath Falls High School yearbook and picked out five of the girls' graduation pictures. These were matched in size and

appearance to one of the pictures of Carrie he had
received from Connie Love.

On August 20, Cooper drove to Woodland and
took eighteen-year-old Jeff Warren to lunch. After
hearing the young man's story for a second time,
the investigator brought out his male lineup.

"See anybody who looks familiar?" Cooper
checked his watch.

Jeff Warren sat there silently, staring at the lineup
for four minutes, thirty-seven seconds, the detective's
report notes. Cooper tried to look calm. Finally, Warren put his finger on one of the pictures.

"There's your man."

Cooper began to breathe again.

"What took you so long?"

"Well, you said this was a murder case and it was
important, didn't you? Besides, these are lousy pictures. They're not even in color. And his hair isn't
really this dark."

"Okay, I'm going to give you a photo lineup of females. Let me know if you see anybody who looks
familiar."

He took only twelve seconds this time.

"There's your girl."

The detective believes the young man's remark-
able memory was enhanced "because it was such an
unlikely, ridiculous contrast. Here's this fat, ugly,
grotesque-looking guy with a naked belly so big he
can't button his shirt over it—a beard down to his
chest—and he's with this cute, petite little girl."

Later, back at his desk in Klamath Falls, digging
through the contents of the briefcase once again,
Ken Cooper discovered what appeared to be a sales

slip for food. Receipt #472252, like the gas receipt, was also dated 6-16-86. And it was for *two* people.

In Seattle, Cooper met with trucker Louis Randolph, an owner-operator trucker who had done some contract hauling for Northern Star. Randolph had called the detective upon returning from the East Coast when he got caught up on the news about Pratt's company.

On June 16, Randolph explained, he had stopped in at the Northern Star office to pick up a check for the $400 Pratt owed him. His request had precipitated a loud argument that he couldn't help overhearing between Carrie Love and her boss. Carrie insisted the Northern Star account didn't have $400 in it, and she didn't want to be responsible for writing a bad check. Randolph ended up getting a check drawn on the Double Jack account (a check that was nevertheless returned for insufficient funds).

Pratt then asked Randolph to follow him to California and to meet him there, but the trucker was delayed until the next morning because of a broken brake shoe. When he got to the Bingo Truck Stop in Dunnigan, California, about 4:00 A.M. on June 18, Randolph said, "Two different people told me, 'Your boss is running only two hours ahead of you.'"

"Pratt must have made quite a stop with his passenger," Randolph said he thought at the time.

Unable to locate Pratt, trucker Randolph called dispatcher Bennett at Northern Star later the same day. Mona first told Randolph "to hold—stay put," he remembered. When she was contacted later, how-

ever, she told Randolph to go to Phoenix to pick up
the Northern Star trailer being held there in the Department of Public Safety impound lot in Buckeye.
But when Randolph got to Phoenix, he discovered
the trailer was gone, so he called the Northern Star
office again.

Bennett told him that Jesse Pratt now wanted
him to go to Fresno and pick up a load of toma-
toes for a destination in Philadelphia—in which
city, Jesse had suggested, Randolph could "make
some money on [his] own to help pay for [his]
own new Kenworth before returning." Louis Randolph did as he was told.

But when he got to Philadelphia with the toma-
toes, Randolph's load was refused. And this time,
when he called Northern Star, the office was
closed and the phone was disconnected.

"I realized I was hung out to dry and stranded
back east," the trucker told Cooper. It was a Pratt
strategy, Cooper was sure, designed to keep Randolph from helping the police. It took Randolph
eight weeks to work his way back to Seattle, where,
for the first time, he learned that Jesse Pratt had
been arrested for murder. He called Ken Cooper
the next day.

Back in Klamath Falls, Ken Cooper completed
his chronology:

06-16-86, MONDAY 375 MILES
3:30/4:00 PM *Pratt & Love leave Northern Star
Office*
5:00 PM *Leave Seattle*
6:30/7:00 PM *Redd's Tire, Woodland*

Pratt & Love seen together
Fuel Receipt 06-17-86 #K0937775, Redd's Tire
Food Receipt for two 06-17-86 #472252

06-17-86, **TUESDAY** 335 MILES
9:00 AM *Leave Eugene*
10:30/11:00 AM *Mona said Pratt called from Klamath Falls, said he dropped Love @ Sea-Tac Airport*
11:20 AM *PNB [phone] receipt; call from Klamath Falls*
1:00 PM *Klamath Falls, OFF 1 Hour*
2:00 PM *Leave Klamath Falls*
2:30 PM *Mona said Pratt called from unknown location*
Texaco receipt 06-17-86 #6431526, Mt Shasta
4:00 PM *Weed, OFF*
6:00 PM *Leave Weed*
7:40 PM *PNB receipt, Red Bluff to Kent 206-631-1932*
7:46 PM *PNB receipt; from Red Bluff to Cypress*
7:48 PM *PNB receipt; from Red Bluff to Seattle*
9:00 PM *Log quits at Dunnigan*
Fuel Receipt 06-17-86 #0777433
9:22 PM *Corning Truck & Radiator Receipt 06-17-86 #11888AT*
Corning Burns Bro Receipt 06-17-86 #30159020
Davis Trip Permits TRK #8472869 TRL #4929500

06-18-86, **WEDNESDAY** 279 MILES
8:30 AM *Mona said Pratt called from Dunnigan, asked if anyone had heard from Love*
10:30 AM *Mona said Pratt called from unknown location*

2:30 PM *Mona said Pratt called twice from
unknown location, advised he will take load from
Hayward to Phoenix*
4:00 PM *Leave Dunnigan*
7:00 PM *Hayward, OFF 1 Hour*
7:55 PM *Citation #X322386 06-18-86*
Livermore, CA
11:00 PM *Log quits at Fresno*
*5th Wheel Truck Stop Receipt #14820 for
2 Padlocks, 2 Air Fresheners (date changed)*

06-19-86, **THURSDAY**
8:00 AM *Leave Fresno*
1:00 PM *San Bernardino, OFF 1 Hour*
10:30 AM *Pratt calls Mona, talks to Hein*
2:00 PM *Leave San Bernardino*
*Colton, CA Terminal Station Receipts
06-19-86 #080312 & #080313
No Further Entries
Ehrenberg, AZ 06-19-93 trip permits*
8:00 PM *Arrest—Conley, on I-10, MP 117, AZ*

ELEVEN

He sat with me in the front seat of the cab, and he told me to go past a house on Southwest 306th Street. On the way, he asked me where he could get a gun. I told him I didn't know. When I drove past the house, the guy suddenly ducked down under the dash. He told me he was spying on a blond woman.

—Tukwila taxi driver

After reviewing the evidence accumulated to date, together with the list of witnesses who had agreed to testify, Klamath County district attorney Ed Caleb believed that relevant background on the character of the defendant and his modus operandi could be helpful. Had Pratt's earlier felony conviction for kidnapping been a similar crime? Historical evidence of this kind had been accepted in previous trials where an eyewitness could not be found.

Caleb asked his staff to research Oregon legal precedent as it related to the case at hand. Briefs were prepared for the judge assigned to the case, and these were submitted to the Oregon attorney general for his review. Encouraged by the results of his research, Caleb asked Ken Cooper to locate the victim of the assault, rape, and kidnapping for which Jesse Pratt had been sentenced to prison in Walla Walla, Washington, in 1980. The earlier case was legally complicated because the kidnapping was committed in Tukwila, Washington, while the rape had occurred in Lane County, Oregon. In that same episode, Caleb learned, Pratt had also been charged with robbery in the first degree.

To protect the victim's identity, she is called "Thelma Adams" here. Cooper set out to find her. Thelma's story would turn out to be a prototype for Pratt's abusive relationships with women.

Beginning his new assignment on October 2, Ken Cooper called Rose Mary Barnes, wife of Lorie Barnes, owner of the L.A. Barnes Truck Brokerage in Tukwila, Washington, where the kidnapping had taken place. It was immediately apparent to Cooper that his call had alarmed the woman. She was so terrified of Pratt that she refused to give the detective her husband's telephone number, but she did agree to ask him to return the officer's call.

Suspecting that the caller might be a friend of Jesse Pratt's who had been assigned to check up on him, Rose Mary's husband, Lorie Barnes, phoned the Tukwila Police Department before calling Cooper. Barnes wasn't much help, though, when he finally returned the call. The investigating officer in 1980, he said, had since quit the Tukwila Police Department and Barnes didn't know where he was. He had heard, however, that Thelma Adams had moved back to Missouri, but he didn't know where she was living. He hadn't seen her since the kidnapping trial. And yes, he, too, was terrified of Jesse Pratt.

"Even though Pratt's in jail," Barnes observed, "he's capable of contacting friends, and he could ask them to do whatever he wants them to do."

Next, Cooper called Thelma's ex-husband, Charles, in Lebanon, Missouri. Charles told the detective that Thelma had assumed her maiden name and that he believed she was living in Richland, Missouri. It was October 21 before Cooper finally tracked her down. He dialed the telephone number.

Thelma Adams's voice registered shock. She didn't trust Cooper, and she didn't trust the system. She was scared to death that Pratt or one of his friends would do something terrible to her if she cooperated in any way.

The following morning, Cooper boarded a plane for St. Louis, where he rented a car and drove to Richland—a town of 1,900 about halfway between St. Louis and Springfield. There, he actually managed to talk Thelma Adams into testifying in the upcoming trial. When she later told her story on the witness stand, it would reveal a courageous streak that for once derailed the classic Jesse Pratt odyssey of a woman initially entrapped by the man's inexplicable charm, only to become imprisoned in the relationship, terrified of what might happen if she left him. For Thelma managed to escape—barely.

Twenty-five years old at the time and more than a little insecure, Thelma Adams had left her husband, Charles, and fled to Washington, where she had friends—hoping to start her life over. There, James and Linda Combs took her in. The couple had recently been hired by Pratt to drive "his" Freightliner—the truck he had borrowed from his half sister Cecilia and her husband. This is how Thelma happened to meet Jesse Pratt.

But the Combses' new job hadn't started because the truck had "disappeared." (It was the truck Pratt had wrecked in a fit of rage when its owners tried to get it back.) Changing his story, Pratt later told the Combses he was losing the title to the truck in an unfair court hearing. On the eve of the trial (actually a lawsuit by Cecilia and Gary to get their truck back from him), he told his hard-luck story so well, eliciting so much tearful sympathy from Thelma, that they spent the night in bed together comforting each other. Shortly afterward, Thelma moved in with Pratt at his place in Kent, Washington. She soon learned, she told Cooper, that whenever things didn't go well for Pratt (as, for example, when he was incapable of fixing her ailing pickup truck), he got "really angry. . . . He'd just fly off the handle. He'd call me a 'bitch' and 'cunt,' and tell me I could go back to Jamie and Linda's if I wanted to. But then in a span of ten minutes or so, it was over."

In an interview with the Lane County Sheriff's Department in 1980, Thelma Adams provided several vignettes revealing how it was to live with Jesse Pratt:

"Jesse was scheduled to have an operation. He thought it was going to be on his heart. One day, he was asleep and his doctor called. His doctor said no, he wasn't going to do anything to his heart. It was the thing behind it. So I went to tell Jesse that. But Jesse was asleep. So, after he woke up, I told him that Dr. Vogue called and what he said. That made him mad. Jesse was just bound and determined that they was going to do something to his heart.

"He got very upset and he started out of the house, but then he asked me if I wanted to go with him. And then he tells me that he wasn't going to put up with my little 'ruse.' Why didn't I wake him up and tell him what the doctor said? And he calls me a 'bitch' and a 'whore' and 'trash.'" (By now, the two of them were in Pratt's truck.)

"We're roaring down the road—awfully fast. And all of a sudden, he hits the brakes. And here goes the briefcase and my purse—and I grabbed the dashboard so I wouldn't hit the windshield. And he turned around and looked at me funny and said, 'If you want to have this out right here, we will.' And he calls me a 'bitch' and a 'whore' and everything again, and I just sit there. And, finally, I says, 'Jesse, I didn't want to upset you. You was asleep. That's the reason I didn't wake you up.'

"But then we went home and went to bed and made mad, passionate love. In his opinion, it was good. But, all of a sudden, in a state of rage right then, he got very upset with me. He put his hand around my throat, and he said I could just go home."

After that episode, Thelma called her husband back in Missouri, and Charles wired her some money. But "because I didn't think it would be fair to either Chuck or Jesse, I never picked up the money. Sometimes he'd be peaches and cream, and my pickup was tore up, so I stayed with him."

But, when Thelma met some of Jesse's friends, she began to have serious misgivings. When the couple drove to Sacramento, they stayed at the apartment of Martha and Leroy Lantz, who, as it turned out, were dealers in both narcotics and prostitution. Leroy, in fact, had just gotten out of prison.

Martha casually asked Thelma whether she was going to "work" for Jesse—like his wife Nancy had.

"I says, 'Stick it in your ear; I'm not working for nobody!'"

Pratt broached the subject later that night when he and Thelma were watching television.

"There was this prostitute in the story. I made the remark that I didn't see how they could do that if they didn't love somebody. He just went, 'Ha!' And he told me there wasn't nothing to it. It was just a job. He explained about the benefits 'working ladies' had, and he told me he used to have some working ladies in Alaska—and that there was a difference between streetwalkers and private house-girls."

When they returned to Kent, Pratt was no longer indirect about the matter. Thelma had just returned from a job interview with Lorie Barnes and his partner, Roger Burnett, seeking a job at their truck brokerage firm. She got the job.

When she got home, Pratt told her there would be more to the job than office work. He claimed to have talked to her new employers and said Barnes needed someone "to work a couple of clients so he could get a contract." And on evenings when Barnes didn't need her, Thelma could work for *him*. Pratt offered inducements. He would spend $500 on new clothes for Thelma, and he "could make a very nice-looking lady out of you." He would even buy her a white fur.

"'You wouldn't have to be by yourself,'" she quoted him as saying. "'I would be wherever you were at to make sure you were not hurt or anything—and I would call men on it to make sure you was fixed up right. I could buy you a nice apartment pretty close, and I could be selective. You wouldn't have to do this with just anybody, and it wouldn't be like walking the street—taking what was offered to you. You would have a choice in picking. I would also be with you so you wouldn't be hurt.'

"But I kept telling him I just couldn't do this," Thelma said, "because I don't love just everybody. I mean, how was you supposed to go to bed with somebody you didn't love or didn't feel for? And he would say to me, 'Well, it doesn't make any difference. It's just a job.' And then he'd go, 'Well, I'd love you anyway.'

"And I said, 'Well, I can't see how you could love me and ask me to do something like this. I thought if you loved a person, you didn't share it.' And he says, 'Well, I can love you and hold you and take care of you and be your main man—and when you need it, you could come to me.'

"This went on every day, and it would go on for hours at a time. When I got back from my job interview that day, I told him, 'Let's not discuss this anymore. I'm not a working lady and I'm not going to be a working lady. Just forget it!'

"He says, 'Well, even if I would ask you to?' And I said, 'If you love me, you wouldn't ask.'"

What Thelma said she just couldn't understand was that "later that same evening, lying on that fold-out divan we was using for a bed, he said that if I would ever leave him, run away from him, or go to bed with another man, he wouldn't hesitate at all to cut my heart out or blow me away. It would mean nothing to him."

Matters got worse later on that night as Thelma packed a lunch for Jesse while he was getting ready to go to work.

"I was cutting cheese with a wrinkled [serrated edge] knife. I didn't know that was a 'no-no.' He comes off the divan in a rage and calls me a 'bitch' and a 'whore' and all this kind of thing. Then he says, 'You better get out of your damn fucking mood and act right!' And here *he* was, the one upset about my cutting his cheese.

"And so I put the wrinkled knife in the sink and picked up a smaller, straight-edge knife and he says to me, 'Don't even fix me anything to eat!'

"So I just left it. But in a little bit, he picked up a piece. When I started to go back to cut the cheese and finish packing his lunch, he took the wedge of cheese and threw it at me. It missed me and landed in the sink.

"By this time, I was dumbfounded. He goes back to his room and picks up a chair and throws it around. Then he goes out the door and slams it. But then, in a little bit, he comes back and says he wants some supper before he leaves. I fixed it and he ate it—including the sandwiches I had started for his lunch.

"He said he wanted his big butcher knives." (Jesse, Thelma explained, preferred to eat his food with two knives instead of with a fork or a spoon.) "So I took them out of the drawer and handed them to him, and he cut an onion and he also cut the cheese— and then he flopped the knives around real close to my face.

"I sat down after he left and collected my thoughts, and thought how dumb I was. I knew Jesse had a gun. And he'd talked about blowing me away. That's all I could think of.

"I made a phone call to Mr. Barnes. He came and

picked me up in fifteen or twenty minutes. We packed up my things and he took me to a small motel room in Renton, Washington, where we stayed maybe an hour. I took a shower and changed my clothes and then we went out to a Jack in the Box and got a sandwich."

It was then that Thelma learned for the first time that she had been offered a legitimate office job after all. Jesse's line about related prostitution was simply not true. The following morning, Barnes's partner, Burnett, proposed that Thelma come live temporarily with him and his wife and children. And, if she wished, they could send her away for a time if Pratt pursued her. She liked the idea and later accepted Burnett's offer.

"Before I left," Thelma explained, "I wrote a letter to Jesse. In it, I told him that he had killed my love and I am not taking his being mad and yelling at me all the time, and I just couldn't live with that."

Thelma's departure did not sit well with Jesse Pratt. On July 13, 1980, she telephoned the Tukwila police to report that Pratt had been harassing her at the brokerage office. The police went to see him, and warned him, and with the cooperation of Barnes and Burnett, they got a court order directing him to stay away from Thelma's place of employment and restraining him from having any contact with her.

On the evening of July 20, 1980, Jesse Pratt hailed a taxi. Sitting in the right front seat, he ordered the driver to go past the Burnett residence on Southwest 306th Street.

Sitting in the front seat, Pratt casually asked the

driver where he could get a gun. The driver told him he didn't know. As they passed the Burnett residence, Pratt suddenly ducked down under the taxi's dashboard, explaining that he was "spying on a blond woman." Noting the address, the taxi driver elected to get involved. After finding out who lived at the address the next morning, he drove his cab to the L.A. Barnes office, found Thelma, and told her what had happened the night before. She called the police.

The police tried unsuccessfully to locate Pratt. He had disappeared.

TWELVE

You don't want to make me mad. I'm the closest thing to the Devil you'll ever see.

— Jesse Clarence Pratt

It was in late July 1980, in a cellblock in the Rio Cosumnes Correctional Center at Elk Grove, California, that a convict by the name of David Whaley received a scribbled note from another inmate. It read, "Job with Jesse Pratt in Seattle." Whaley was due for release at the end of the month.

Whaley made a phone call. The job, it seemed, was a simple one. He was "to beat up a guy," for which he would "receive $3,000."

Upon his release, using a prepaid United Airlines ticket he had received at the prison, Whaley flew to Seattle and was met at the Sea-Tac International Airport by Jesse Clarence Pratt. He arrived on August 3.

As they drove out of the airport parking lot, Pratt opened his glove box, silently pointing to a handgun lying inside. Before taking Whaley to the place where he was now staying in Puyallup, Washington, Pratt drove by the L.A. Barnes Truck Brokerage in Tukwila.

On Tuesday afternoon, August 5, the pair pulled into the L.A. Barnes parking lot in a blue station wagon. David Whaley walked into the building with a jacket over his arm, concealing the pistol. There were four people in the offices at the time: Lorie Barnes, Linda Barnes, Roger Burnett, and Thelma Adams. Spotting Thelma as the receptionist, Whaley casually asked her a question about the business.

At that point, Jesse Pratt walked through the door. Noting Thelma's alarm, Whaley removed the coat from his arm, exposing the handgun. Pratt took it from him and pointed it at Burnett, who stood up at another desk when he saw what was going on.

Pratt told Burnett to keep his hands on the desk. He then herded everyone but Thelma from the front room into Barnes's back office, ordering them to turn their backs and to place their hands behind them. With the gun on them, they complied.

Producing a roll of duct tape, Pratt and Whaley bound the hands and feet of each of their prisoners, put gags into their mouths, and taped the gags in place, passing the gun back and forth between them. They pulled wallets out of the pockets of the two men. It was a little after 2:00 P.M.

Someone rattled the locked door. Dispatcher Geoffrey Valentine was trying to get back into the office. Rattling the door again, he managed to open it—and was confronted by Whaley with the drawn gun. Whaley motioned him inside and closed the door, revealing Pratt standing behind it with his hand over Thelma's mouth.

Pratt ordered Valentine into the back room where the others lay, and told him to lie down on the floor. He pulled off the man's boots and taped his feet together.

"Don't remember me, or I'll be back," he warned.

The two men left with Thelma.

Valentine was able to free himself in a few minutes and untied the others. They called the police.

After obtaining a search warrant, the Tukwila police went to Pratt's apartment, where they seized a number of documents, including his telephone bill showing calls to Elk Grove, California, and a note with Whaley's name and the United Airlines flight number. They also found an envelope containing a letter with the return address of Leroy Lantz of Georgetown, California. The Tukwila, Washington, police notified law enforcement agencies in both Oregon and California.

Thelma Adams picked up the story in a detailed statement she recorded on August 7, 1980, at the Tukwila Police Department:

"On August fifth, a Mexican male, I'd say about five feet six, black hair with no part, one hundred fifty pounds, wearing jeans and a cotton pullover, came into the office carrying a tan leather coat. He stood in front of my desk and asked something about a southbound load. He said his name was 'Bill.' I had the name Bill written on my scratch pad, so he may have gotten it off there.

"I started going to the back office, and the Mexican said, 'I need to talk to you.'

"When I turned around, the guy was holding a long-barreled, large-caliber gun. It had been covered by his coat. He told me not to do anything stupid—

and he smiled. He wanted to know how many people were in the office and where they were.

"Jesse then came through the door. I didn't say a word. Everybody got up and we walked into Roger's and Lorie's office. The Mexican told me to close the blinds. Then he told everybody to turn around and close their eyes—and he told everybody, again, not to do anything stupid.

"Jesse taped everybody up and placed them on the floor. Roger was first, Linda next, and then Lorie. He gagged everybody also. He took off the guys' boots.

"Roger asked Jesse if he was going to kill everybody. Jesse said he was going to put me on a plane and send me home. Jesse went through Mr. Barnes's wallet and called him a 'broke son of a bitch.' The Mexican took fifteen dollars from Roger's desk.

"During the time Jesse was gagging everybody, the Mexican asked if I was expecting anybody else. I told him a guy was out there changing tires.

"When the Mexican got through taping, Geoffrey came back, and they were waiting for him when he walked in. When Geoffrey knocked on the door, Jesse unlocked it, keeping me behind it.

"The door opened, the Mexican put the gun to Jeff's head and made him go into the back office. Jesse taped and gagged Jeff. The Mexican asked if I had anything to get, and Jesse asked where my purse was. I picked up my purse and was again told not to do anything stupid.

"Jesse put his hand around my neck with a lot of pressure and commented not to do anything stupid or I'd get blown away. The Mexican said I should 'act normal' when we left. 'Smile.' Jesse had ahold of my neck from the back, and the Mexican was walking behind me with the gun.

"We walked around to the back of the building, where we got into Jesse's blue station wagon. Again I was told to smile. Jesse drove—me in the middle and the Mexican on the passenger side.

"We turned left on Strander and got on I-5, southbound. The Mexican unloaded the gun and put it in the glove box. The Mexican also took the ten-dollar bill out of my purse, telling me I wouldn't need it. We drove to Federal Way, the Evergreen truck stop, and pulled in behind the Plymouth that was parked there.

"The Mexican reloaded the gun and told me not to do anything stupid. Jesse and I got out and got into the Plymouth. He held my hand.

"During the ride on I-5 to the truck stop, Jesse said he was taking me to meet Chuck. There were also comments made by the Mexican about my looks, the size of my breasts, and so forth. The Mexican fondled my breasts and rubbed my vagina through my pants. The Mexican took my hand and placed it on the crotch of his pants.

"I asked Jesse if that's what he wanted, and Jesse said, 'Do what the man tells you.'

"We left the truck stop with the Mexican driving the blue car in the lead. Jesse and I were in the Plymouth. Jesse turned on the CB to Channel 19 and said, 'Don't do anything foolish. Gene [David Whaley, Thelma's 'Mexican'] still has a gun.'

"When we left the truck stop, Jesse called me a 'lying cunt' and accused me of sleeping with my husband while I went home. He hit me in the face and accused me of sleeping with Roger. There was two other times in the car that I was slapped, but I don't recall what led up to these.

"Jesse told me that we should sit down and talk about our problems and that I shouldn't run from him. Jesse then hit me with his elbow in the chest. It stunned me. He said, 'Talk to me, bitch!'

"I said, 'I was just listening.' He pulled out a pocketknife, put it under his left leg, and said if anything happened, he would gut me. Jesse explained to me what kidnapping was, and he knew that was what he was doing. He said if we got stopped to say nothing was wrong. He said this several times.

"A lot of the conversation was Jesse stating we would get back together and do things his way—coming back in a couple of days and starting over and getting me an apartment. Throughout the trip to Eugene, I was continually told not to do anything stupid or I'd be blown away. Jesse said he knew where I'd been and what I'd done these last two weeks.

"We arrived in Eugene after seven P.M. but before eight P.M. Prior to that, we stopped at a rest station. Jesse took me into the stall with him while I went to the bathroom. And then he went while still holding my hand.

The blue station wagon now followed us. We pulled into the Country Squire Motel and checked into rooms one twenty-nine and one thirty. The doors were locked and the drapes were pulled. Jesse told me to leave the bathroom door open.

"He started talking about running away from problems, and Jesse accused me of calling him 'Chuck.' Jesse struck me twice in the face, and then a third time pertaining to the same thing. He called me 'bitch' and struck me again. Jesse wanted me to work as a prostitute. Reno was mentioned. I told him I didn't want to.

"Jesse told me he thought I ought to see a psychiatrist, and I agreed. He told me he loved me—wanted me—couldn't live without me. I played along with him so he wouldn't hurt me. I told him to hold me, which he did.

"Jesse told me that 'Gene' was coming over in a bit and Jesse wanted me to go to bed with him. I said, 'I don't love him.' Jesse said, 'Do it anyway.'

"Gene came in and told Jesse the gun was loaded and ready to go. Jesse forced me to have sex with Gene. The loaded gun was now there on the nightstand, and I was very scared that either of them would use the gun.

"After that, I took a shower, and then Jesse and I talked. After a couple of hours, Jesse wanted to have sex. Again the gun was moved to the nightstand, where it was very accessible. Jesse made me stay in bed with him, and if I moved a little, he would squeeze me around the neck or other body parts. Neither of us slept.

"In the morning, about seven-thirty A.M., he wanted me to play with him. Later in the morning, about half an hour later, Jesse wanted to have intercourse again. Again the gun was on the nightstand. Jesse fell asleep, but I didn't want to try to get away because of the way he had ahold of me.

"About eleven o'clock, he woke up. He still wanted to make things work—even to the point of wanting to get married in Reno. Before leaving, he put the gun in his suitcase, I think, as I was getting up to go to the bathroom.

"About eleven fifty-five that morning we went to

the restaurant and ordered breakfast. As we were going in, I seen two women entering the rest room. I told Jesse I was sick and going to throw up, and to come to the women's bathroom door and wait, which he did.

"When I entered, all the stalls were full. Pretty soon a little girl came out. I told her I wanted to talk to someone else—older. Finally, an older woman, her mother, came out.

"I touched her, handed her the [Barnes] company business card, whispered to her that I'd been kidnapped from Washington State and to call the owner of the business.

"The woman had a foreign accent, but I thought she understood. She took the card and put it in her daughter's purse. She said she would call, but not from here. Then she repeated, 'Thelma, room number 129.'

"No sooner had she done this when Jesse came through the door and asked me if I was all right. He grabbed me by the arm and took me back to the table. I don't think Jesse knew that I'd talked with the woman. We ate and went back to the room. I wasn't feeling well, and we sat and laid on the bed, and watched TV for a while. Jesse said he would have to call Reno because people there were waiting for him or expecting him. I told Jesse before he went to sleep that if I didn't feel better, I wanted to go to the lobby and get some aspirin.

"We got up, got dressed, left the room to go to the lobby to get some aspirin or Rolaids. I'd decided to get him outside so I could run away from him if I had to.

"There were a few people in the lobby as we walked in. I walked up to the medicine counter.

"A man walked up to Pratt, grabbed him by the neck, stuck a gun to the side of his head and identified himself as a police officer.

"I was pushed into a room. I was later taken to the police department by Officer Jim Walcott, where I gave him a taped statement."

THIRTEEN

RASHOMON (1950-Japanese) 88m.
**** . . . *Superlative study of truth and human nature; four people involved in a rape-murder tell varying accounts of what happened.*
 —Film critic Leonard Maltin

After having his Miranda rights read to him at the Eugene police station, Jesse Pratt was invited to tell the officers what happened. His story was at variance with that of Thelma Adams.

"I decided that I needed to see Thelma to talk to her. Now, I went into the office with a friend. I took Thelma out of the office.

"I tied Mr. Barnes and Roger and Linda. I tied them up so that way they aren't—nobody would get hurt—there was no sense in anybody getting hurt over this.

"When I took and put Thelma in my car and brought her down here, now, I told her coming down that if she wanted to go home, that she had the free right. I told her that anytime she wanted to go home, I'd let her go or I would take her. And I took her against her will because if I didn't—if I went in there by myself—that she wouldn't come out and talk to me. And the love between her and me had to be brought out so we knew what was going to happen.

"And so I brought her down here. She was no way—she was no way hurt. I took her to the hotel room, and we sat there and we talked for about three hours last night, and this morning, too. We talked about getting married the last of the month, and we pretty well had our differences straightened out between us.

"The reason that I didn't push the issue about us leaving today is that I didn't want no officer to stop us on the road and have her or anybody else get hurt." Pratt's interviewer challenged his claim that he didn't want anyone to get hurt.

"As far as I'm concerned, and pardon my French on this, but that's bullshit," Pratt responded. "There was no harm intended on my part to hurt anybody in the office up there. Now, I know there's hard feelings over it—which I really can't blame them. And I—if she wants to go back up there now, she can. She's got the right to take the car and, you know, I'll give her the keys and stuff; and you guys and she can drive my car back and give her a hundred dollars to go back on. But my main concern is that she's all right.

"And I know that Mr. Barnes is probably mad about what happened and I really can't blame him."

Pratt was asked whether he had taken anything from the L.A. Barnes office, or from the personnel there.

"No. I deliberately did take and look at both of their wallets to see if they had any money. They go around acting like they always got—like some kind of million-dollar people. Their attitudes and stuff since Mr. Barnes got his office going—the man is completely changed. Before, you could talk to him. And he would sit down and talk to you just like you and I are. But since he got his office now and everything, the man's completely changed. But that's—as far as anything taken out of the office, *no.* There was nothing taken."

Pratt was asked why, if he had meant no harm and didn't want to see anyone get hurt, he had brought a gun.

"Okay, the reason that my pistol was involved is because if I went in there to see Thelma and wanted to take her out of the office and talk to her, I was afraid that Roger would pull his gun and somebody would get hurt. Okay, now, Roger, as I told you, has pulled his gun on me before. I knew he had one with him, so we walked in there at gunpoint 'cause I didn't want anybody to get hurt.

"I took 'em. I laid 'em out on the floor real good. We didn't force them. I mean, we didn't hit 'em or anything like that."

The interview went on for some time. Skipping ahead to the events that later transpired in the Country Squire Motel, Pratt was finally asked, point-blank, "Did you rape Thelma?"

"No. Nobody did."

"Okay, did you have sexual intercourse with Thelma?"

"Yeah."

"She consented to that?"

"Yeah."

"Why?"

Pratt's rambling response replayed most of the

topics he claimed they had talked about during the evening at the motel.

"We made love to each other," he finally concluded, "and we talked about what we were going to do about our future. We talked about us going to get married the first of next month—and that, you know, just basically *us* and how my feelings were toward her and how her feelings were toward me. And we both sat there and talked to each other like we've always. We've always talked to each other. And I told her, 'Now, you're sure this is what you want to do?' I says, 'If you want to go home, you can go home.' And she said no, she didn't want to go home."

The jury didn't buy it when Pratt's case came to trial. He was charged only with kidnapping, since the rape had occurred in Oregon. It was the responsibility of Lane County, Oregon, to pursue the rape charge, but Lane County never followed up.

Sentenced to ten years in prison, Jesse Clarence Pratt became Inmate #274387 at the Washington State Penitentiary in Walla Walla on March 20, 1981. He would be released in 1984 after serving only thirty-nine months.

FOURTEEN

sadism n. [Fr., after marquis de SADE] 1. the getting of sexual pleasure from dominating, mistreating or hurting one's partner. 2. the getting of pleasure from inflicting physical or psychological pain on another or others
                    —Webster's New World Dictionary

Thelma Adams was by no means the only abused woman Ken Cooper would find during his investigation. He managed to persuade nearly all of them to come forward as character witnesses—often having to promise that the location of the woman's home would be kept secret. Before Jesse Pratt's trial began, Cooper would have traveled to Louisiana, Alabama, Missouri, California, Washington, Oregon, and Alaska, interviewing former wives, girlfriends, and family members.

Their stories were very similar. When he first met an impressionable woman, Jesse Pratt would manage to con her—coming off as this rich, charismatic, macho, big-time trucker from Alaska who owned land in that state, and whose truck fleet regularly scheduled runs from Fairbanks and Anchorage all the way to southern California. By the time they discovered he was really a cruel, sleazy, small-time, self-centered deadbeat, most of them had been humiliated, slapped, punched, choked, and scared to death.

Sometimes Pratt struck the children of his wives and girlfriends or tore up their toys. He threatened mothers with rape of their daughters, and he is on record as fondling one eleven-year-old girl—whose head he had earlier shoved into a metal bathtub faucet because she was not cleaning the bathroom properly. The same child told of seeing Pratt throw a fork at her mother with such force that it stuck in her arm, the tines buried in the woman's shoulder.

Paradoxically, although he sold one of his wives to a pimp for $1,000 dollars, and tried to persuade most of his girlfriends to earn money for him as "working ladies," Pratt made it clear that he hated prostitutes.

"They're not fit to walk the face of the earth and should all be in hell," he was quoted as saying.

Sadly, and amazingly, although a number of Pratt's women left him after being repeatedly beaten, he somehow managed to persuade most of them to come back to him—sometimes more than once. His first wife, Linda, who married Jesse when she was sixteen, walked out on him eight times.

In October 1987, three months before Jesse Pratt's trial was to begin, Ken Cooper interviewed Pratt's half sister Cecilia. Because she had gone to great pains to keep her address a secret, Cooper had asked the assistance of a local police officer in her town. When Sergeant Rasmussen went to see her, identifying himself as a police officer, Cecilia panicked. As she later explained to him, she had lived for years with the fear that a policeman would come to her door to tell her that her brother had killed their mother.

Cecilia was two years younger than her brother, "Clarence," as she called him. When his father, Jesse Clarence Pratt Sr., failed to return from World War II, their mother had remarried, and Cecilia was born during that second marriage. When that marriage ended in divorce, the children were separated. She and her sister, Judy, were raised by their father; Clarence lived with Elizabeth, their mother. Cecilia was seven years old at the time of this separation, and Clarence was nine. As she remembered her brother then, there was never any mean streak in him. She even recalled having good times together playing hide-and-seek.

Sister and brother didn't see each other for the next ten years, although Cecilia sometimes talked to him on the telephone. When Cecilia did, he often talked about their someday looking up his other half sister, Judy, and reuniting the family.

Sharing such a goal when she turned seventeen, Cecilia traveled from Oregon to Anchorage on her own to find her nineteen-year-old brother—hoping it would be a surprise and a happy reunion.

Cecilia waited for Jesse on his front porch and identified herself when he finally showed up.

"As far as I'm concerned you're dead—or should be dead," he blurted as he brushed past her and slammed the door behind him.

"It really hurt me. Before I left Alaska, I went back to see Jesse to ask him, 'What's the problem?' And he was a totally different person. He was glad to see me. He never said he was sorry for saying that, but he didn't want to talk about it."

Cecilia didn't see her brother again until he was thirty-two years old, when he came down to Oregon to talk her and her husband, Gary, out of their Freightliner.

Cooper asked about their efforts to recover the truck.

"I'm gonna leave out all his dirty mouth," Cecilia said, "but he was gonna take me over in the field and beat me to a bloody pulp, and he didn't care if the cops were there. His main threat was 'I'm coming down there—or maybe for fifty dollars I'm gonna have one of my buddies come down there. *You* don't know which.'

"First of all, he was going to kill the kids in front of me; then he was going to kill Mom. Then [he] was going to have 'fun' with me before he killed me. Sometimes he'd go into more detail. Sometimes he was gonna 'play with' the kids before he killed 'em. If you've talked to Clarence, you know he's got a dirty, vulgar, filthy mouth, so you can imagine the words that he used. I'm not even going to repeat 'em, but if you've talked to him, you know how he would describe what he was going to do.

"His threats were so often and so strong that I even practiced with my kids. I told them if they saw him or someone we didn't know—out on our property or behind the animal pens—to *hide*. And we practiced that drill. That's how terrified I was."

Cecilia said that she knew she had committed the unpardonable by confronting her brother on the issue of the truck instead of being cowed by him.

And she had concealed her whereabouts from him ever since.

Jesse's sister Cecilia offered an opinion about the death of Carrie Love:

"I'd say there's no way that anyone could convince me that this is the first girl that he's killed. And the way he talks, it's not like Clarence would enjoy just shooting somebody. Clarence would have to do something ugly first."

"Like what?" Cooper asked.

"If it was a female, he would probably viciously rape. And he would enjoy as much pain as he could inflict. That's just the way he is. If the facts are proven that he committed this crime, I think he should get the chair. I know that probably sounds awful since he's my half brother, but the way the laws are, just locking him up—in five years maybe he'll get out. He's a perfect example of someone that can *not* be rehabilitated. I'd like to see him get the chair."

Cooper asked her about their childhood—specifically about Jesse Pratt's claims that he was raised in an atmosphere of drugs and prostitution, that his mother physically abused him, and that he was sexually assaulted many times by his stepfathers. Cecilia insisted he made up all this stuff to gain sympathy from defense lawyers, psychologists, and juries.

"Remember," she reminded him, "I had the same mother."

Sure, it was true that her mother had a number of husbands, Cecilia admitted, but she had only one divorce. Jesse's father failed to return from World War II, one husband died in an auto accident, another died from cancer, and an army retiree, unable to adapt to civilian life, committed suicide. Some of Jesse's stepfathers were distant. Others lavished affection on him. But none, she was certain, ever did anything improper to the boy.

Cecilia confirmed that "when we lived in Valdese, [Alaska], Clarence had a prostitution house, and he had some girls at the Forty-niner Truck Stop out of Sacramento. A lot of drivers were being clubbed on the head. And that was Clarence that was doing that. And he ran drugs. In Alaska, the drivers didn't want anything to do with him.

"But whenever he got into trouble and went to jail," Cecilia said, "he would become a model prisoner, building up brownie points with everybody, while at the same time he was making money running drugs, selling them in jail and laughing about it.

"Clarence is really good at conning people. He really knows how to 'play' our mom. Whenever he gets in trouble, he always calls her collect from jail. And it's 'Oh, woe is me and they're framing me. And I didn't do this. I'm innocent. Everybody's against me, and you're the only one that'll help me.'"

Her brother had, in fact, called their mother from the Klamath County Jail, Cecilia said, but "when he realized that she wasn't going to lie for him, he blew it. He started threatening her and ranting and raving and cussing at her. You just can't *believe* how he talks. And she told him at that point that she would accept no more collect calls."

Cecilia was now worried about her mother's safety, she said.

"He has threatened my family to the point where if he knew I was talking to you, he would come unglued. He's gonna absolutely flip his dipper."

***

Cooper left for Alaska the next day. In Kenai, he met Elizabeth Kathleen Helle, mother of Cecilia, Judy, and Jesse. It was really too bad about Jesse's father, she told Cooper. He was a really good mechanic, but he was deathly afraid of guns. "And when he was drafted in World War II, he begged to be put in the mechanical part of it. But the army put him in the Infantry. And he died on the battlefield in Germany."

Young Jesse never finished high school, Helle said. He quit when he was about sixteen, never having learned to read. She had asked the principal in grade school to hold him back until he learned how to read, but "they just passed him along." Jesse lived with her until he was eighteen or nineteen, she said.

Cooper asked about his childhood.

"He was a very compassionate boy," his mother said. "He didn't want to see me sick; he never forgot my birthday. He never forgot Mother's Day—there was always a box of candy. He was a very considerate, very compassionate person. He couldn't see animals or anything hurt.

"He always found himself a job, and he worked. He'd come home at night happy-go-lucky. I came home one night—he worked for a chicken farm then—and he had a sick chicken for me. Another time he brought home this puppy with a bottle of milk for me to raise this day-old puppy because the mother had been killed. He brought home a cat that the dogs had got ahold of for me to nurse back to health.

"These terrible cusswords, these four-letter words that he uses all the time now, he couldn't stand anybody to say that in front of me years ago. If somebody used a word like that in front of me, he jumped right up and informed them that I was his mother and they weren't to talk that way."

Elizabeth described her son's concern for her during the 1964 Alaskan earthquake. By then, she was assistant field director for the Red Cross at Elmendorf Air Force Base. She was making a list of earthquake casualties when Clarence showed up with tears in his eyes, she said. "He put his arms around me, wanted to know how Don [Elizabeth's husband] was, to make sure we were both fine." He would have been twenty years old at the time.

After Jesse married Linda, they moved to Anchorage, Elizabeth said. One of his first jobs in that city was with a house-moving company. He got along well with the owners and they liked him. One day, when one of the jacks fell, he suffered a broken leg. While he was recuperating in a cast, the business was sold. It was during this same period that Jesse's son was born to Linda. When he returned to work, he found he didn't get along with the new owners and he abruptly quit.

"That was when he started driving trucks. And it was at that point that he started turning bad. He come down here and he'd demand money. If there was no one around, he'd push me, shove me, hit at me. I got a place on my arm where he had hit me and it still hasn't healed right.

"I discovered he was going around with different people, including colored people, and he just started changing. That was when he started beating his wife.

I got a call from Linda one day and she was crying. I went to Anchorage to see her and she was all black and blue. She just wanted to go home to her parents, so I bought her a plane ticket and helped her get on the plane with the baby.

"After Clarence was arrested a couple of times, I didn't see much of him, except when all of a sudden he'd show up on my doorstep." These surprise visits were always accompanied by demands for money. At one point, he wanted her to buy him a truck—not a pickup, but an eighteen-wheeler.

When she explained that she simply didn't have the money, "he'd get mad, he'd cuss, and then the next thing I knew, he'd start pounding on me or shove me up against the wall. He never would do this when there was anybody else around. And as soon as anybody'd show up, then he'd calm back down again. But he, in his mind, started 'weaving'—going somewhere in his mind. I don't know; his eyes would even be strange. He wasn't the boy that I had known before. He had totally changed."

Helle confirmed that she had accepted telephone calls from her son while he was in jail. When he was in Walla Walla, she accepted nearly five hundred dollars' worth of collect calls from him. She also sent him money and such packages as were permitted.

When she began to feel guilty about what had become of her son and had difficulty sleeping, her daughter Judy took her to their minister for counseling and also to a psychiatrist.

"It was just a one-visit thing. The psychiatrist told me that after they get grown up, you have no control over them—that I was just gonna have to try to put it out of my mind.

"The last time I talked to Clarence, I told him *he* had some serious problems and he should go try to find a counselor. And he started on those four-letter words and I hung up on him and I wouldn't take any more calls. I wrote him a long letter explaining that if he would straighten himself up, I would agree to talk to him again."

Despite what she had said, Helle had relented when Pratt called from the Klamath County Jail. He was well behaved, she said, during the first of these calls.

"There were no four-letter words, no swear words." But when she told him she couldn't come down and testify that he was "an upright citizen who owned a trucking company in Alaska"—because it wasn't true—his attitude changed.

"He says, 'If you don't come down and testify for me, I will have you killed. I have people that I can contact. All I have to do is pick up the phone and I can have you killed.'"

Like her daughter Cecilia, Elizabeth said she now lived in fear of her life. She had put dead bolts on her doors. When her friends dropped her off, they would wait in their cars until she had turned on the interior lights before they drove away. When a car pulled into her driveway at night, she said, it was a terrifying experience. She had actually been to a lawyer, telling him that if she died under suspicious circumstances, that her son should be the first suspect investigated.

Cooper asked her to repeat what she had said earlier.

"He flat out told me if he couldn't do it himself, he

would have me killed. I was nothing but a . . . I don't want to say it. I was nothing but a 'fucking, no-good bitch.' It was very hard to take. It hurts terrible."

What else hurt, she said, was when she learned that Jesse was now denying that she was his mother. He was claiming he had been adopted, that he had been raised in a filthy environment, that he had been sexually abused, and that his mother was a prostitute and a drug addict.

"Still, he *is* my son. I tell you, it would have been a lot easier if I had gotten word that he had been killed. If I had gotten a phone call and they said he was in a truck accident and he had been killed, I could have coped with that. But this . . ."

Elizabeth Helle agreed to fly down to Klamath Falls to testify in her son's trial—for the prosecution.

PART THREE

FIFTEEN

*Mr. Pratt, as the evidence will show, is not a
particularly nice individual. His vocabulary is
foul and vulgar. He is not the sort of person you
would want to invite home to dinner to meet your
family. But that is not what he is on trial for. He is
on trial for murder, and his personality is not, or
should not be, an issue.*

—Defense Counsel Peter Richard

Although Jesse Clarence Pratt's trial for the murder of Carrie Love was originally scheduled to begin on December 2, 1986, more than a year would elapse before it actually got under way. Part of the delay was due to a series of motions filed by his initial defense counsel, Klamath Falls attorney Enver Bozgoz. The first of these motions sought a continuance on the contention that Pratt had been deprived of a preliminary hearing before being indicted on two counts of aggravated murder. If a postindictment preliminary hearing could not be granted, the defense counsel moved that the two charges against his client be dismissed.

Bozgoz filed other motions. Each erected another legal obstacle that temporarily postponed the inevitable, but the additional time would be useful in preparing the defense's case. And, in the meantime, newspaper coverage in Klamath Falls, Seattle, and Spokane could be expected to subside.

The court-appointed defense attorney's vigorous defense of Jesse Pratt was not a surprise. Oregon's laws are designed to avoid the stereotypical inexperienced or incompetent public defender that is occasionally portrayed on television. Law firms that meet the rigid qualifications prescribed by the state are retained on contract, assuring that indigent clients get a fair shake. Bozgoz seemed dedicated to that end.

An extended delay ensued when the defense asked for time to repeat all of the forensic testing that had originally been conducted by the Oregon State Crime Laboratory, using independent experts hired by the defense—at additional state expense.

There were several "omnibus" pretrial sessions in 1987, as well as hearings for "motions in limine" (motions to limit testimony), during which Jesse Pratt appeared in the courtroom in shackles and jail garb. By this time, for unknown reasons, Bozgoz had resigned from the case, and Klamath Falls attorneys Peter Richard and Myron Gitnes had been appointed in his place. Richard had once been senior deputy district attorney for Klamath County. He had run at the time for the office of district attorney and lost—after which he had gone into private law practice and was now representing some of the criminal defendants he might otherwise have prosecuted.

The defense counsels had been busy. Sticking to the alibi he had repeatedly planted in the minds of the police, as well as that of his loyal employee, Mona Bennett, Pratt told his lawyers that he had dropped off Carrie Love at My Place Tavern near the Seattle-Tacoma International Airport the afternoon of June 16, after she decided she preferred to fly to Los Angeles. And that was the last he had seen of her.

So, just as Ken Cooper had done, Richard and Gitnes drove to Seattle and retraced their client's tracks over the route he claimed to have taken. Under the rules of discovery, they also had access to all of the state's evidence, including the contents of the black briefcase, as well as what the prosecution had learned as a result of its investigation.

When Richard and Gitnes interviewed young Jeff Warren at Redd's Tire Service in Woodland, Washington, they confirmed Cooper's findings: Carrie Love was still in the truck when Pratt headed across the Oregon border.

Returning to the Klamath Falls Jail, the defense lawyers had a heart-to-heart talk with their client. Never at a loss for creating a new alibi, Pratt told them what he now said "really" happened: He and Carrie had argued over what he claimed was some missing company money after she cashed a check at the bank that morning. Angrily, he had shoved her out of the truck on Highway 58, north of Chemult, and threw her things after her. And that's the last he had seen of her. The defense lawyers were now stuck with their client's new story as they headed into the trial.

On Monday, January 11, 1988, the case was finally called, and the trial got under way in the brick-and-limestone Klamath County Courthouse—a modified Greek revival structure at 316 Main Street in Klamath

Falls, a town of 17,700 at the southern tip of Upper Klamath Lake. The criminal trial would be conducted in the courtroom of the Honorable Donald A. W. Piper. The sixty-six-year-old circuit judge had recently been honored at a ceremony celebrating his twenty-fifth year on the bench.

Appointed by District Attorney Ed Caleb, the prosecution team was headed by Senior Administrator/Deputy District Attorney Roxanne Osborne, a thirty-four-year-old Klamath Falls native, a graduate of Oregon State University Law School who was active in community affairs, and had recently returned from Lagos, Nigeria, under a cultural exchange program sponsored by Rotary International.

Deputy District Attorney Bob Foltyn would assist Osborne. Early in the trial, Osborne would receive Judge Piper's permission to seat Detective Ken Cooper at the prosecution table as an additional cocounsel.

Because the charges against Jesse Pratt carried a potential death sentence, jury selection was a slow, painstaking process in which some fifty potential jurors were interviewed by both the prosecution and defense lawyers. In Oregon, criminal trials involving a possible death penalty consist of an initial "guilt phase," followed by a separate "penalty phase." If Jesse Pratt should be found guilty of aggravated murder, the same jury would then be required to make the decision as to whether his sentence should be life in prison or death by lethal injection.

Jurors' individual attitudes about Oregon's recently reestablished death penalty were, therefore, of considerable importance to both sides. Two weeks would elapse before this voir dire process was complete and a jury of eight women and four men, plus two alternate jurors, was impaneled. Jesse Pratt, no longer in shackles, sat through the process, his eyes hidden behind large, tinted glasses. At six feet two and weighing 230 pounds, he was both taller and substantially heavier than the sheriff's deputies who brought him in each day. His hair, beard, and mustache had been trimmed a bit, but they could hardly be described as neat. Above the tinted glasses, rope-like strands of matted hair fell forward over the naked scalp exposed by his receding hairline.

Pratt's lawyers had bought him a brown corduroy jacket, which he wore every day throughout the trial, over either the single white shirt or the other (green) shirt he had also been given. His shirts were unbuttoned at the neck, revealing a white T-shirt underneath. The defendant's substantial stomach prevented his buttoning the jacket. A low-slung belt on his pants supported the paunch—after the manner of a stereotypical Texas sheriff in a B-grade western movie. The defendant was also wearing black tooled-leather Durango boots. According to all who knew him, Jesse was never seen without his cowboy boots.

The scene was a high-ceilinged courtroom with two-story wood-paneled walls and an elevated judge's bench and witness stand. The latter was so high that each witness had to walk up five steps to the witness chair, which was situated on the judge's right. The witness-box, thus, overlooked the jury.

Near the front of the spectators' gallery sat Carrie's mother, Connie Love, accompanied by Charlene Divine, coordinator for the Klamath

County District Attorney's Victim Assistance Services. The pair would be seen together in almost the same spot every day of the trial.

Sitting under the great seal of the state of Oregon, flanked by U.S. and Oregon flags, Judge Piper instructed the jury members at length. Tall, balding, and wearing black horn-rim glasses, he was an imposing figure. The judge would permit the jury to take notes, he said, but he cautioned that they should not allow their note taking to interfere with their ability to observe, listen, and evaluate. Their notes were to be left in the courtroom each night. During the trial, they were not to discuss the case with anyone, including one another.

In her opening statement, prosecuting attorney Roxanne Osborne told the jury who would be called as witnesses and what she expected their testimony to prove—emphasizing the forensic details to be presented by Dr. Robert Jamison, Lieutenant Michael Howard, and criminalist Larry Dickenson.

Reporting on the opening session of the trial, staff writer Doug Higgs of the *Klamath Falls Herald and News* picked up on a part of the prosecutor's opening statement that would become a major issue in the trial's outcome:

> Osborne said she intended to call as a witness a woman who had "a brief relationship" with Pratt in 1980. However, when the woman attempted to break off with Pratt, he abducted her and took her from Seattle to Eugene, Oregon, where he had "forcible intercourse" with her and compelled her to have intercourse

with another man, the woman would testify,
according to Osborne.

This, obviously, was to be Thelma Adams's story.
The defense got off to a bad start. Defense counsel
Peter Richard's opening statement was interrupted
by an objection from prosecutor Osborne, who
claimed that Richard "was going into argument and
even testifying, making statements well beyond what
is permitted in opening remarks." Judge Piper sustained her objection and Richard started over.

This time Pratt's defense counsel began by telling
the jury that because his client "was not a particularly nice individual," the investigation of the case
by the Oregon State Police had been biased. Instead of attempting to learn the truth, the police
set out single-mindedly to incriminate Pratt because of their unfair, prejudiced, preconceived
notion that he was the culprit—a not unfamiliar defense strategy.

After the lawyers' opening statements, the first
witness called by the prosecution was Bruce Mc-
Donald. He testified to finding the sleeping bag
and pillowcase in the ditch beside the road about
10:00 A.M. on June 17, 1986, and that he had put
the pillowcase in a wooden box behind the cab of
his Toyota pickup. He also described his meeting
with investigating officers the next day and his unsuccessful attempts to help them locate the exact
spot where he had found the evidence.

When it was the defense's turn, McDonald was
first asked about the jeeplike vehicle abandoned in
the area—the International Scout with California
license plates. The defense would later suggest that

its driver might have been the killer. In fact, they would establish that red stains had been found on the floor of the vehicle.

When assistant defense counsel Gitnes attempted to challenge the accuracy of his recollections, McDonald, a practical man devoid of pretense, quickly grew impatient with court protocol.

"How do you know it was ten o'clock in the morning?" Gitnes asked.

"Because I knew what time I left."

"What time did you leave?"

"I left Chemult about nine-thirty. I had breakfast down there."

"And you had breakfast where?"

"The Chalet."

"How do you know you left at nine-thirty? Did you look at a clock? Did you look at your watch?"

"Like I said, I had my watch on."

"Well, you looked at it then?"

"Yes."

"And it takes about half an hour to where you saw the sleeping bag?"

"Yes."

"And you were traveling at the speed limit? Fifty-five?"

"This is ridiculous. Yes!"

"What's ridiculous, sir?"

"All these stupid questions! I'm not gonna tell you I'm driving ninety miles an hour."

"Well, I want you to tell me the truth, sir."

"Well, I *am* telling you the truth!"

"I am trying to find out if you were traveling at fifty miles an hour so I can figure out how far you went. Can you tell me how fast you were averaging?"

"About fifty miles—fifty-five miles an hour."

"I have no more questions."

Bruce McDonald was excused.

Troopers Eric Brown and Ray Rathke followed McDonald to the witness stand. Rathke testified that the Scout on Highway 97 was reported by California State Police to be a stolen vehicle.

When Detective Ken Cooper was called, his testimony covered much of the ground detailed in the early chapters of this book, including his finding some green paper towels by the side of the road that seemed to match the ones in the pillowcase— *and* ones later found in Pratt's truck. He also described the white Pro Wings tennis shoes found in the pillowcase. But when he showed the jury photographs of the area where the body was found at Milepost 206, he suddenly galvanized the defense by describing a furrow in the gravel as a "drag mark."

Defense counsel Richard's objection stopped the trial. Lawyers for both sides repaired to Judge Piper's chambers. There Richard claimed that calling it a "drag mark" was "an "inflammatory characterization designed to prejudice the jury." Warming to this theme, he also objected to the videotapes officers had made at the scene and to pictures documenting the autopsy, insisting that these graphics "depict gruesome photography."

Judge Piper explained that he had already screened the material and that he had instructed the prosecution to delete some scenes as being too gruesome.

On its front page, the *Klamath Falls Herald and News* summarized the events of the day:

He [Richard] has failed, thus far, though, to prove that police were biased in their investigation—as he contended in his opening statements to the jury Tuesday. . . . At one point in Wednesday's proceedings, Richard sought a mistrial on the basis that the prosecutors and Cooper were trying to sway the jury through a number of unethical tactics.

The defense's motion for a mistrial, the first of several, was denied.

Carrie's father, William Eckhart, testified briefly the following day. Other witnesses, including Mel McClintock, Cody Kupferer, and Carrie's Air National Guard unit commander, appeared long enough to confirm the timing of when Jesse Pratt and Carrie Love had left Seattle and when Carrie was expected to return.

When news spread that Mona Bennett, a loyal supporter of her boss, had arrived in Klamath Falls, it created some excitement in the courthouse because Jesse Pratt had told other prisoners in the county jail that he had a "blond chick friend who would be bringing in a gun to blow some people away." The rumor, which quickly leaked out, proved groundless—although sheriff's deputies equipped with portable metal detectors quietly checked both witnesses and spectators as they entered the courtroom for several days.

When she took the witness stand on Thursday, January 28, 1988, Mona Bennett confirmed Northern Star's location, told the court who worked there, and introduced the fact that it was originally she who was to have gone to Los Angeles to help set

up the new office and the new business having to
do with fish shipped from Seattle. But, since she
had not been able to find a baby-sitter for her son,
the plans had been changed on Thursday, June 12,
1986. She seemed oblivious to the possibility that
she might have been the murder victim instead of
Carrie Love.

Mona's testimony that Carrie was concerned that
"Jesse might make a pass at her" led to another defense objection that sent the lawyers and the
judge—and Jesse Pratt—back into Judge Piper's
chambers for more than an hour. The defense
counsel claimed that the witness was testifying to
hearsay. Endless wrangles over arcane points of law
(e.g., whether Bennett's testimony "fell under the
exception to the hearsay rule, in 803, Subsection 3,
making it valid evidence"), doubtless lost on the defendant, would interrupt the proceedings again
and again—causing the trial to last seven weeks.

When questioning of Mona Bennett resumed,
she volunteered the information that during one of
her telephone conversations with her boss on the
day after the murder, Jesse told her "he had received some scratches on his back, caused by
making love with Carrie."

When Mel McClintock testified, he admitted
(over defense objections that were overruled) that
Jesse had asked him to lie about the pillows in the
truck. His wife, Connie, was shown one of the pillows and asked to identify it.

"It is a bed pillow from my house," she said, "or
one of two. We had two of them. One of them I
gave to the officers on the day they came to the
house, and one of them we left in the truck, when

Jesse and Carrie left. And yes, we had a pillow just like that in the truck." Connie also confirmed that she remembered kicking a roll of silver duct tape lying on the floor of the truck when she and Mel turned it over to Jesse.

When her turn came, Kelley Eberle testified about Pratt offering Carrie a job early in May, the day she and her roommate had lunch at Flynn's Café on Airport Way. A waitress, Ramona Smith, had been a catalyst in Carrie's moving into the next booth to talk to Jesse Pratt for her brief "interview."

Eberle was asked what kinds of questions Carrie had been asked about her qualifications for the job.

"None. She sat down; she had the job. All she had to do is show up and see if she liked it." Eberle was asked how Carrie later felt about the job.

"She would come home crying to me in regards to working there with Mr. Pratt and stuff he wanted her to do. And I would continually tell her, 'Don't go back there.' But she needed the money, and she felt she would be safe as long as she—"

Her testimony was interrupted by Gitnes's motion to strike. It was denied. Kelley went on to state that the first time she met Pratt, she thought "he was a snake." And she had never altered that opinion.

The next witness, Louis Randolph, seemed to enjoy presenting himself as a very professional trucker. He was obviously proud to testify that he owned an "FW Kenworth, twin screw, Airide, with conventional fifth wheel, and a sleeper on the back." Unlike Pratt's dirty green Kenworth, his was "Rolls-Royce gray and Rolls-Royce white."

"I have a picture of it if you'd like to see it," the witness offered, pulling one out of an inside pocket like a proud parent. He seemed pleased to have the photo of his truck accepted as Exhibit 214.

Louis Randolph was supposed to follow Jesse Pratt on the trip to Los Angeles, he explained. Except Jesse preferred to travel Highway 97, and Randolph hated that route. He would travel I-5 as he always did, but he couldn't leave on June16 because his truck had a broken brake shoe. He had come into the office, he said, to collect some money Northern Star owed him so he could get his truck repaired.

"That's when Jesse's son came in," Randolph said. (Pratt had sometimes denied that the black youth was his son.) "He got a check." When Randolph told the young man that he, too, had come in to get a check, "Pratt's son told me to be sure I got a good check because Pratt's known to give out rubber checks."

That brought Gitnes to his feet with another objection. The counsel didn't want Randolph's check introduced into evidence, since it was written on the Double Jack account, and the defense had hoped to avoid any discussion about Double Jack deriving its income as an escort service. A compromise was reached in Judge Piper's chambers. Although the check would be introduced in evidence, the jury would be told simply that it "was drawn on the First Line Bank." The prosecution was instructed not to question Randolph about the loud argument in the back office between Carrie and Jesse in which Pratt had reduced his bookkeeper to tears and had threatened to cancel her trip to Los Angeles.

The defense's cross-questioning of Randolph had a heavy, accusatory air, many of the questions centering around the validity of his log sheets. Louis Randolph's time on the witness stand consumed more than one hundred pages in the trial record. Growing tired of the protracted cross-examination, Judge Piper finally called the lawyers into his chambers, asking, "What does any of this contribute to the story?"

The answer, the defense said, was (1) questionable entries in the log sheets went to the credibility of the witness, and (2), an apparent discrepancy of two hundred miles in the days subsequent to June 16 could have provided *Randolph* an opportunity to commit the murder. The defense seemed to be short on motive, however. Roxanne Osborne put the matter to rest when she returned for redirect examination:

"Mr. Randolph, did you kill Carrie Love?"

"No, I did not. I wasn't even around her until that day on the sixteenth. And then I couldn't go nowhere. My rig was dead in the water."

The next witness, Officer William Conley of the Arizona Highway Patrol, described the arrest of Pratt and the impounding of his rig.

The jury now had the logistics of the case.

SIXTEEN

Tape marks were found below the ear. They were found in front of the ear. They were found along the jawline—underneath the jaw. And they proceeded across, over onto the side of the cheek. Tape marks were not found on the other side of the face due to its having been essentially crushed—macerated.
                                    —Dr. Robert Jamison, pathologist

The prosecution now began its effort to establish that aggravated murder had occurred. Klamath County medical examiner Dr. Robert Jamison was called to the witness stand. The pathologist revealed that he was a graduate of UCLA Medical School and that he had also done his four-year pathology residency in California.

Questioned by assistant prosecutor Bob Foltyn, the doctor testified that he had arrived on the scene shortly after the body was discovered in the gravel pile and that he had assisted in uncovering it. Foltyn asked about a "depression in the parking lot and a trail with bloodstains in it and bits of brain material." He avoided calling it a "drag mark."

The assistant prosecutor then turned to the pathologist's subsequent autopsy. His questions led Dr.

Jamison to observe that "these color photographs demonstrate clearly the large streaks of tape residue that were present on the face and neck of Carrie Love." The residue marks had been brought out more clearly, he explained, by black fingerprint marking dust applied to the body.

"Objection!"

Peter Richard was on his feet again at the defense table. He had a number of complaints about the pictures, which were taken up in chambers. He claimed that "Exhibit 6, which shows the side of the skull crushed in, with a lot of extra damage, is simply being introduced primarily to prejudice the defendant for whatever value the gore has." He wanted the photograph to be cropped. He lost.

Back in the courtroom, Foltyn asked the doctor whether the tape marks along the jaw of the victim had assisted him in his analysis. Pointing at the tape residue on one of the photographs, the pathologist said they helped in concluding the *cause* of death.

"These tape marks point to an asphyxiation," the witness explained. "And when taken in combination with the presence of pulmonary edema [fluid in the lungs], these tape marks indicate that the deceased underwent a period of quite *prolonged* asphyxiation, measuring, I would say at the extreme least, half an hour, at the reasonable least, an hour, and probably *several* hours during a period when the deceased was unable to get enough air to carry on normal bodily functions. This asphyxiation occurred over a very prolonged period of, apparently, several hours." The prosecution seemed to be successfully establishing one of the criteria for aggravated murder, namely that "the homicide occurred in the course of, or as a result of, intentional maiming or torture of the victim."

Asked whether there were any other tape marks on the body, Dr. Jamison selected another photograph and pointed out "tape marks around both wrists of Carrie Love—and in the region of the small of the back."

In what seemed an effort to divert attention from the pathologist's devastating testimony, Richard interrupted with a question "in aid of an objection." The doctor's lengthy, pedantic answer made it clear that Carrie's hands had, without a doubt, been taped behind her back. Angrily, Richard appealed to the judge, complaining that the doctor's testimony "had gone beyond answering the questions put to him." He moved for a mistrial. His motion was denied.

Foltyn now asked the witness to turn his attention to the puncture wounds on the body. There were sixteen such wounds, Dr. Jamison said. They were about an eighth of an inch in diameter, and they had been inflicted with a "sharp object with a point on the end—an instrument such as an ice pick."

The doctor went over the wounds on a photograph. Number 1, he said, was located directly over the spine in the mid to lower back; Number 2 was also over the spine, slightly above the first, in the mid back, and Number 3 was a little higher. Number 4 was over the spine, below the base of the skull, as was Number 5, which was "on the neck below the skull." Number 6 was "approximately in the midline over the abdomen—a quite deep puncture wound several inches deep. The seventh is over the heart. . . ." Some of the jurors averted their eyes at times.

When he returned to the witness stand on the following Monday, the medical examiner was asked what he believed to be the ultimate cause of death. Although the death certificate he had signed read simply, "Stab wounds to heart and great vessels," Dr. Jamison testified that the victim probably died from a *combination* of suffocation and loss of blood as a result of the stab wounds. He added that the victim had also suffered a crushed skull, broken cartilage, and broken ribs on the left side, as well as a broken neck, but he believed these injuries were inflicted after Carrie Love was dead.

Ken Cooper returned to the witness stand to testify about his having seized the "first tire on the Number 5 axle" on Pratt's rig after the trucker's arrest in Arizona. He had chosen this tire because he noticed that it had a tread pattern similar to the "burnt-in pattern of a side tire tread on the victim's left arm." It appeared, he said, that "she had been run over from right to left by this tire, crushing the right side of the skull, and embedding several large rocks into its left side as the skull was crushed by the tire." He had asked Lieutenant Howard to peel off a portion of the tread for examination in the crime lab, he said.

While he was on the witness stand, Cooper, who happened to be a skilled avocational sculptor, introduced a mask he had reconstructed over a molded Styrofoam head using paper towels and duct tape. This creativity on the part of the witness precipitated an immediate reaction at the defense table. Richard complained that there was no way of knowing whether the Styrofoam head Cooper had used exactly matched the contour of the victim's head. Besides, he complained, "it was extremely prejudicial to the jury." He would not have objected to the introduction of the original mask, he said, and "saw no reason why it had to be torn to pieces."

The defense counsel went on to criticize Detective Cooper as case agent for failing to have a battery of forensic tests run on the blue Scout vehicle found by the side of the road near Milepost 230, suggesting that its driver could well have been Carrie Love's murderer. Cooper said he didn't understand the lawyer's logic, since this vehicle was nine miles from where the evidence had been found—*but*, as a matter of fact, fingerprint tests *had* been run as a matter of standard police procedure, since the vehicle had been reported stolen.

Undeterred, Richard then argued that Cooper's reporting of the positive identification of the defendant and the victim in the photo lineups the detective had shown to attendant Jeff Warren in Woodland should be thrown out as hearsay. Judge Piper was willing to let the defense have that one, since the next witness would be Jeff Warren of Redd's Tires.

Although it had been a year and a half since Ken Cooper had first come to see him, fuel stop attendant Jeff Warren's memory remained impressive. He clearly recalled identifying the pictures he had been shown at the time.

"On the guys' photo lineup, it was Number 4; and the girls' was Number 2."

Had Cooper asked him for a description of those

two people when the detective had first called him on the telephone? He had.

"What do you remember about them now?"

"Oh yeah—the guy. Pot gut. Scrawny arms. About my height, maybe a little taller."

"What kind of vehicle were they in?"

"A green Kenworth semi truck–tractor—whatever."

"How is it that you happen to remember these people?"

"Coincidence, I guess." But he then added he also remembered that when the pair came through in June, it was a sunny day, and it was late afternoon. And yes, he had his glasses on and could see clearly.

"What were they wearing, if you recall?"

"The girl had a light coat, jeans, no shoes—she had booties on. A striped shirt, I think it was black and white. And that was about all. It had fur—or whatever you want to call it—on the front of the coat. Not bushy. And it was cut real short." He went on to describe the woman's hair coloring.

"What about the man?"

"I guess it would be a plaid shirt—unbuttoned. Either short sleeved or rolled-up sleeves. And a pair of jeans."

"Did he have something on under the shirt if it was unbuttoned?"

"No. That's how come I realized the pot gut."

"Do you recall anything else about him?"

"Big, bushy beard. And if I remember, he was wearing a pair of cowboy boots."

Asked whether the man was in the courtroom, Jeff Warren identified Jesse Pratt.

SEVENTEEN

The difference between the right word and the almost right word is the difference between the lightning and the lightning bug.
— Samuel Clemens (aka "Mark Twain," 1835–1910)

Sergeant Loren Laird of the Oregon State Police Fingerprint Identification Bureau began by explaining to the jury what fingerprints are. They are caused, he said, by minute amounts of perspiration that are exuded from the fingertips and left on the surfaces they touch. Usually they are invisible.

Laird described some of the techniques he used for making these "latent" prints appear. These vary with the surface material to be treated, he explained. A steel surface, for example, may be dusted with a magnetic powder, which is available in either black or white. But the iron filings it contains negate tests for blood type.

In examining Pratt's truck cab and sleeper, Laird said he had used a more reliable method. He had fumed Super Glue in the closed interior. The cyanoacrylate ester in the Super Glue reacts with the moisture in the latent fingerprint residue, he explained, and this results in a white frosting effect on the latent print. But since these fumes are toxic, the vehicle must be "bagged" to contain them. He usually did this overnight when no one was present in the area to avoid accidental breathing of any fumes that might escape.

Sergeant Laird testified that he had found at least four fingerprints of value on the cab side of the window separating the sleeper and the cab compartment. He found another on the interior of the driver's windshield, and two more on the interior of the driver's rear-door window. He was able to match these with samples from Jesse Pratt, Mel McClintock, and arresting officer Conley.

Fingerprints on the checkbook in the black briefcase had been made by Carrie Love.

When Sergeant Laird got to the "mask" he had been asked to examine, Richard succeeded in preventing him from calling it that. It became a "cup-shaped object." Laird explained that it had to be taken apart so he could soak the masking tape in a solution to bring out any fingerprints. The forensic scientist didn't find any prints, but he did find hair samples and fibers that were red, yellow, and white, as well as a length of white thread—all stuck to the tape. He had sent these to the crime lab.

Criminalist Larry Dickenson of the Oregon State Crime Laboratory told the court he had been able to identify the blood on the pillowcase as belonging to Carrie Love. It was *not* consistent with Jesse Pratt's blood type. A smear of blood on the defendant's jeans had been too small to type, but Dickenson *was* able to determine that it was human blood.

To prepare the jury for upcoming testimony, the criminalist explained that 80 percent of people are "secretors." That is, they secrete evidence of their blood type in other bodily fluids, such as saliva or semen.

Forensic testimony was briefly interrupted to permit a witness from Weed, California, to record his testimony and go home. To dispel any suspicion that might still cling to the 1974 blue International Scout found on Highway 97 on the morning of June 18, the prosecution brought its owner, Howard Neill, to the witness stand. His vehicle had been stolen the night of June 16, he said.

The Scout had two gas tanks, Neill explained, and there was a selector switch on the dash that had been turned to Auxiliary when Neill got it back four days later. Since there had been no fuel in this spare tank, the thieves had apparently run out of gas and abandoned the vehicle on the shoulder of the road. The witness said there had been about ten gallons of gas in the primary tank, which would have taken it about 160 miles—just about the distance to the Oregon location where it was found.

He had to clean up the interior, the owner said, because it was full of fingerprint dust. As to the red stains, those were not blood. Neill explained that he was a surveyor, and he had spilled some of the red marking paint he used in his work.

Lieutenant Michael Howard, director of the Oregon State Crime Laboratory in Bend, was called. He had been a criminalist for twelve years, he said. "A *criminologist*," he explained, "is a sociologist or psychologist who studies crime and criminals. A *criminalist* is a person who uses scientific means and procedures for the analysis of all types of evidence. We do analysis of hair, blood and tissue, paint, glass, guns, drugs—anything that comes into the lab that needs forensic analysis. We do not do fingerprints, and we do not do handwriting analysis.

"When I arrived at the crime scene on June seventeenth," Howard said, "there were some small bits of paper and a carpet sample on the ground. There was an area where some of the gravel had been cleared away. There was bloodstaining, some tissue, and hair around on the ground there. There was an obvious *drag mark* through the ground."

The forbidden words propelled Richard out of his chair, and the lawyers repaired once again to Judge Piper's chambers. Richard was upset:

"In Officer Cooper's case, it was a 'mask.' Now, in Officer Howard's testimony, it's an 'obvious drag mark'! It's apparent that the state is either advising these people to testify in this fashion or incompletely advising them on the court's rulings. In either case, it's prejudicial."

For the third time, the defense counsel moved for a mistrial, then asked that the witness be instructed "not to *characterize* this so-called 'drag mark,' or any other item of evidence unless he has some basis— some *scientific* basis—for his opinion." Foltyn cited, "Rule 705, which states that an expert may testify in terms of opinion or inference and gives the reasons therefore." The arguments went on for nearly twenty minutes.

When the trial was recalled to order, Howard was instructed not to call it a "drag mark" anymore. But when he referred to it as a "depression in the gravel from the stained area toward the photographer who took this picture, a depression in the gravel from one point to another, to its terminal end," the dispute resumed. This time the defense lost. Before the end of his testimony, Lieutenant Howard would twice more revert to calling it a "drag mark," each time precipitating an unsuccessful motion for a mistrial.

The defense counsel later had cause to regret having made such an issue of the words when assistant prosecutor Foltyn, as prescribed in Rule 705, first qualified Lieutenant Howard as an expert in the area of forensic science, then spent nearly ten minutes having his witness define this standard forensic term. Thereafter, "drag mark" was used all the time—in both the prosecution's questions as well as in Mike Howard's answers. The unpopular words were repeated six times in seven sentences as criminalist Howard detailed how far along the drag mark each of the numbered exhibits of hair samples, blood, and tissue had been collected.

When the prosecution's inquiry moved on to processing of the truck and trailer in the impound lot near Phoenix, Arizona, the jury learned that the outside temperature had been 105 degrees—so the investigators had done the exterior first. When the interior had cooled down enough to enable a driver to move the truck into the shade, Howard and Dickenson photographed the interior of the cab as well as that of the sleeper, and, using a small portable vacuum cleaner equipped with interchangeable bags, meticulously collected and labeled the trace evidence entrapped in the bags.

Toward the end of the day, Lieutenant Howard explained, they prepared a Luminol test, spraying the inside of the truck with a chemical that reacts with blood and causes it to become fluorescent. Returning after dark with an ultraviolet lamp, they looked for the telltale blue glow of latent bloodstains—finding one on the driver's inside door handle. With a phenolphthalein indicator dye kit, they confirmed chemically that it was blood. Many previously unseen fibers and "fuzz balls" also showed up under ultraviolet, glowing colorfully in the dark interior.

They did similar UV tests on the Number 1. tire of the Number 5 axle, which may have run over the victim. But there was so much iron rust in the dust on the tire that they got a false positive glow on the entire circumference of the tread.

Lieutenant Howard described the meticulous photography of the tires on the impounded rig and the seizing of the suspected Number 1 tire on the Number 5 axle. Although he corroborated Detective Cooper's testimony that the tread pattern on this tire was *consistent with* the marks on the victim's arm, he could not establish a *positive identification* that would prove that Carrie Love had been run over by Jesse Pratt's rig.

By the end of Mike Howard's three days of testimony, over frequent objections by the defense, the criminalist's damaging findings included:

- Hair and blood in the drag marks was that of Carrie Love.
- Hair on the tape and mask was Carrie's.
- The silver duct tape on the mask was consistent with the silver roll Mel McClintock had left on the floor of the cab.
- Cross contamination by identical fibers in

the sleeping bag and in the truck sleeper cast doubt on Pratt's denial that the sleeping bag found by witness McDonald was his.

- Fibers in the victim's fingernail scrapings matched positively with those from the red T-shirt Jesse Pratt had been wearing at the time.
- There were rents in the red polyester T-shirt where Carrie's fingernails had broken the threads; the location of these rents matched the scratches on the defendant's body.
- The mask that had been found in the sleeping bag by the side of the road was made out of paper towels positively identified as coming from the roll found in the truck's sleeping compartment; the plastic wrapper for this newly opened roll was still in the truck.

Mike Howard later explained how it was possible to identify a single roll of paper towels as being identical with those in the mask.

"In my investigation, I learned that every paper company has its own design pattern that they emboss on the product. So if you can make out the pattern, you can even go to a grocery store and look at all the embossed patterns and you can tell what brand it is. This time it was pretty easy because the unopened roll had a Bounty label right on it.

"In this case, the machine that puts the embossing on the paper was worn enough that it was making little holes along one edge every so often. The manufacturer told me those are called 'pinholes.' They don't like for them to be there, but it

154   *Jack Gieck*

does occur sometimes. And it just so happened that one of the big steel rolls [of the paper calender that squeezes water out the absorbent sheet and embosses the pattern] was producing these pinholes once every time it went around.

"The paper towels that had been used in the mask had the same pinholes along one edge as the ones found in the sleeper—*and* the ones found on the side of the road at Milepost 221.4 as well. In addition, they were the same color; they had the same embossing pattern [thereby making them the same brand]; and they had the same dye in them. I stripped out the dye and ran a chromatography test and found the dyes were consistent between the ones found at the scene in the mask *and* the ones found in the truck."

Howard was followed to the witness stand by serologist Lori Rawlinson, who testified that the semen in the vaginal swabs that she had tested was of Blood Type A and Blood Enzyme PGM Type One, which was consistent with Pratt's blood type. But since Pratt never denied having had (he claimed consensual) sex with Carrie Love, and, in fact, bragged about it, this did not constitute damning testimony.

Roxanne Osborne's final witness was Thelma Adams. Because there were no eyewitnesses to the crime for which Jesse Pratt was being charged, Thelma's testimony would be presented, as Doug Higgs explained in the *Klamath Falls Herald and News*, "to demonstrate definite similarities between incidents involving [Adams] and the murder of Love."

Thelma told the story of her kidnapping and

rape by Jesse Pratt, a crime assisted by convicted
felon David Whaley, as detailed in earlier chapters
of this book. It was difficult for her, and it obviously
impressed Higgs, who wrote in the paper's Sunday
edition:

> Jesse Clarence Pratt's lurid past could prove
> fatal. The testimony of Thelma Adams, who
> rendered an emotional account of a series of
> incidents involving Pratt in August, 1980, was
> devastating to the defense.
> The account including acts of kidnapping,
> assault and rape, was provided Friday during
> the 19th day of the death penalty jury trial of
> Pratt in the Klamath County Circuit Court.

EIGHTEEN

*Since we are near Valentine's Day, we draw a
heart.*

　　　　　　　　　　　　—Dr. William J. Brady

It was now the defense's turn. Peter Richard's first
witness was Raymond Davis, a chemist and professional expert witness from Seattle. He had been
asked to analyze the evidence assembled by the prosecution—which included pictures of the tire marks
on Carrie Love's arm, photographs of the suspected
tire, and the piece of tire tread excised by Mike
Howard. He had also read criminalist Howard's field
notes, and he had examined the tire itself.

In his direct examination, Davis testified that the
marks were a mystery to him at first because "it just
didn't look like a direct impression. I was just at a
loss to figure out how these marks got there." This
was, he said, because a "blow or impression leaves
blank spaces where the pressure is applied, and the
blood runs into the spaces in the tire where the
blood was forced into." But because the injury was
inflicted after death, he explained, there was no
blood pressure, so the result was, to him, a "very

confusing impression." It was, as he put it, an "indirect" impression.

"The wounds were irregular," he said. "They weren't evenly spaced like you'd expect to find on any tire. Tires all have different tread designs and patterns and wear characteristics, but they are reproduced every couple of inches. But the postmortem wounds on the arm are *irregular*."

Davis went into a complex personal theory about how "the tire had pushed the skin, but after releasing the pressure, the skin had snapped back." He had not tried to fit the tire with the wounds, he said, because he had not been given a one-to-one full-scale picture of the marks on the victim's arm. Nevertheless, he stated, "it is my opinion that this tire is inconsistent with the marks made." But he could not be certain, he said, for two reasons that his testimony did not make altogether clear:

"Number 1, this is not a direct impression. Number 2, this is a reverse, and a *poor* reverse impression. The blood is in the areas where there is no pressure, so this is not a direct impression, and number two, the depression is irregular. There is no way to determine whether it was this tire, a 'semi' truck tire—or even a pickup truck tire—that could have made this mark."

"You think a pickup tire could have made this mark?" Richard asked.

"Certainly."

"Well, a pickup tire is a lot smaller in circumference, isn't it?"

"Yes."

"But you think a pickup truck could have made this?" the defense attorney repeated.

"Sure. The actual length of this bruise could have fit *any* tire. It doesn't take much pressure on just pushing your thumb for a few seconds on your hand [he demonstrated], and releasing it squeezes the blood away. If you do that with my thumb, certainly with any kind of tire it would do the same."

Richard zeroed in.

"Was Lieutenant Howard's conclusion correct that the red marks on the arm were similar in tread design to this tire? Is that conclusion correct?"

"It is *not* correct. Again, this is not a direct impression. Only way for that to happen is if some material—blood, dust, dirt from the tire—based on the tire. That's a direct contact print. The evidence here is that the blood was forced to the interstitial spaces within the arm where there was no pressure, left marks where there was pressure marks where the tire was. This is a reverse and indirect impression. And irregular, I might add."

It sounded highly technical, if somewhat unclear. But the defense had heard what it wanted to hear—and what it wanted the jury to believe. Their expert had said the Oregon State Crime Laboratory was wrong.

Forensic scientist Davis was also shown photomicrographs of several fibers, which he identified as being cotton and polyester, respectively—the mixture of fibers he had concluded Jesse Pratt's shirt was made of. But he had also concluded that the red fibers in the photomicrographs (collected from under the victim's fingernails) did not match fibers in the shirt. There was a difference in color, he said.

Davis emphasized his preference for comparing color "photographs" (prints) rather than slides because slides "tend to wash out." The prosecution did not contest Davis's declaration, which is technically unsound. (Since color prints from negatives are one generation down compared with slides, and since prints are routinely "corrected" in the processing laboratory by personnel adjusting the settings of color filters in the enlarger, the potential for error in comparing colors in prints is far greater than in original 35mm slides.) Davis's technique of comparing photographs seemed less sophisticated than the techniques employed by the state crime lab, where Mike Howard had used a binocular comparison microscope equipped with polarizing filters to control surface luster while examining the actual fibers side by side.

On Tuesday morning, the defense called its own pathologist, Dr. William J. Brady. Dr. Brady began by giving the jury an anatomy lesson:

"Our blood is circulated by a pump. And it pumps through a pump. Really two pumps. And we call that pump 'the heart.' And the heart, in order to keep pumping, the little pump sends blood into the lungs (the right side of the heart), and the big pump (the left side of the heart) pumps blood all through your head, body, and so forth, is operated from the material that nourishes it."

Brady was asked to step down from the witness-box and to draw a diagram of the heart, showing the pericardial sac and the pericardial space that had accumulated blood from the victim's stab wounds. The doctor complied, opening with a little joke that drew no smiles from his audience.

"Since we are all near Valentine's Day, we draw a heart."

When asked how long a heart could continue to function if stabbed, he likened the bleeding to "how long it takes to fill the sink in our bathroom." He reminded the jury that "if we turn the faucets on too fast, the sink will overflow." Dr. Brady challenged Medical Examiner Jamison's autopsy report, which had concluded that death was caused by "stab wounds to the heart and great vessels." Brady believed that these were not necessarily the immediate cause of death of the victim.

Dr. Jamison's autopsy protocol had concluded that asphyxiation had also contributed to Carrie Love's death, as evidenced by pulmonary edema, or fluid in the lungs, and the foam discovered in the trachea of the victim. Asked about this conclusion, Dr. Brady's new anatomy lesson became a lengthy monologue.

"Asphyxiation is a very common thing. It's trapped air. We can't breathe. The balloon. That's all the lung is: a collection of little balloons. If the balloon is all blown up and we can't breathe, the air stays in the balloon, because—if it goes out of the balloon—then, of course, we are breathing. And the lungs are exactly the same thing in asphyxiation. They are all blown up. So if a person is asphyxiated, you have millions and millions of great big blown-up balloons. Open the chest and there are the typical lungs of asphyxiation: the lungs filled with these tiny blown-up balloons."

But, the pathologist said, the photographs he had seen showed that Carrie Love's lungs were not all blown up. They were, in fact, retracted. They certainly didn't look like classic textbook examples of asphyxiation.

The defense's motive for presenting the doctor's testimony had been an effort to deny that the killing was *aggravated* murder, as would be implied by the victim having been choked.

"This lady did not die of asphyxiation," the doctor bluntly declared. "And she did not die as a result of a truck driving over her head, because this had occurred after she was already dead."

He said it with the same breezy air that had characterized his earlier testimony.

NINETEEN

So we pulls off, went down Airport Way, got up I-5 headed southbound. I could see traffic was so-so. So I just dropped the hammer on the old girl. I stuck my foot in the pump. And I walked up against a shlonk a couple of times. That's like when you put your foot on the brake. But on a truck, you got a shlonk brake. Coming off, I walked up against it. Carrie looked at me kind of funny. She never been in a moving truck before. Never down the highway in one of 'em. Not a big eighteen-wheeler. So we walked down through there, and we wasn't havin' any trouble with anything.

—Jesse Clarence Pratt

It was a moment that both spectators and the press had been waiting for. Defense counsel Peter Richard had made the decision to put his client on the witness stand.

Jesse Pratt seemed to enjoy the limelight. Relishing his role as a trucker, he rambled on about such technical details as adequate overhead clearances at fuel stops, how an engine tends to sputter while going uphill when the fuel tanks are nearly empty, and other mechanical details. More than once his defense lawyer had to interrupt him, refocusing his attention on information pertaining to his own murder trial.

When he was asked about the start of his trip with Carrie Love, Pratt described how he had helped her climb into the sleeper behind the cab. Almost immediately, he said, "she asked if we have time to fool around a little bit." So he drove to the Evergreen Truck Stop, he said, "and we had sex." He said it as a matter of fact, his eyes invisible behind his tinted glasses.

Before they left on Monday morning, Pratt related, he had sent Carrie to the bank with the company checkbook to withdraw $600. He had $230 of his own personal money at the time, he testified. At the prosecutor's table, cocounsel Cooper noted that this did not square with the defendant's having over a thousand dollars in his wallet when he was arrested in Arizona several days later.

Defense counsel Richard had his client recount how after the pair had been under way for a time, he pulled into a truck stop in Longview, Washington, to refuel. Here, Pratt said, he discovered that the metal cap on one of his fuel tanks was missing. He replaced it with a cup-shaped cluster of paper towels and tape, he said, making it sound like Cooper's description of the cup-shaped mask found in the pillowcase.

To pay for the fuel, Pratt said, he asked Carrie for the $600 she had withdrawn that morning, and to his dismay, "it was two hundred dollars short and Carrie wouldn't tell me who she gave the other two hundred to." The shortage made him "real mad," he said—especially after all he had done for her. So he ordered her back into the sleeper and "I told her I didn't want to hear another word out of her."

When they stopped for dinner at Oak Ridge, they argued over the money again. Here, Pratt said, he noticed that his handmade fuel cap had come off, so he made another one. Farther along, when he stopped the truck at a ski area to relieve himself beside the road, he noticed that his replacement cap had also disappeared, and he made a third cup-shaped paper-and-tape fuel cap.

Pratt said he began getting angrier as he drove down Highway 58.

"I comes on down and I'm runnin' pretty fast down through here, and I can see the brush and stuff down where 97 comes across, and right about then is when I shut the old truck down. As I was squonkin' her down, I told Carrie, I says, 'Get up here!' And so I stopped the truck in the middle of the road, and I locked the dynamiters up. It's like a parking or emergency brake on you guys' cars. An' I locked up both gauges and I says, 'We're gonna have it out right now. I want to know where my money is—an' right now.' An' there was some few words said between us, and then she told me to take everything I have and shove it up my ass."

So he struck her in the chest, he admitted, then pulled her out of the cab and threw her luggage after her.

With that, he pulled away, he said, leaving her standing in the darkness in the middle of the road with some headlights approaching in the distance behind her. Pratt's new alibi was not a very endearing one.

Prosecutor Roxanne Osborne took over cross-questioning of the witness. First, for the record, she attempted to straighten out the matter of Jesse Pratt's age, handing him a copy of his birth certificate—which listed his date of birth as July 3, 1944. Although he admitted "it's got my name on it," he denied it was his birth certificate.

"You know I was adopted to a woman named Elizabeth Helle at the time when I was ten. I've fought with you people ever since I've been here. You and I just had this discussion. Don't get me wrong, but how my name was spelled and where I was born at, and who I was born to—I know you don't understand. But I been goin' through this ever since I been here. This says I was born in '44. I was not born in '44. My dad and mother are *deceased*. I never saw them. The woman claimed as my mother is my stepmother. I don't know how to tell you this, but my dad was black and my mama was white. My dad got killed in the service."

The motivation for presenting this odd testimony may have been the defense's knowledge that Jesse Pratt's mother was scheduled to be called as a witness by the prosecution in the penalty phase of the trial.

Jesse Pratt's testimony had produced a front-page article in the *Herald and News* the following morning:

ACCUSED MURDERER DENIES EVERYTHING
By Doug Higgs, Staff Writer
Accused murderer Jesse Clarence Pratt denied almost everything, including his age.

The last time he saw her was when, in a fit of anger, he put her out of his truck on a lonely stretch of Highway 58 between Oakridge and

Highway 97 during the late night hours of June 16, 1986, Pratt testified during the 20th day of his death penalty jury trial in Klamath County Circuit Court.

He also insisted he is not, as a birth certificate states, 43 years of age. Instead, he is 53, he said.

In the process of his extensive denial of any implication in Love's murder, Pratt admitted having lied on a number of occasions. The most prominent lie was the one he told a number of people, including Arizona Highway Patrol officers following his arrest near Phoenix, Ariz., June 19, 1986.

Pratt falsely represented that, after he and Love left Seattle from Pratt's place of business, Northern Star, a trucking company, he "dropped her [Love] off in the Seattle area so she could take a cab to the airport and fly to Los Angeles."

He also confessed that he lied in the records kept by him in his truck log book for the period of time he left Seattle on June 16, 1986, until his arrest June 19, 1986.

He also verified his criminal record. Pratt revealed he served time in the penitentiary in the state of Washington on charges of kidnapping and assault, and, before that, "I also did eight years in the state of Alaska."

He said in court the reason he lied to the Arizona Highway Patrol officers was because "I don't have a very good past. I had just been out of the penitentiary in the state of Washington about one and a half years at the time."

In his relatively short closing statement, assistant prosecutor Foltyn emphasized that running over the victim's head was almost certainly done to prevent identification, as was taking off her rings. He reviewed the elements of the case from the prosecution's perspective, telling the jury that, taken together, they proved the defendant's guilt.

Summations for the defense by Myron Gitnes and Peter Richard run more than two hundred pages of court transcript. Their statements, designed to discount the evidence presented by the prosecution, reminded the jury of such previously expressed defense positions as:

- The entire case is circumstantial evidence— insubstantial evidence flawed by inference and innuendo.
- The police investigation had been biased against Jesse Pratt from the beginning, as exemplified by their doing only a superficial examination of the Scout vehicle found near Milepost 230.
- Expert witnesses presented by the defense had challenged the accuracy of the state's laboratory tests.
- Although the victim scratched completely through Jesse Pratt's red T-shirt, there was no blood under her fingernails; thus, she must have washed her hands afterward and, therefore, was still alive after their sexual encounter.
- Defense expert Dr. Brady said it would not take someone two hours to die if the person was asphyxiated, as the medical examiner,

Dr. Jamison, had suggested. Brady had insisted it would be more like three to five minutes.

This last was an inaccurate characterization, prosecutor Osborne later reminded the jury. Dr. Jamison had estimated the asphyxiation time as lasting anywhere from thirty minutes to two hours.

In her final summation for the prosecution, Roxanne Osborne began by telling the jurors she didn't want them to vote for a conviction just because they didn't like Jesse Pratt—or just because Thelma Adams testified that he kidnapped and raped her.

"He must be guilty of *this* crime," she explained. Thelma Adams's testimony should be considered only "when you decide whether the defendant had the *intent* to commit the crime of rape." It was a fine point, legally. But she drove it home with an emotional underscore. "Thelma got on the stand and said, 'Yes, he did rape me.' Carrie can't do that."

Prosecutor Osborne complimented the defense attorneys. They had done a good job, she said. But her generosity was limited.

"One of the things that happens in a defense situation is like an octopus. When a predator starts to come after an octopus, it shoots out this big cloud of black ink to confuse the predator so that it can get away in the confusion. And that's what the defense has done in this case, ladies and gentlemen. I'm not faulting them for it. That's their job. But don't buy it. Look at the evidence. Think logically."

Osborne went on to point out what she believed were major holes in the defense's position. Pratt's excuse for lying to the Arizona State Police, for example (claiming he had dropped Carrie off at My Place Tavern), might have made some sense at the time of his arrest. But his telling such a yarn to Mona Bennett two full days "before he knew Carrie Love was dead" made no sense at all. In attempting to build his alibi too soon, she said, Pratt had trapped himself.

"The reason he lied so much—he even altered some of the stories he told while still on the witness stand—is simple. It's because he's guilty."

Although she had no formal medical training, the prosecutor presented a persuasive attack on Dr. Brady's expert testimony.

"For him to insist that the alveoli, his 'millions of little balloons' in the lungs, had to remain inflated and distended in a dead body in order to prove the victim had died of asphyxiation is ridiculous—unless the victim had a trachea with a one-way valve."

Osborne pointed up internal inconsistencies in the defense's logistics. If Pratt had slept nine hours on the night of June 16 as he testified, "how come he needed a two-hour nap when he got to Weed? And then he has to buy a new blanket because his sleeping bag wasn't there anymore. He had to throw the old blanket away because it was full of blood!"

Osborne reviewed each piece of evidence the prosecution had introduced:

- They presented the tire that was believed to have run over the victim and the corresponding marks on Carrie's arm.
- Fibers and "fuzz balls" found in the sleeping bag showed cross contamination with ones in the truck cab.

- The fibers under Carrie's fingernails matched the fabric in Pratt's shirt.
- The silver duct tape and the particularly damaging roll of green Bounty paper towels in the truck positively matched the materials out of which the mask was made.

She discussed the defendant's hatred of women, how he doesn't see women as real people, giving them an example from the defendant's testimony:

"Although everyone else in this courtroom views Carrie's death as a tragedy, the defendant, while professing his innocence, obviously feels no remorse about his having contributed to her death by shoving her out of the truck on a lonely road in the middle of the night in a fit of anger—thus leading to her being killed by 'someone else.'

"But there was no 'someone else.' There is no phantom killer in this case, ladies and gentlemen."

TWENTY

It was one of the worst times of my life. I'd screwed up the jury!

—Detective Ken Cooper

On Thursday morning, February 11, 1988, Judge Donald Piper charged the jury. Once again, the judge defined the elements of *aggravated* murder. For the defendant to be guilty of this charge, he reminded them, they would have to find intentional torture or maiming in the process of killing the victim. For the record, the defense complained that the judge had not told the jury about the importance of an eyewitness. And, indeed, when the jury retired for its deliberation, it not only had no eyewitness to the crime, it didn't even have a murder weapon.

Detective Ken Cooper, however, was certain it had been an ice pick that had killed Carrie Love. "All truckers carry them to pop stones out of their tires," he maintained. The fact that they found no ice pick in Jesse Pratt's toolbox was itself evidence, he believed. It was a little like "the unusual activity of the dog"—the dog that *didn't* bark in

Arthur Conan Doyle's famous Sherlock Holmes story "Silver Blaze."

At 9:35 P.M., after ten hours of deliberation, the jury returned to the courtroom. Juror Robert Tucker reported that they had reached a verdict.

The judge reminded the spectators in the courtroom that "there is a uniform rule in force in all Oregon courts which requires all persons to remain seated without any reaction or display of emotion until the jury has returned to the jury room." He then asked Mr. Tucker to hand the verdict to the bailiff, who read the contents of the paper.

"We, the jury, being duly impaneled and sworn, do find the defendant on the charge of aggravated murder, Count One, guilty of the crime of aggravated murder, all of our number concurring.

"We, the jury, being duly impaneled and sworn, do find the defendant on the charge of aggravated murder, Count Two, guilty of the crime of aggravated murder, all of our number concurring."

Jesse Pratt just sat there impassively. Not a flicker of emotion crossed his bearded face.

The "guilt phase" of the trial was over. The judge thanked the jury members for their work but reminded them that they would be recalled "to proceed with the next phase as soon as practicable."

"I feel fantastic," Connie Love told a reporter from her hometown Spokane newspaper. "It's like he didn't get away with it. I'm emotionally drained; but I feel relief. I feel like I can let Carrie rest now."

But the day wasn't over yet.

* * *

In an unscheduled session, the court reconvened five days later—but not to begin the penalty phase of the trial. The jury was not present.

Detective Ken Cooper was called to the witness stand to testify about a matter that caused the defense, in his words, "to go ballistic." The event had occurred after the jury had been dismissed the previous Thursday evening. Cooper was obviously tense as he began his testimony.

"I was asked to help take some of the jurors out to their cars. When we got out into the hall, a couple of the male jurors said they could walk with some of the women. Several other police officers and I took the rest of the jurors out. I was walking out to the cars by the Modoc Lumber lot.

"I was thinking about what had just occurred, and I heard a comment from one of the female jurors.

"'He's a dangerous man, isn't he?' she asked me. And I gave a reflex answer of 'Yes, he's probably the most dangerous person I've ever worked.'"

It was after he had escorted the woman to her car and walked back across the street that it hit him, he later explained. He could have let it go. Instead, he went to District Attorney Ed Caleb and reported the exchange.

Cooper was excoriated by defense counsel Peter Richard, who promptly moved for a mistrial. Before ruling on the matter, Judge Piper elected to call in the members of the jury one by one. When the poll was complete, it was established that only two jurors had heard the exchange: the woman who asked the question and a companion walking beside her.

Two alternate jurors had sat through the trial—and only two. Judge Piper excused the two women who had been involved in the conversation and the two alternates were substituted. He denied Richard's motion for a mistrial.

There were audible sighs of relief in the courtroom.

TWENTY-ONE

The quality of mercy is not strain'd.
It droppeth as the gentle rain from heaven
Upon the place beneath. It is twice blessed:
It blesseth him that gives and him that takes.
— William Shakespeare (1564–1616),
The Merchant of Venice

It was time for the penalty phase of Jesse Clarence Pratt's trial to begin. Judge Donald Piper addressed the members of the jury.

In order to made their critical decision, he explained, they would first have to answer two questions: One, was the conduct of the defendant that caused the death of Carrie Lynette Love committed deliberately and with a reasonable expectation that the death of Carrie Lynette Love would result? And Two, was there a probability (meaning it is more likely than not) that the defendant will commit similar acts of violence that will constitute a continuing threat to society?

Having found him guilty of aggravated murder in the guilt phase, the jury was now being asked to decide whether Jesse Pratt should be sentenced to life in prison, life in prison without the possibility of release or parole, or to death by lethal injection. In the process of making this decision, the defendant's character and background would be explored, as would the possibility of his constituting a threat to others while in prison.

The first witness in the penalty phase of trial was Detective Ken Cooper. His response to the prosecution's very first question suddenly put the earlier flap into perspective.

"If released, I believe Jesse Pratt will commit a crime worse than the one we're doing right now," the detective testified. But this time it was on the record for all the jurors to hear.

Elizabeth Kathleen Helle, Jesse Pratt's mother, was sworn in. She had flown in from Alaska to testify.

Helle confirmed that Jesse Clarence Pratt's birth certificate was correct as written. He was born in Tyler, Texas, on July 3, 1944. After her husband, Jesse Clarence Pratt Sr., was killed in battle during World War II, she had subsequently married Donald Hudson. Jesse, as a result, had two half sisters and a half brother, who died in infancy. When Helle's marriage to Hudson ended in divorce, the two girls were raised by their father. Young Clarence, as she always called him, lived with her.

Her son did not graduate from high school, she said. His last schooling was in King City, California, before the family moved to Alaska.

When he was in prison in Walla Walla for kidnapping Thelma Adams, his mother had talked to him on the phone on several occasions. During one of these calls, she asked him why he did it and whether he was sorry he did it.

"He said, 'No.' So I said, 'Well, why did you do it?'

The ditch along Oregon State Highway 97, near milepost 220.4. It was here that witness Bruce McDonald found a sleeping bag and pillowcase that led to finding the body of Carrie Love.
(Photo by the author)

Witnesses Bruce and Dorothy McDonald, who found critical evidence in the murder of Carrie Love.
(Photo by the author)

Sand Creek, a general store, diner, and filling station south of Military Crossing, where Bruce McDonald met with Oregon State police officers after turning in the evidence he found. *(Photo by the author)*

Interior of Sand Creek; the store's mini-diner, where witness Bruce McDonald met with police officers for his interview the morning after he found evidence in a nearby ditch. *(Photo by the author)*

Military Crossing, south of Chemult, where gravel for winter highway maintenance is stored by the state – one of the areas unsuccessfully scouted in the search for a murder victim.
(Photo by the author)

Loop Road at Milepost 206 as it looks today. It was an unimproved turnoff from highway 97 when the crime took place in 1986. *(Photo by the author)*

Carrie Lynette Love, 1966-1986, at the prom she attended with Cody Kupferer. *(Courtesy Connie Love)*

A 1986 photo of
Carrie Love,
at age 20.
(Courtesy Connie Love)

Jesse Clarence Pratt;
a mug shot shortly
after his arrest
in June, 1986.
(Courtesy Ken Cooper)

The many faces of Jesse Pratt. *(Courtesy Connie Love)*

Jesse Pratt's 1976 Kenworth truck, in which the murder was committed. *(Courtesy Pete McDonald)*

Side view of Pratt's Kenworth tractor, showing right front tire. *(Courtesy Pete McDonald)*

8465 Perimeter Road on the east edge of Seattle's Boeing Field, the building in which Northern Star Trucking rented office space. The company had no garage or maintenance facilities. *(Photo by the author)*

Oregon State Police Detective Kenneth D. Cooper, at his home in Klamath Falls.
(Photo by the author)

Using tiny diamond grinding wheels, avocational sculptor Ken Cooper works in his unusual medium, the marrow in the bony webbing between moose antlers. "Since the moose shed their antlers every year," he says, " the raw material is free."
(Photo by the author)

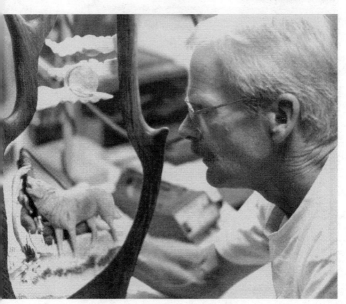

The Klamath County Courthouse on Klamath Falls' Main Street,
where the Pratt trials were held. The Greek Revival structure
was later destroyed by an earthquake in September, 1993.
(Photo by the author)

Klamath County's Circuit Court No. 1, the courtroom in which
Jesse Pratt was tried twice for the murder of Carrie Love.
Jury box is at left; there are five steps up to the witness chair.
(Photo by the author)

Cell in Klamath County's "Old Jail," where Jesse Pratt twice awaited trial. *(Photo by the author)*

Criminal Investigator Bill Carroll in his office at the Department of Justice in Salem, Oregon. *(Photo by the author)*

Forensic scientist Peter McDonald studies off-tracking geometry on the drawing board of his office as he maneuvers his model of a tractor-trailer rig to study how the tandem axles run over the tiny cardboard model placed between the rear wheels of the trailer. The stained-glass window behind McDonald's head (with the drawing board motif) is one of his own pieces of artwork.

(Photo by the author)

A highway trailer tire on which McDonald has marked "accidental characteristics" that make it possible for forensic scientist to positively identify a tire that has made a given tire track.
(Courtesy Pete McDonald)

Peter McDonald's diagram showing how the rear tire of the Northern Star trailer could have produced the marks found on Carrie Love's left arm and chest after passing over her head.
(Courtesy Pete McDonald)

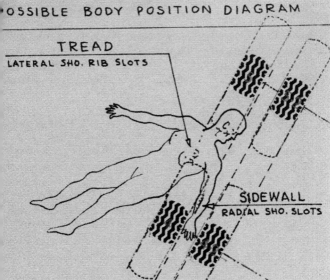

POSSIBLE BODY POSITION DIAGRAM

TREAD
LATERAL SHO. RIB SLOTS

SIDEWALL
RADIAL SHO. SLOTS

Pete McDonald's gloved hands measure the contusions on Carrie Love's arm produced by the side treatment of the #1 tire on the #5 axle of Jesse Pratt's trailer. *(Courtesy Pete McDonald)*

Moments after being sentenced to death, Jesse Pratt rises with his lawyers, Co-counsel Ever Bosgos, center, and Defense Counsel Kenneth Hadley on the right. *(Photo by Lou Sennick, Courtesy Klamath Falls Herald and News)*

Oregon State Penitentiary at Salem, Oregon – where Jesse Pratt remains on Death Row fifteen years after the rape/murder of Carrie Love. *(Photo by the author)*

Death row at Oregon State Penitentiary, Salem, Oregon. Pratt's cell is one of the nine along the right wall of this intensive management unit. *(Courtesy Oregon State Penitentiary)*

Connie Love, Carrie's mother, entertains her grandson.
(Photo by the author)

"And he said, 'Because I wanted her.'

"And I said, 'Well, there's other fish in the sea.'

"And he said, 'When I want something, I get it.'"

Elizabeth Helle told the court that she had been "slapped around by Clarence on a number of occasions because I wouldn't loan him large amounts of money, or I wouldn't do what he wanted me to do. He'd get very unhappy and slam me around."

"Was Mr. Pratt always like that?" Roxanne Osborne asked.

"No. Until he was about eighteen years old, he was a very compassionate person, a very loving person. Then he started living in Anchorage and driving trucks and he associated with people he was working with. He became a roustabout—just the complete opposite of what he grew up as."

Myron Gitnes conducted Helle's cross-examination. The assistant defense counsel asked her whether it wasn't a "fair statement that he runs off at the mouth and threatens people, but he really doesn't carry through with them?"

"He runs off at the mouth, but he *can* carry through with them, too," Pratt's mother responded, "especially if it's a woman."

It was not the response Gitnes had hoped for. Changing the subject, he asked how she felt as a mother about the sentence the court must now decide. Helle took a deep breath.

"I don't want him to be out in society anymore," she said. "But I don't want him put to death." She paused again—longer this time. "I can't say I want my son put to death. I feel he should have life in prison without any parole."

Cecilia Gunn, Pratt's half sister, followed their

mother to the witness stand. Sitting down nervously, and carefully avoiding her brother's contemptuous stare, Cecilia testified that she was "terrified" of her brother. In fact, because of his threats, she said, she had dropped out of sight in an effort to make her whereabouts unknown.

"I don't think he deserves to live," she declared for the record.

Seeking to establish that Pratt's continuing to live could cause *others* to commit violence, the prosecution now called convicted felon David Whaley. The witness did not help his partner's cause when he confirmed that Pratt had solicited him while he was still in prison in Sacramento—offering him $3,000 "to do a job."

In its initial summation, the defense complained about "prosecutorial misconduct." Gitnes pleaded that there is "reasonable doubt" in the case. He reminded the jury that "you are deciding the ultimate fate of a human being."

Prosecutor Roxanne Osborne's summation surprised both the jury and spectators in the court. She opened by reciting the famous quatrain from Shakespeare's *The Merchant of Venice*, Portia's plea on behalf of Antonio concerning the pound of flesh Shylock sought to claim—the lines beginning, "The quality of mercy is not strained."

"Now, you might think that's an odd way for the prosecution to begin its closing remarks in the penalty phase of this trial," she said. "But I do so for two reasons: Isn't that really the only single argument left to the defense in this case? Isn't it clear that the answer to those two questions you have been asked to decide *must*, in fact, be yes?"

Osborne went on to warn the members of the jury that it would be difficult for them to make those decisions. "But," she declared, "you have a *moral* duty." To illustrate what she meant, she told them a personal story. When she was in junior high school, she said, she had the painful experience of seeing her father kill a kitten that had been run over by a car.

"The only moral choice for him was to kill it. It was very sad, but it stuck with me all these years. There are some things that are our *duty*. If you really believe that Jesse Pratt will commit further acts of violence that constitute a threat to society, either by himself or at his bidding—if you really believe there will be even *one* more victim of Mr. Pratt— then your duty is clear. Thank you."

It was a hard act to follow. In Peter Richard's final summation for the defense, he appealed for sympathy for "this poor person who had no male influence in his life until he was twelve years old." He stated, "There isn't any real evidence that when the defendant has been imprisoned he was violent or a threat to society inside the prison. The appropriate thing is to put the defendant in prison for the rest of his life."

Assistant prosecutor Bob Foltyn had the last word. "There comes a time for talking to stop. There is no laughter in this place, because this is the place where *death* is required for the benefit of the living. And the answer to these questions, beyond any doubt, is simply yes."

The penalty phase of the trial had lasted only half a day. The jury retired to the jury room at 11:30 A.M.

Two hours and forty-five minutes later, the jury

reappeared. As the word went out, almost the entire staff of the Klamath County District Attorney's Office filed into the courtroom. Looking apprehensive, several women held hands.

"Some of us prayed," Melina Johnson, Ed Caleb's administrative secretary, remembered. "It was strange. It didn't seem right to pray for somebody to die."

The banner headline in the February 18, 1988, issue of the *Klamath Falls Herald and News* said it all:

PRATT RECEIVES THE DEATH PENALTY
By Doug Higgs
Jesse Clarence Pratt, 43, Seattle, received the death penalty Wednesday.

The death penalty finding by a jury of six men and six women concluded a twenty-four day trial in Klamath County Circuit Court. Formal imposition of the fatal sentences will be by Judge Donald A. W. Piper at 1:30 PM Monday.

The two aggravated murder counts on which Pratt was convicted alleged he caused Carrie Love's death by asphyxiating her, stabbing her in the heart, and running over her head with a motor vehicle while trying to rape and maim her.

Klamath County District Attorney Edwin Caleb said he was "extremely proud of the two deputies [Foltyn and Osborne] who prosecuted this case. They handled themselves in a very professional manner under very difficult circumstances." Caleb also thanked the jury for what he considered to be "a just verdict."

On the following Monday, after Judge Piper imposed the prescribed sentence of death by lethal injection, he ordered the sheriff of Klamath County to "deliver the defendant to the superintendent of the Oregon State Penitentiary at Salem, Oregon, pending the determination of the automatic and direct review by the Supreme Court of Oregon"— for every death sentence in Oregon carries an automatic appeal.

So, it wasn't over yet.

PART FOUR

TWENTY-TWO

Inmates on death row status are responsible for cleanliness of their cells. All cells must be clean and in a sanitary condition at all times. Items issued at each meal must be consumed during that meal. No foodstuffs may be stored in cells.

Because of security and safety concerns, no metal items or glass containers shall be permitted. Radio batteries shall be exchanged on a one-for-one basis only.

A clean set of outer garments and undergarments shall be provided on an exchange basis three times per week.

Coats may be issued for yard or escort purposes only. Issued coats shall not be permitted in the cell.

Each inmate may be provided an opportunity for inside exercise a minimum of 30 minutes per day (which may include shaving and showering) seven days per week.

Television viewing may be available to inmates; but if an inmate is using any service or activity in a destructive manner, the service may be suspended.

—Operation of Death Row Housing Unit, Oregon Department of Corrections

Jesse Clarence Pratt now took up residence in one of the nine cells on Death Row in the Oregon State Penitentiary at Salem, a facility first established in 1866—only seven years after Oregon became a state.

The present prison complex houses nineteen hundred inmates in a tight cluster of very plain three-story and four-story rectangular concrete structures with flat tarpaper roofs. A double grid of heavy steel bars covers all of the windows. The bare yellow ocher buildings are surrounded by a thirty-foot reinforced concrete wall punctuated by classic guard towers equipped with loudspeakers.

A separate Women's Unit is enclosed by a twelve-foot chain-link fence topped by two parallel coils of stainless-steel razor wire. Inside this fence, for the convenience of the ladies' visiting children, a small, pathetic collection of playground equipment is provided in a tiny razor-wire-enclosed quadrangle.

The stark inner corridor that provides access to the nine cells in death row is spotless. Images of the shielded lights in the ceiling are reflected in the polished surface of the bare waxed floor. The facility is utterly devoid of anything visually interesting. It is the essence of boredom.

As Jesse Pratt settled into life on death row, his automatic appeal process began. The thrust of the defense's appeal would center on its motion during the trial to exclude the testimony of Thelma Adams, detailing her abduction and rape by the same defendant six years before the rape-murder of Carrie Love—the "similar crimes" premise of the prosecution.

Adams's testimony had cast doubt on Pratt's claim that he had consensual sex with Carrie Love, and it helped "establish the identity of the person who had caused the death of Carrie Love," as the prosecution put it.

In hearing the defense's appeals at the local level, Judge Piper sided with the state. This earlier crime demonstrated intent, he concluded. And there were many similarities in the crimes. The victim was in the "same class of victims as in the present case." They were both acquaintances of the defendant. They were both relatively young and relatively attractive. They both had a relationship with the defendant. Both women were taken from the state of Washington to the state of Oregon. Both were sexually assaulted. Victims were bound and gagged with paper towels and duct tape. They were similar crimes.

Judge Piper ruled that since the victim in the present crime was deceased, there was a need for this evidence: "It showed that this similar crime had been committed, that the defendant did it, and Thelma Adams was here in court to establish that. This is evidence of modus operandi, or a common feature of both crimes."

The defense's appeal was therefore denied by the Klamath County court. But the next hurdle would be the Oregon Supreme Court. Putting that appeal together would take more than a year. Running hundreds of pages, the appellant's brief would be prepared in Salem by public defenders Gary Babcock and Stephen Williams. The document was received by the Oregon Supreme Court in June 1989, but would not be acted upon for six months.

Ambivalent about the death penalty, in its 135-year history, Oregon has repealed capital punishment twice and reinstated it twice. Since Pratt's appeal closely followed a five-to-two decision in February 1988, when the court had ruled that the death penalty was not in violation of the constitution of the state of Oregon nor of the U.S. Constitution, prosecution personnel had cause to feel comfortable about the current appeals process.

But when the Oregon Supreme Court finally ruled on Pratt's case on January 11, 1990, its decision produced shock waves that were felt as far away as Seattle and Spokane. The testimony of Thelma Adams might have been permissible, the court ruled, in the penalty phase of the trial as evidence of the defendant's character, but it was unacceptable as means to establish his guilt. Reversing the decision of the lower court, the body voted unanimously that Jesse Pratt was entitled to a new trial.

"This entire office is stunned by the supreme court decision," Ed Caleb told the *Klamath Falls Herald and News.* "The issue on the admissibility of prior crimes in the Pratt trial was researched thoroughly, at the local level and by the Oregon Department of Justice. This decision will cause immeasurable grief to the mother of Carrie Love and will put a huge financial burden on the taxpayers of Klamath County to retry this case." (Trial costs to date had been estimated at $150,000, not including police time and related travel expenses.)

"He *will* be retried!" the district attorney declared.

In Spokane, where nurse Connie Love had by now founded her own hundred-member Violent Crime Victims support group to help others, the news reversed members' roles as Connie's charges now offered their sympathy and support in their leader's new crisis.

"I felt like I did the night the deputy came and told me Carrie had been killed," Connie told the *Spokane Chronicle.* "It was like someone hit me in the middle of the abdomen. There's frustration, pain, and it just makes you want to cry." But she would go to Klamath Falls for the new trial, she declared.

At 5:30 P.M. on March 2, 1990, Jesse Clarence Pratt, having been returned from the Oregon State Penitentiary under heavy guard, was booked once again into the Klamath County Jail. He would be held without bail.

TWENTY-THREE

All the followers of science are fully persuaded that the processes of investigation, if only pushed far enough, will give one certain solution to each question to which they can be applied. . . .
—Charles Sanders Peirce (1839–1914),
founder of pragmatism

Three months after Jesse Pratt was transferred back to the Klamath County Jail for his second trial, Peter McDonald (no relation to Bruce McDonald) received a telephone call from Roxanne Osborne.

McDonald is an architect by training, and it shows in the stunning originality manifested in his home, which overlooks a tree-lined lake in Northeast Ohio. Pete took the call in his office. It is decorated by some of his own artwork in such diverse media as oils, watercolor on birch bark, wood sculpture, and stained glass.

For the last half of his first twenty-eight-year career, Peter McDonald was Director of Tire Design for the Firestone Tire & Rubber Company. He estimates that perhaps 100 million tires bear his personal imprint.

In his second career as a forensic scientist, McDonald's ability to sort out arcane subtleties in tire design has become the nemesis of at least a dozen convicted felons who made the mistake of leaving tire tracks at the scenes of their crimes—nailing themselves as surely as if they had left a set of fingerprints on a murder weapon. He has helped put away thieves, murderers, rapists—and sometimes he has helped exonerate an innocent defendant.

Typically, given a photograph or a plaster cast of a tire track found at the scene of a crime, McDonald can usually identify the manufacturer, the tire size and model, and what kind of vehicle it is likely to be on. His book on the subject, *Tire Imprint Evidence,* is a standard reference.

Osborne told McDonald about the Love murder case, which was now to be retried. She would not, however, be able to serve as prosecutor this time because she was currently running for district judge. District Attorney Caleb had, therefore, requested help from the Oregon Department of Justice, and McDonald would be hearing from the new lead counsel for the prosecution, Deputy Attorney General Byron Chatfield of the state's District Attorney Assistance Division in Salem.

Detective Ken Cooper and criminalist Mike Howard had suggested that McDonald might be able to help analyze the tire marks found on the victim's arm. In the first trial, these had not been convincingly tied to the tires on the defendant's tractor-trailer rig, Osborne explained.

McDonald arrived in Klamath Falls on June 17, 1990—four years to the day after the murder had been committed. At her office in the Klamath County Courthouse, Roxanne Osborne introduced the Ohio forensic scientist to Byron Chatfield, who had driven down from Salem.

On Osborne's desk was a stack of documents that included photographs of each of the thirty-four tires on Jesse Pratt's rig, as well as pictures of his truck. Because they had tire relevance, McDonald was also shown pictures of the crime scene and autopsy photos, including a life-size print of Carrie Love's left arm, bearing the marks that Ken Cooper had characterized as a "partial tire impression—the burnt-in pattern of a side tire tread."

McDonald asked if he could take the evidence somewhere where he could spread it out and study it more carefully. Osborne found him an office in the courthouse whose regular occupant was out of town. McDonald spent the next several hours going over the materials.

"When I get started on a new case," he later explained, "I don't like to prejudice my mind by reading other people's reports before I study photographs and any other materials related to the tires involved. I need to kind of absorb that first."

He laid out the materials on the desktop. When he is working, the Churchillian reading glasses perched on Pete McDonald's nose might give him an owlish look if he weren't bald. He began losing his hair while still in college, but he hasn't aged significantly since.

In his early sixties at the time, his fringe of gray hair matched a tailored mustache. Slightly built, he swam daily and looked it. The few lines on his face revealed that he laughed often.

Because the marks on Carrie Love's arm had been characterized as a "tire imprint," McDonald was expecting to see a *tread* pattern—the standard forensic "fingerprint" of tire footprint analysis. Instead, it looked to him as if the purple contusions on the victim's flesh had been made by the "side treatment" of a tire, the *edge* of the tread and the shoulder area of the tire sidewall as suggested in Ken Cooper's report—which McDonald had yet to read.

On one of the autopsy photos, McDonald had noticed something else. Amid the bruised tissue on the victim's upper chest, there appeared to be a faint diagonal pattern barely recognizable as the imprint of a truck tire tread. When he came out of the office, Pete asked if he could see the "Number 1 tire" in the real world and make some imprints from it.

The following morning, Chatfield and McDonald met Ken Cooper and Mike Howard at the Oregon State Highway Department Garage on Altamont Drive in Klamath Falls. Knowing that McDonald would want to run some tests, Cooper had borrowed a ThermoKing refrigerated trailer similar to the one rented by Northern Star and having about the same empty weight. The Pratt murder trials having been the news item they were in the Klamath Falls community, the owner-operator was pleased to let the police use his unit for their forensic experiments.

Already mounted on the trailer's rear "Number 5" axle in the outside right "Number 1" position, and pressurized to 70 pounds per square inch, was the tire Cooper had saved.

Pete McDonald immediately recognized it as a retread. Assisted by Ken Cooper, he wrote down all of the tire identification data molded into the sidewalls of the original carcass as well as marks added by the retreader. Because the tire sidewall had been abraded, the lettering branded into it during the recapping process was difficult to read—even when edge-lit with the flashlight Cooper had brought along.

McDonald laid out two twelve-foot strips of white cardboard on the smooth concrete floor of the garage. He coated one of them with fingerprint ink. After having a driver pull the trailer slowly over this sheet, McDonald asked him to roll the inked tire over the clean sheet—making an imprint of the entire circumference of the tire. The two small sections where the tread had been cut away were readily apparent in the inked imprint, but that wouldn't create a problem, McDonald assured the others.

The group then helped Pete unbolt the heavy wheel-tire assembly, lifting it up and laying it on its side on top of a fifty-five-gallon drum. Sandwiching a piece of carbon paper, carbon side out, between the tire and successive sheets of white paper, McDonald moved around the circumference, making carbon rubbings of all 360 degrees of the tire's side treatment. After the group turned it over, he repeated the operation on the inside of the tire.

That was it for now, McDonald announced. Thanking his fellow investigators, Pete folded his cardboard sheet into rectangles of a size he could carry back on the plane, packed up the rest of his evidence, which included the prosecution's photos, and returned to his home in Ohio.

Ken Cooper, meanwhile, had embarked on an expedition that would take him from Texas to

Alaska, with the objective of persuading all of the witnesses who had testified in the first trial to come back to Klamath Falls and testify once again. It would not be an easy task, particularly with the terrified women who had been abused by Pratt.

At least one witness was dead. Louis Randolph (the material witness who was proud of being the very professional trucker in the first trial) had been killed by a drifter hired by his allegedly abused wife. The woman, Cooper learned, had paid off the hit man in installments, using cash advances on her Visa card. While this spin-off murder had nothing to do with the case at hand, Cooper emphasized, it was perhaps an indication of the kind of people with whom Pratt surrounded himself.

TWENTY-FOUR

When I investigate a suspect in a murder case, I try to go back to when the defendant was in second grade.

—Criminal Investigator Bill Carroll

Returning to his office on Cottage Street in Salem, Chatfield briefed veteran criminal investigator Bill Carroll, who had been assigned to the case. Carroll, together with Ken Cooper, would assemble the evidence and locate the witnesses for Jesse Pratt's second trial. A former undercover drug investigator, Carroll was elected Narcotics Officer of the Year in 1984. A dogged investigator, Bill Carroll prided himself on having the highest telephone bill in the Criminal Justice Division. His office had several phone lines so he could receive incoming collect calls on one line while placing outgoing calls on another.

As was typical, when he got hold of the black address book found in Jesse Pratt's briefcase, Carroll called every telephone number in the book, using Pacific Bell's directory service when the number was no longer in service. He also checked each of the numbers against Northern Star's 1986 telephone bills—which included calls charged to Pratt's credit card.

Finding the "April" in Jesse Pratt's address book was a typical exercise. Like many entries in Pratt's little black book, hers was a first name only, reading simply, "April, black lady." Pratt had called this Seattle prostitute at 7:48 P.M. on June 17—about fifteen hours after the murder.

"From the telephone exchange, I could guess where she lived at the time," Carroll later explained. "So I called Seattle Police and I talked to the director of [the] vice [division] and told him, 'I'm looking for a black prostitute who works streets in that area who goes by the name of April—and that's all I know about her.'

"They had like four Aprils, and they gave me the names of everybody. So I just started calling the last known phone numbers that they had for them, and I just happened to hit it. A lot of these people are transients, and you lose 'em. And just because somebody was able to find them to be witnesses for one trial, if there is a second trial, you have to find them all over again."

When Ken Cooper visited April in Seattle, she admitted having been a prostitute and a drug addict in 1986 and that she had been arrested for prostitution twelve times. April remembered Jesse Pratt well. When she later took the witness stand, her testimony would reveal what the weapon used to stab Carrie Love might have been.

Another entry in Pratt's little black book was "Diane," a black girl from Seattle's inner city who grew up in a family of eight sisters, two brothers, and a few stray children from other families—one of whom was the mother of the youngest child in the house. Diane wanted Cooper and Carroll to understand that she was never really a career prostitute, but sex was an easy way to get enough money for a fix—and she was heavily addicted at the time. So, she was more of a call girl than a streetwalker, she said. This was how she met Jesse Pratt, through her friend "Sunshine."

"Sunshine's the weirdest person you'd ever expect to meet," she told them. "We grew up together in the same neighborhood, went to the same grade school. His real name is Leonard junior; so he was Sonny at first." But when Leonard became a transvestite, "Sonny" became "Sunshine."

A six-foot-tall black man, with skinny legs encased in nylons and wearing size 13 high heels, Sunshine looked a little ridiculous, she said. But not only did the two remain friends after his "transition," but Diane managed to accept and adjust to her friend's new lifestyle. During an interview with the author, Diane frequently spoke of Leonard as "she," explaining that she thinks of "her" that way.

Sunshine had introduced Diane to Jesse Pratt when he stopped by to pick up the two of them in his gold-speckled Cadillac with fur on the dash. "It was kind of a double date," she said, "but with just one guy." For openers, Pratt gave each of them a handful of money and generously passed around a variety of drugs.

"He was this big, domineering man who just acted like the perfect host. He took us to this house in Kent that he said was his. We all started undressing and so forth, and I was kind of in shock because although me and Sunshine were friends, we never went this direction before, and I didn't know what was going to happen. And when Jesse told Sunshine, 'Go get the rod,' it kind of freaked me out because I thought we were gonna get beat or something.

"But Sunshine comes back with this welding rod and Jesse had him put Vaseline on it. And after Jesse got hard, he had Sunshine stick it down his penis. And it started bleeding—and that *really* freaked me. But he got off on that!

"After that was over, Jesse and I had sex (without the welding rod in place, she was relieved to note), and the thing that really scared me was when I told him he was hurting me, he didn't move or anything. He just kind of smiled. He just loved it. And I started crying—and he seemed to get *more* of a thrill out of it.

"He kept welding rods—or sometimes knitting needles—in the glove box of his car or his truck to be used that way," Diane explained. It turned out, she said, to have been a regular routine carried out between Pratt and prostitutes of both sexes.

"He would give Sunshine as much as five hundred dollars for one of those sessions," Carroll reported. "And sometimes there was more to it. Leonard would give oral sex to Pratt to give him an erection, then insert knitting needles into his urethral canal until they bottomed out. After they were inserted, he would squeeze the tip of the penis and squirt rubbing alcohol along the knitting needles down the urethral canal and then masturbate his penis until he ejaculated along the needle. Or sometimes it was a welding rod. A new twist there."

It may have been a practice he invented while he was in Washington State Penitentiary, Carroll said.

Digging into Pratt's prison file, the investigator discovered that as a prisoner Jesse had worked in the Walla Walla welding shop for a time and that he had gone to sick bay for urethral bleeding.

Perhaps the most surprising thing Carroll and Cooper learned from Diane was that Jesse Pratt had offered *her* $1,500 to go to Los Angeles with him—on the trip he eventually took with Carrie Love. But, like Mona Bennett, Diane couldn't find a baby-sitter, or she "might never have had this interview," she now realized. After she told Pratt she couldn't make it, he offered the same deal to Sunshine. But Sunshine, who had also been smart enough to refuse previous bondage requests from Pratt, demurred.

When Ken Cooper later located Thelma Adams, she told him that she had also helped Jesse achieve his kinky reverse penetration orgasms—only with a "reefer thermometer." Every refrigerated trailer, or reefer, has one of these instruments inside the little trapdoor on the back of the unit so the driver can monitor the temperature of the chilled interior. The thermometer has a slender metal probe like a meat thermometer, with a round temperature-dial disc mounted on the end. Jesse would have her put this shaft into his urethral canal, she said, and he enjoyed watching the temperature go up.

The trailer Pratt had been pulling on the trip to Los Angeles with Carrie was a reefer.

TWENTY-FIVE

Pratt may be technically crazy, but he certainly knew right from wrong, or he wouldn't have built all those elaborate alibis.

— A Pratt defense counsel

Back in Klamath Falls, preparations were being made for Jesse Pratt's second trial. Donald A. W. Piper, the judge at Pratt's first trial, would preside at this one as well. Byron Chatfield would be lead counsel for the prosecution, assisted by Klamath County deputy district attorney Mark Runnels.

Defense counsel in the new trial would be Kenneth Hadley of Newport, Oregon. Assistant defense counsel was to be Klamath Falls lawyer Enver Bozgoz, who had been the author of a number of the motions filed early on in Pratt's first trial—before he suddenly resigned as defense counsel. The two defense counsels in the second trial would prove to have very different styles.

Pratt's new defense team had commissioned a psychological consultant to evaluate the personality and the intelligence of the defendant. He was Dr. Faulder Colby, a specialist in mental testing.

Excerpts from the clinician's detailed report would be presented in court.

Dr. Colby found Jesse Pratt to be "in the border-line range of intelligence. He has probably suffered some degree of severe cognitive impairment." The doctor, in fact, thought it was likely that Pratt had suffered a head injury.

"Mr. Pratt has problems with memory, tracking, concept formation, and general cognitive inflexibility. He has severe memory deficits, and his memory tends to confabulate older and newer information, leading him to generate new memories to fill in gaps. He has bizarre sensory experiences, mental confusion, and a rich fantasy life. He has an organic personality disorder in addition to whatever other disorders he may also have."

When given a standard Rorschach inkblot test, Pratt came up with very few interpretations of these enigmatic designs, and he surprised Dr. Colby by finding *no* shapes that looked like human beings. This, the psychologist said, generally indicates a person "who has difficulty in establishing close personal relationships—a person who is socially isolated." Colby found Pratt "full of hostility" and probably a person who tends to be "excessively sensitive to any inferred slight." In fact, the subject had quit abruptly in the middle of one test.

When the psychologist gave "this overweight, guarded, suspicious man" some standard intelligence tests, he found him to be "in the low average range. His insight and judgment were poor. He had trouble paying attention and concentrating to tasks." Dr. Colby scored Pratt as having an IQ of 77 in the "full-scale range" and 78 in the "verbal range." (These numbers were higher than the one Bill Carroll had found when young Jesse Pratt took a similar test at King School in California. At that time, his IQ was measured at 70.5.)

During the interview, Jesse Pratt told the psychologist that he had been sexually abused by a number of his stepfathers. Dr. Colby's report contains a discussion about the effects of sexual abuse on males, offering a possible explanation for the man's behavior. In a paragraph that seems designed to elicit sympathy for the defendant, Colby wrote:

"One can imagine the difficulties this young man had in adolescence. He was of borderline intelligence and unable to read, and would have been seen by other children as stupid. This, along with his history of sexual abuse, exacerbated the normal stress adolescents experience as they struggle with their developing sexuality and their desire to fit in with their peers. It is likely that adolescence was extremely painful, and was characterized by rejection, cruelty, teasing, and social isolation. It is not surprising that Mr. Pratt currently shows many of the more serious problems reported in male sexually abused victims."

The psychologist was not optimistic about Jesse Pratt's future. Dr. Colby seemed resigned to the defendant's losing in the guilt phase of his trial, and the report appears to be striving merely to save him from the death penalty:

"Mr. Pratt will likely do all right in highly structured and undemanding situations which conform to his previously conceived notions about the natural order of things; however, once he realizes he has no chance of parole, he may behave less docilely. . . . He is apt to lose control in conflicted situations. . . . He can be predicted to be violent and assaultive in the wrong situations. . . . Mr. Pratt's history strongly argues in favor of being kept under tight and rigidly supervised control for the remainder of his life."

This was not the kind of report Pratt's defense team had hoped to get. Noting the psychologist's speculation about possible sexual abuse, Enver Bozgoz went to the county jail to see his client. There, according to Bozgoz's account of the meeting, Pratt tearfully confirmed what he claimed was frequent anal rape by *two* of his stepfathers as well as by a male friend of his mother's, *and* heterosexual molestation by a woman who also was a friend of his mother.

As it happened, counselor Bozgoz had recently served as defense counsel for a Klamath County father who had been indicted for sexually molesting his own daughter. In preparation for that trial, the attorney had met another psychologist, a Dr. Ralph C. Underwager of Northview, Minnesota. Underwager had written several books about child sexual abuse and billed himself as an expert witness on the subject. Bozgoz called Underwager and invited him to evaluate Jesse Pratt at state expense.

Dr. Underwager arrived in Klamath Falls in February, 1991, a month before Pratt's second trial was to begin, and was introduced to the defendant by Bozgoz. Cleaned up for the occasion, Pratt was described in Underwager's resulting report as "clean and well groomed, sandy hair, short and combed forward to cover baldness; fingernails long but clean." He noted that Pratt had quick, jerky movements indicating a "high energy level" and that he "speaks clearly, with a slight nasal twang."

Dr. Underwager's report is somewhat more sympathetic than the one written by Dr. Colby. He quotes Pratt's characterization of Elizabeth Helle as "drunk, mean, cool, rejecting." He states he called her a stepmother because he cannot think of her as a mother. It is apparent that he sees her as sexually promiscuous, possibly whoring, with a steady succession of men coming through her life.

"He presents himself as aggressive, not backing down, angry, and able to intimidate at least some other people. He appears to have some pride in his independence, aggression, and readiness to stand up for himself. He sees this as 'manly' behavior. He was adamant that he would not let women dominate him. He apparently believes that women will always attempt to dominate males, and that 'a true man must resist at all costs.'"

Both psychologists would testify in Jesse Pratt's second trial. Neither knew that, at the same time, Ken Cooper was building his own profile of Jesse Pratt's personality based on complaints from his fellow prisoners in the Klamath County Jail—where Pratt found himself in disciplinary lockdown after threatening to kill two other inmates. Sample inmate quotes:

"Pratt thinks he's the head of the pecking order by bragging that he was in for murder, and everyone else was just a peon."

"Pratt's demeanor when he walks in a room is all high and mighty. Pratt treats everyone else like they are shit. Pratt's favorite words are 'This is *my* hotel.'"

"Pratt likes to continually threaten and harass and bully everyone around."

"Pratt makes life miserable for everyone in here."

"He told me, 'I've heard someone ratted on me. If I find out it was you, what I did to that little girl is nothing compared to what I will do to you.'"

"Pratt told me he was 'in for murder, for killing some broad. It was neat,' he said, 'I put her head under the back wheels and drove over her. You should've heard her head pop.'"

TWENTY-SIX

Consistent with the macho image Pratt sought to maintain, the pin-striped Kenworth tractor was equipped with quality tires in good condition: Bridgestone radials on the front steering axle and Michelins on the four drive wheels. The rented Utility trailer, by contrast, was fitted entirely with bias tires, all of which had been retreaded—the cheapest thing going.
>   —Forensic scientist Peter McDonald

Back in his high-ceilinged studio-office overlooking the tree-lined lake in Northeast Ohio (through a stained-glass window whose leading forms the pattern of a tire tread), Peter McDonald laid out the graphics he had collected. With the aid of his library of tire catalogs, he had been able to identify every one of the 34 tires on Jesse Pratt's rig. The two pairs of tires on the right side of the trailer's tandem axles, the ones suspected of having left their marks on the victim, were all of the same tread design. Although the tire carcasses, the "body" of the tire made by the original manufacturer, included two Generals, a Cordovan, and a Goodyear, all had been recapped with the same tread design. Looking up the tread pattern in his industry reference, McDonald identified the brand as a "Long Mile Highway Rib."

Unfolding the tire imprint he had made in the Klamath Falls garage, laying it out on the floor and comparing it with photographs of the victim, it was apparent to McDonald that the configuration of macula running diagonally across Carrie Love's naked chest had been made by the tread of a Long Mile Highway Rib recap.

In the familiar jargon of the forensic scientist, Pete noted that the tread pattern on Carrie Love's body was "consistent with" the Long Mile Highway Rib pattern of the tires on the Northern Star trailer. However, there was not enough detail in the contusions to tie the pattern of bruises positively to a particular tire. Stronger evidence would be needed to convince a jury.

McDonald pulled out Mike Howard's and Ken Cooper's pictures of the tires and studied them intently. He could see that three of the four trailer tires were worn much more severely than the one on the outside right of the rear axle—the "Number 1 tire on the Number 5 axle."

This was the tire Ken Cooper had saved. Pete noted that its carcass was a Goodyear Custom Cross Rib 11-22.5 "Hi-Miler" truck tire, and that the top cap on the retread was nearly new. Unlike its three siblings, which had circumferential cracks between the base of the tread and the tire body, the Number 1 Number 5 tire showed no such separation, further indicating its limited service on the road.

Examining his carbon rubbings of the side treatment of this tire, McDonald noted a succession of

molded "bars and pockets" on the edge of the tread
and that the pockets between the bars (where a tire
groove runs out to the tread edge) alternated round-
square, round-sqare. In the life-size photograph of
the victim's left forearm, the pattern of these alternating round and square pockets was clearly visible
in the bloody macula on Carrie Love's body.

Evident in the bruise pattern on the victim's arm
was that one of the bars was shorter than the others, possibly caused by the splice in the recap tread
stock. Such a splice interrupts the pattern in both
the tread and its side treatment.

Going back to his carbon rubbings of both sides
of the Number 1–Number 5 tire, McDonald found
what he was looking for. The rubbing pattern from
the inside surface of that tire clearly exhibited
a short bar in the corresponding round-square
sequence.

From this rubbing, Pete McDonald traced the pattern of this part of the tire's side treatment onto a
sheet of clear acetate, making a transparent "template" that showed the alternating round and square
pockets between the bars—including the short bar.
Turning over the acetate sheet, producing a mirror
image of the pattern, he placed it over the full-size
photo of Carrie Love's bruised forearm.

"I could see there was a consistency there," Mc-
Donald later explained with characteristic
understatement. It looked like Ken Cooper had
saved the correct tire.

McDonald felt that his analytical procedure
might be too technical for a jury to visualize merely
from his description, so he tried an experiment.
In his first career as a tire designer, he had often

sculpted tire treads out of modeling clay. Now he did something similar. After gluing his plastic template to a piece of Foamcore (a rigid styrene foam sheet used for mounting photographs) and cutting away the acetate from the recessed (pocket) areas of the side treatment pattern, he carved a model of the part of the tire segment that highlighted the tread splice. The result was "a partial replica of the Number 1—Number 5 tire on Pratt's trailer."

Coating his sculpture with Carter's red stamp-pad ink, he applied it to his own left arm, using the model like a big rubber stamp. The result looked eerily close to the life-size image of the arm in the picture in front of him. He now knew how to explain his findings to the jury. When Bill Carroll called later that day, Pete McDonald told him about his demonstration.

"But, as I told him," McDonald later recounted, "there was one thing that bothered me about it. How was it that the right rear tire on the trailer should turn out to be the *only* tire to leave marks on the victim's body, recognizing how close together the tires are on a tandem axle trailer suspension? Bill suggested that it could have something to do with the way the wheels on those rigid axles react when the truck tractor is turned sharply."

McDonald remembered he had a 1/25-scale model of an 18-wheeler tractor-trailer in the attic— a gift he had purchased some years ago in hopeful anticipation of a grandchild, who had yet to arrive. Or at least that had been his excuse when he saw it on display at the Firestone store.

Bringing the truck model downstairs and putting it on his drawing board, Pete made a tiny cardboard cutout of the victim's body to the same scale. Reenacting the crime in miniature on his desktop, he repeatedly drove the toy tractor-trailer rig over the 2½-inch figure, and he began to understand the dynamics of tire movement on tandem axles during a turn.

"The trailer often pivots around one of the forward wheels during the turn," he later explained to Carroll and Chatfield. "The result is what truck engineers call 'off tracking.' The rear tire 'scuds' sideways. You see it sometimes when the rear tire of a trailer tears up over a curb as the rig turns a corner, sometimes with enough sideways force to actually tear *off* a retread."

McDonald thought it might be helpful to locate the retreader of the Number 1–Number 5 tire to see if there might be a record of its sale to Northern Star. Referring to the notes he and Detective Cooper had taken in the Klamath Falls garage, he found the seven-digit code "debossed" (indented) into the tire sidewall by the tin identification strip inserted into the mold by the retreader.

Because the sidewall had scraped against curbs, these recessed letters and numbers were somewhat worn. They had been recorded by McDonald and Cooper as R XVH 034. The R stood for "retread"; the next three letters in the code identified the retread shop, and the numbers following designated the date of manufacture.

Pete looked up XVH in one of his references, *Who Retreads Tires.* He came up with Blue Grass Bandag, Inc., of Winchester, Kentucky. Checking the area code list in his phone book, he dialed Kentucky Bell Directory Service.

It proved to be a dead end. The retread shop

didn't use Long Mile treads. As implied in its name, Blue Grass Bandag purchased its tread stock from the Bandag Company and used Bandag's completely different retreading process.

McDonald put in a call to Bill Carroll to talk about it. Carroll volunteered to have the sidewall rephotographed with a "diopter" close-up lens with edge lighting to bring out the identification number more clearly. But it would take a day or two.

They talked about the part of the debossed code that had been indistinct—the critical letters in the middle. Could they be XVN rather than XVH? McDonald looked up XVN in the book. That one stood for the Puget Sound Tire Company, a Seattle retreader. Bingo!

He made another telephone call. Puget Sound's operations manager, Rick Wooten, was glad to help. Wooten not only confirmed that he had sold such a tire to Northern Star, but he managed to locate the sales slip. He even offered to send McDonald an old retread marking tin, reading "R XVN 081," that McDonald could show the court.

Wooten promised to obtain from his company's bank a photocopy of the Northern Star check in payment for the tire. It was in McDonald's mailbox a week later.

Written for the amount of $163.88 and dated June 4, 1986, the check was signed by Carrie L. Love.

TWENTY-SEVEN

The plot thickens. . . .
    —Arthur Conan Doyle (1859–1930),
                    A Study in Scarlet

After agonizing weeks of voir dire jury selection, the guilt phase of Jesse Clarence Pratt's second trial finally got under way on Wednesday morning, March 13, 1991. Seated at the defense table was a very different-looking Jesse Pratt. Gone was the bushy sphere of Afro-style hair. Instead, a short, conservative haircut exposed more of his advancing baldness. His trademark mass of unkempt facial hair had disappeared. A clean-shaven, unfamiliar face had emerged—so unfamiliar that criminalist Mike Howard, sitting in the courtroom before the trial began, failed to recognize the defendant when he walked in.

As Pete McDonald observed after he testified, "Those pictures that Ken Cooper shot of an un-shaven truck driver in the nude with a big belly hanging out looked very different from how the defendant looked in the courtroom." Pratt was also better dressed than when last seen. Over a dark sport shirt, he wore a beige corduroy jacket. He would wear it every day. He might have been a scholarly author—or the trucking executive he aspired to be.

Pratt's current predicament seemed to have little effect on his demeanor. During breaks in the trial while the jury was out, he chatted cheerfully and flirted with court reporter Carol O'Brion.

"Despite his obvious frustration, he was full of friendly jokes," O'Brion remembers. "Lots of sexual overtones, but he never crossed the line. He loves attention—an egomaniac really. But he can be very endearing. He knows how to get'cha. He can really suck you in—make you feel sorry for him. Although he has poor grammar, he can be very manipulative. He's *got* to be in charge.

"He had an odd posture as he sat at the defense table," O'Brion continued. "Sitting kind of hunched forward, he seemed to have no neck. He was bent over as if he had a back problem and he had an off-center hump on his back that prevented his jacket from fitting properly. The skin on his hands was pure white—probably because he had spent so much time in jail. He had long fingers that were bent inward as he sat there—as if he were arthritic, but I don't think he was. He did have hypoglycemia, I understand."

Connie Love, Carrie's mother, had a different impression as she sat rigidly in the spectators' gallery with victim's advocate Charlene Divine.

"He had enormous hands—hands like an ape. I couldn't take my eyes off them, knowing they had killed my daughter."

After Judge Piper gave the jury its initial instructions, he called on the prosecution. Lead counsel Byron Chatfield told the jury that his opening statement would be like a table of contents to familiarize them with the evidence he would present. Chatfield told the jurors that Bruce McDonald would testify about finding the sleeping bag and pillowcase in the ditch and how he and the officers tried to find the spot the next day. They would hear evidence about later finding the body and about forensic work that would tie the crime to the defendant—including testimony from a tire expert who had analyzed tire marks on the body.

It was a short, straightforward preface devoid of histrionics. Chatfield's manner was that of a teacher explaining a new computer program to a class whose intelligence he respected. When he completed what he called "this overview of our evidence," the prosecutor's voice softened. His tone became compassionate as he seemed to sympathize with the personal distress some jurors might feel as they faced up to their responsibility.

Cocounsel Enver Bozgoz presented the opening statement for the defense. He invited the jury to be suspicious—to be skeptical of the prosecution's "so-called evidence." Bozgoz began by giving the jury a sympathetic biography of Jesse Pratt, opening with the tragic loss of his father in World War II.

Speaking with a Russian accent familiar to those who knew him, Bozgoz frequently put down the prosecutor's "overview of the evidence." He claimed that the evidence to be presented by the prosecution was tainted by police prejudice, which ignored any evidentiary trails that led away from Jesse Pratt. It was a long, detailed opening statement. Items he complained about included:

• Bruce McDonald's wife, Dorothy, had recognized the purse in the sleeping bag as looking like one a young woman had when Dottie waited on her at Manley's Tavern in Crescent Lake Junction on the evening of June 16. The woman had been with a gray-haired man who might have been driving the dark-colored Kenworth that Dottie McDonald had also noticed in the tavern's parking lot. Why wasn't the gray-haired man investigated as a suspect?

- There was a footprint on the shoulder of the road where Bruce McDonald had found the initial evidence. Why wasn't a cast made for comparison with the shoes of the defendant—or other suspects?
- There was a Merit cigarette butt found in the same area. But as soon as they learned that neither Jesse Pratt nor Carrie Love smoked, the police didn't bother to check it.
- There were cigarettes in the gravel in the area where Carrie Love had been run over. And there was a glove. Why were these ignored?
- Why hadn't the Oregon State Police photographed the tires of the blue Scout found abandoned on Highway 97 a few miles from where the evidence was found?

Speaking of tires, Bozgoz added, the defense's expert witness would explain that the tire marks on Carrie Love's body could have been made by *any* tire. This last statement may have been intended to discount in advance the testimony of prosecution witness Peter McDonald—whom Bozgoz inadvertently called "*Paul* McDonald," and later "McFarland," in his opening statement. Bozgoz seemed bent on denigrating the forensic scientist:

"He's from Ohio. And apparently, a number of years ago, he was workin' for—uh—I don't know—Firestone or Goodyear Tire Company, an' he'll testify." The cocounsel spoke of the "overlay" McDonald would present as fitting the marks on Carrie Love's arm or body and told the jury they would have to decide whether that proved that the tire that ran over her belonged to Jesse Pratt. Then he told the jury the answer:

"No! It does *not* belong to Jesse Pratt. Never been on Jesse Pratt's truck." The prosecution failed to object.

Although cocounsel Bozgoz displayed an excellent command of the English language in his well-written pretrial motions, his oral manner was disconcerting. Not only were his words submerged in a Russian accent that got heavier whenever tension mounted, but he also omitted articles ahead of nouns. His aggressive, finger-pointing interrogation style was not enhanced by his habit of filling his own thoughtful pauses with a single explosive, throat-clearing cough, often modulated to express his mood at the moment. Bozgoz concluded his opening statement with a plea for skepticism.

"We will present the evidence, and then you take a look—the 'overview of the evidence' that Mr. Chatfield said—and ask yourself, 'What kind of evidence do you call this? You ask us to convict this man of aggravated murder so you can get death penalty and then you don't investigate your case?' They are asking you for a scapegoat. And that will be up to you—whether you want to use Jesse Pratt for scapegoat or not. Thank you."

Bozgoz then moved to exclude all witnesses from the courtroom so they could not hear each other's testimony. The judge granted the sequester motion, and a number of people in the audience stood up and exited.

The first witness, as in the first trial, was Bruce McDonald, who told his story once again about finding the sleeping bag and pillowcase and turning them over to the Oregon State Police in Klamath Falls.

During cross-examination, Enver Bozgoz attempted to confirm that Bruce's wife had worked at Manley's Tavern the previous evening and that she had noticed the couple to which he had referred in his opening statement. But McDonald said he didn't think Manley's Tavern was open on Monday nights. The defense counsel also asked some questions about the Scout vehicle that Bruce remembered seeing. The witness said it was "way past" the area where he had found the evidence. In redirect examination, Byron Chatfield had McDonald quantify the distance. He estimated that the Scout was "eight or nine miles away."

Troopers Eric Brown and Raymond Rathke followed Bruce McDonald to the witness stand, confirming receipt of McDonald's evidence and police attempts the next day to locate the spot where he had found it. During cross-examination, Kenneth Hadley concentrated on the attention the officers had given the stolen Scout vehicle.

When Chatfield called Detective Ken Cooper to the witness stand to testify about his analysis of Bruce McDonald's evidence, both questioner and witness were careful not to characterize the "ball of paper towels and duct tape" as being a "mask." Cooper repeatedly called it an "item." After he opened it up, it became a "bowl." It was "cup shaped," he said. The detective described the hexagonal black earring he found inside. He spoke of "indentations" in the bowl's interior, describing the molded impression of a face merely as a "configuration."

When Chatfield asked if the indentations in the configuration appeared to have the shape of a nose or chin, the defense objected at once. The objection was sustained.

Defense counsel Hadley's cross-examination was uneventful. In contrast to Bozgoz's accusatory tone, the questions asked by Pratt's lead counsel were gentlemanly. They seemed to be intended merely to clarify the physical details about which the witness was testifying.

When he took the witness stand, criminalist Mike Howard was similarly careful to avoid the use of "drag mark," the term that had caused so much trouble during the first trial. As he went through the prosecution's evidentiary photographs, he spoke of a "depression in the gravel" containing bloodstains and human tissue, an "impression in the gravel leading toward the photographer," an "impression that looks like something has been dragged through the gravel." Getting away with these phrases, he finally ventured to point out a "drag mark much more obvious where the gravel has been parted and pushed to the sides."

There was no objection. Indeed, during cross-examination, even Bozgoz began calling it a "drag mark," to the prosecution's surprise. After that, the

expression became a standard reference that everyone in the courtroom understood.

When Enver Bozgoz cross-questioned Lieutenant
Howard, he asked questions to which he hoped to
receive uniformly negative answers: Had the criminalist analyzed the Merit cigarette butt found in the
ditch? How about the cigarette package found in
the truck stop at Milepost 206? What had been
done with that? Wasn't it possible to get DNA identification from residual saliva on cigarettes? Or
from the dried tear on a contact lens collected at
the autopsy? Or from the black earring found inside the ball of paper towels and duct tape?

Such analysis was beyond the state of the art,
Howard stated.

To dramatize the importance of analysis, cocounsel Bozgoz poured a glass of water from the
decanter on the defense table. Turning to the witness, he pointed out that it was impossible to tell
whether the contents of the glass were water or gin
unless they tasted them or analyzed them.

"In the totality of the courtroom," Howard observed dryly, "we would have reason to believe it
was water."

Once again, the defense lawyer focused attention on the blue Scout. Had Howard processed
the vehicle?

No, Howard answered, someone else had.

Bozgoz spent a great deal of time on questions relating to the possibility of matching dust on a
suspect's boots, for example, to the mineral content of gravel found in the area. Specifically he
wanted to know if Mike Howard had analyzed the
dust collected from vacuuming the interior of the

cab and compared it with the mineral formulation of gravel in the truck stop area.

Howard pointed out that dust on a ten-year-old truck would contain a mixture of a multitude of things, and to try to pick out dust from Seattle or from California or from British Columbia would be impossible.

Ken Cooper returned to the witness stand to narrate an edited video showing the jury the truck stop at Milepost 206, the location of the gravel pile where the body was found, and its surroundings.

This time the defense wanted to know whether Cooper had made castings of any of the scores of ruts seen in the heavily traveled gravel surface—and if not, why not?

TWENTY-EIGHT

*A pathologist is a doctor of laboratory medicine,
an M.D., a doctor who specializes in the
examination of tissues, microscopic sections, gross
pathology on larger pieces of tissue with subsequent
microscopic sections. In the hospital, we do the
examination of biopsies—a lung, say, or a portion
of a liver. And we examine chemical pathology
which may go on in patients.*

*We also do autopsies. I think you know what
autopsies are: the examination of a body after
death to determine the cause of death, and the
mechanisms surrounding death, and other
conditions which may have been present at death.*
—Dr. Robert Jamison, Medical Examiner

After lunch on the first day, Dr. Robert Jamison,
Klamath County medical examiner, was sworn in.
The doctor was an impressive witness. He spoke with
simple eloquence. He sounded like the young professor every first-year medical student wishes he
could have for anatomy. His patient, articulate ex-
planations were easy for the layman to understand.
He defined medical terms when it seemed necessary
to use them, and he easily translated metric values

into American units to make it easier for the jury to visualize them (e.g., "200 cc's of blood is about a fifth of a quart").

The intrinsically grisly content of his lecturettes was somehow mitigated by the sincere, caring manner in which they were delivered. As a prosecution witness, Dr. Jamison never referred to the victim as "the body." When he spoke of her injuries, she was always "Carrie Love."

The prosecution spent considerable time on the distribution of duct tape residue on Carrie's body—to establish that something had been taped over her face and that her hands had been taped behind her back.

Because it was difficult to photograph this residue, Dr. Jamison explained, he first had his photographer take close-ups of the deposits as they appeared with normal lighting. Then, after dusting the areas with fingerprint powder, which clung to the sticky residue, these areas were reshot, making their location more obvious. Each time one of these photos was shown to the jury, defense counsel Hadley entered an objection to the "altered" photo; each time he was overruled.

The doctor reviewed the many injuries Carrie Love had sustained. Her head had been crushed, as had her facial bones, and her upper two vertebrae had been dislocated. Her left arm and her chest showed "marks consistent with tire tread marks." There were twelve puncture wounds about an eighth of an inch in diameter in locations ranging from the back of her neck to the front of her abdomen. These had been inflicted by a pointed object, he said. They could have been produced by an ice pick. And yes, in answer to Byron Chatfield's question, they could have been inflicted with a metal knitting needle.

These stab wounds would not have caused much external bleeding, the pathologist explained, "because the smooth sides of the rounded instrument would have compressed the tissue and sealed it to a degree, since there was no cutting edge to it." Internal bleeding, on the other hand, "could have ranged from nonexistent to massive."

Jamison pointed out that at least one fingernail had been "torn from its moorings" and bent backward with considerable force. There was foam in Carrie's trachea, showing the presence of edema, a buildup of fluid in the respiratory system—which, he explained, indicated that suffocation had taken place over a considerable period of time as fluid seeped in from the bloodstream and adjacent tissues.

"She was deprived of air sufficient to prevent her from carrying on normal bodily functions for at least half an hour and, more likely, more than an hour."

The resulting asphyxiation could have caused death by itself, the pathologist said, but once she suffered stab wounds to the large veins adjacent to her heart, death occurred in a matter of five minutes or so as the pericardial sac surrounding the heart became filled with blood and prevented its beating. But, he emphasized, she may still have been alive when she was run over. It was impossible to tell.

This was not good news for the defense. Running over the head of a living person obviously could qualify by itself as "maiming"—one of the criteria that could establish *aggravated* murder.

In his cross-examination, defense counsel

Hadley quoted the opinion expressed by the former state medical examiner, the recently retired Dr. William Brady, who had stated in Pratt's first trial that he believed that this head injury had been inflicted after death.

"There is no way to tell whether she was alive or dead. *But* as soon as her brain stem was severed, her heart would stop beating," Jamison responded, showing no hesitation in disagreeing publicly with the senior doctor. He repeated that this determination was simply unknowable given the pathological evidence available.

In an effort to avoid the connotation of "torture," Kenneth Hadley made an effort to dismiss the medical examiner's suggestion that the victim had been smothered. He asked the witness to read what he had put down on the line labeled "Cause of Death" on the death certificate he had signed.

On a line with the printed instruction "Enter only one cause per line," the document read: "Stab wounds to heart and great vessels." But, the medical examiner pointed out, he had also listed "evidence of asphyxiation (partial)" on the line following.

There was some lengthy discussion about the meaning of "partial." Perhaps that meant, the defense counsel suggested, that the mask had been removed before the stabbing began.

No, the pathologist said, he had meant that asphyxiation was a partial cause of Carrie Love's death, and he still thought so.

Hadley wanted the doctor to estimate Carrie Love's time of death. He criticized the doctor for not bringing his own thermometer to the crime scene to record the body temperature and for permitting someone to step on and crush the only one available.

The police had already taken the temperature of the body, the doctor said, and it was already so cold that there was no way to graph its temperature decrease over time—to extrapolate the time of death. A nude body on a cold night in contact with cold gravel, the doctor explained, was a very different situation than the one an investigator enjoys when a person dies in a warm building.

The degree of rigor mortis was no help, either, Jamison said, since it is caused by the muscles stiffening when the sugar in the muscles turns to lactic acid. But this rate of change is affected by the ambient temperature, by how recently a victim has had a meal, and by other factors.

The defense's final quibble was about the doctor's observation that the weight of a passenger car would not be sufficient to crush Carrie Love's skull, but that the weight of a semi–truck-tractor would. Hadley got the witness to admit that a pickup truck, loaded heavily enough, might be sufficient.

TWENTY-NINE

*Whoso killeth any person, the murderer shall be put
to death by the mouth of witnesses. . . .*
                                        —Numbers 35:30

When Connie McClintock was called to the witness
stand, she described taking their own things out of
the truck as Pratt and Love loaded their belongings.
She confirmed leaving a partial roll of silver duct
tape in the cab, as well as Jesse's sleeping bag, which
she identified when the court exhibit was presented.

Connie McClintock also identified her pillows—
the ones in the truck and their mates, which she
had at home, but which she had subsequently
turned over to Sergeant Hein. Bozgoz objected
because "she didn't look at them for more than
ten seconds," and he didn't understand how she
could recognize them that quickly unless they
were marked in some manner. During cross-
examination, he also got her to admit that since
they had been purchased by Mel at a large discount house, other people probably had some of
the same make and appearance.

New and interesting was her knowledge that Jesse
Pratt kept an ice pick, "about eight inches long with

a wooden handle," in the glove box of his Cadillac
and that Mel and Mona had looked for it in his car
after they heard about the murder, but they didn't
find it. The defense got that last statement dismissed as hearsay, however, because she hadn't
personally looked for the ice pick. Instead, standing next to the pair as they searched, she had
accepted Mel's word for their having been unable
to find it.

The next witness was none other than Leonard
Slack, aka Sunshine, who had recently had his
name legally changed to Sandy Slack. Although he
had grown up in the ghetto, he didn't use ghetto
syntax, nor was there any hint of a Southern accent
in Slack's speech. It was peppered with jive talk,
however, and his voice sometimes sounded unnat-
urally high—until he cleared his throat in a heavy
bass register. Slack seemed to have a hard time taking the court seriously, occasionally breaking into a
nervous giggle.

The witness was asked to identify the defendant.
"He looks a little different, but that's Jesse." He
said it with a lilt reminiscent of Ed McMahon introducing Johnny Carson on the old *Tonight Show.*

Slack had been introduced to Jesse Pratt by April,
he said, and the man had been very kind to him.
They had, he said, "hung out" and "kicked favors."
But he had never acquiesced to his patron's request
to do bondage. I told him, "The only way I'm
gonna do any ropin' is by jumpin' it."

He was willing, reluctantly, to go along with "a
trio, sexualwise," as Diane had described, and he
explained that Jesse Pratt had wanted to set up such
an arrangement with his secretary (Carrie)—whom

Pratt described as a "jazzy lady, cheerleader type of blonde girl, slim waistline." But Pratt's planned assignation had never come off.

The important part of Sandy Slack's testimony was that Jesse Pratt often carried with him metal knitting needles "about twelve inches long and as big around as a pencil." He fitted them into a leather glasses case and they stuck out the end, the witness said. They were used, he said, in Jesse's creative sexual excursions.

The defense had no questions for Slack.

The final witness for the week was Dean Bolton, a thirty-eight-year-old convict who had volunteered his testimony, and who had been brought down from the Oregon State Penitentiary in Salem. He readily admitted he had been convicted of more than one felony. Since 1988, he said, he had been serving a twenty-year term, from which he expected to be paroled in 1994. Instead of saying "I do" when taking the oath, Bolton's response was simply "Yeah." Questioned by assistant prosecutor Mark Runnels, the witness stated that he expected no special treatment for agreeing to testify in this trial.

Bolton had met Jesse Pratt in the Klamath County Jail in 1986, while Pratt was under investigation for murder. He was one of the inmates Ken Cooper had talked to about Pratt's behavior in the county jail. With some misgivings about possible reprisal by Pratt, he had decided to come forward.

"We had a little conversation," the prisoner testified. "I asked him whether he really killed the young lady, and he told me yes, he did."

"Do you remember anything else about it?" Runnels asked.

"He said the funniest thing about killing the young lady was when he run her over with his truck—the sound her head made when he ran over it."

The career criminal apparently didn't quite have the stomach to repeat for the jury the more precise quote he had given to Ken Cooper: "You should have heard her head pop."

That ended the prosecution's questions. The defense counsel asked the prisoner what he had been convicted of. Bolton mentioned "first-degree robbery, first-degree burglary, first-degree theft, driving without a license, and a whole bunch of misdemeanors."

The defense wanted to know if the witness had ever driven a big truck—an eighteen-wheeler. He said he had. Asked for his opinion, he ventured that a driver could probably hear the sound of a fracturing head over the truck's engine noise if the body was under the rear wheel of the tractor, but not if it was run over by the rear wheel of the trailer—as had been the case with Carrie Love.

A procession of familiar witnesses followed. Some had matured since their last appearance in the Klamath County Courthouse. Cody Kupferer was now twenty-two years old and working in a jewelry business. Former tire changer Jeff Warren, who had pumped Jesse Pratt's diesel fuel at Redd's Tires, was a twenty-three-year-old electrician. His memory seemed as sharp as ever as he recalled the oddly mismatched couple whose Kenworth he had serviced five years earlier. He still remembered the man's "bushy hair, full beard, scrawny arms, big gut, that his shirt was unbuttoned" and that he was wearing blue jeans and cowboy boots. He described the girl's shoulder-length hair, estimated that she was about his own age, maybe a little older, and that she was wearing a light coat, jeans, a striped shirt, and no shoes. "She had booties on."

Mona Bennett, now married and with a new last name, still seemed to be a staunch supporter of Jesse Pratt as she reluctantly testified to his giving her his early alibi about having dropped Carrie at My Place Tavern. In cross-examination, Kenneth Hadley grilled her at length about what she knew about Carrie Love's intimate relationships with Jim Hancock and Cody Kupferer—until Byron Chatfield objected to the line of questioning as irrelevant and was sustained. "Demeaning a victim's character can sometimes make a jury care less about her," Chatfield later explained.

Kenneth Griffin, a since-retired trucker who had worked only two months for Jesse Pratt in 1986, testified to having breakfast one morning with Pratt and an unidentified pockmarked man (probably Dan Gates, the elusive manager of Jesse's Double Jack escort service) at a small café on East Marginal Way. The stranger, he said, told Jesse he had "a neat secretary," to which Jesse responded that "he would have to try that out, but would have to be careful about it." Griffin claimed that Pratt's sexual intentions were obvious, but Enver Bozgoz successfully objected to his drawing such a conclusion.

When Ken Cooper returned to the witness stand, he described the processing of Pratt's truck and trailer, including seizure of the right rear outermost tire (Number 1 tire on the Number 5 axle), and his asking Lieutenant Howard to cut out two pieces of its tread. The heavy tire, mounted on the original trailer wheel, was leaning against the wall of the courtroom. It had been submitted as State Exhibit 246.

Photographs of all the other tires on the tractor-trailer rig were also placed in evidence. The number of pieces of state evidence, now numbering in the hundreds, grew further still with submission of the contents of Carrie Love's purse, all of the items in Jesse Pratt's black briefcase, photos of him at the time of his arrest, bits of his hair, and fingernail scrapings, plus other items.

The prosecution's next witness would jolt the court. Again. Danny Randolph (no relation to the late Louis Randolph) had shared an isolation cell with Jesse Pratt in the Klamath Falls jail while awaiting trial for possession of firearms. He reported an experience similar to that of prisoner Dean Bolton, but much more recent.

Thirty-two years old and a convicted felon, Danny Randolph had waived extradition from St. Louis with the approval of his parole officer in that city, and he seemed to be trying to turn his life around. Although he had traveled two thousand miles to voluntarily testify in this trial, he made it clear that he didn't relish residing in the Klamath County Jail while in Oregon. In his hometown of St. Louis, he said, he had been free on probation.

Beginning in August 1990, Randolph testified, he had talked to fellow inmate Jesse Pratt every day for about three months. He identified the defendant in the courtroom. Mark Runnels asked Randolph if Pratt had ever told him he was accused of murder and rape.

"Yes. He said he was in jail for murder and a sexual crime."

"Did he ever tell you who he was supposed to have killed?"

"He never said no name. He just said some girl."

"Did he ever tell you that he did it?"

"Yes, sir. On the Monday before the eleventh. I was going to court on the eleventh, and Jesse said, 'Yeah, I choked her. I ran over her and it felt good to feel and hear her bones crush.' And he looked at me and smiled, and said, 'How do you like me now?'"

"During these discussions," Runnels asked, "did you ever discuss other types of injuries?"

"Yeah. About a stab wound or stab wounds, and they couldn't figure out if they happened when he ran over her with the truck or whether he stabbed her—in the back of the neck."

"And did he discuss with you anything about what type of truck?"

"Yeah. A *big* truck. But he said that him and his lawyers were gonna make it look like a jeep or a little truck that was stolen all the way from California, or somewhere like that."

"Did he ever talk with you about any witness in this case?"

"Yeah. Some kid that worked in a filling station."

"This is a kid who worked in a gas station?"

"Yeah, he was. That's what *I* said, 'A *gas* station?' And he got so heated about it, he said, 'It's not gas; it's *diesel.* Diesel trucks take diesel!' I was supposed to say 'diesel' because Jesse is infatuated with big trucks. And we got into an argument about the 'gas' and 'diesel' thing. And I wondered why he got so mad."

"Did he ever want you to do something concerning this witness?"

"Well, yes. I was supposedly a member of a gang, and he wanted to know if I could have somebody killed. He kept saying, 'If this witness wasn't around'—because he seen him and the girl together the night he supposedly killed the girl."

The witness Jesse Pratt feared was obviously Jeff Warren. Pratt might have shown greater concern for his own mouth.

Danny Randolph insisted that no one had told him anything about this case except Jesse Pratt and that no deals had been made with him—"Or I wouldn't be sittin' in the damn jail here."

The man's testimony seemed to shake up Enver Bozgoz, who inadvertently called him Mr. Pratt when he rose to cross-question him. Quickly correcting himself, the lawyer sought to discredit the witness by having him confirm a string of previous convictions for burglary, robbery, theft, and, in last year's Klamath Falls arrest, possession of firearms.

Randolph readily admitted his record.

Bozgoz then attempted to introduce several exhibits apparently detailing the witness's convictions. But each time Bozgoz tried to get one of his documents admitted, Byron Chatfield objected, stating that admission of such written records was impermissible under Oregon rules of evidence, since the man had not denied his arrests and/or convictions.

Cocounsel Bozgoz tried other tacks to destroy Randolph's credibility. He particularly sought to impeach the witness's claim that his knowledge of Jesse Pratt's crimes had come exclusively from Pratt himself. Despite his limited debating skills, Danny

Randolph successfully parried the lawyer's verbal assaults at every turn.

"Mr. Randolph," Bozgoz asked, "you have indicated you have been in prison in various places, is that correct?"

"Yes."

"Is it true, sir, when a person comes to prison, before he even opens up his mouth, everybody knows what he's been convicted of?"

"Not necessarily, no."

"But generally it is true, isn't it?"

"No, not the way they are nowadays, no."

"Well, [cough], how are they nowadays?"

"They have changed from where inmates, or people in my position or people that's in jail, they don't work around records no more. They don't have access to records. They keep all them jobs with civilian personnel."

"Are you telling us, sir, that when a person goes to jail he can be there for several weeks or months without anybody knowin' anything about him?"

"Yes."

(Long pause) "You watch television?"

"Not while I was in there. No. There was no television there."

"All right. Do they have televisions in jail?"

"Not the part I was in. No, they didn't. Me and Jesse was in the hole together and there was no television, no nothin'."

"Well, you talking about a hole. Uh. What you mean about a hole?"

"It's just a place where, like, if you're violent or, you know, you're in trouble, they put you in the hole. It's a place segregated. You know, TV's considered a privilege, and stuff like that are considered privileges, and I wasn't supposed to get no privileges or nothin' like that."

"And why were you in the hole?"

"'Cause I . . ."

"Objection, your honor." Chatfield's objection was sustained.

"Now you telling us then, sir," Bozgoz resumed, "under oath here that you have never seen prisoners in the county jail, nobody knows why they are there, nobody talks about it in jail?"

"I didn't really care. I was worried about myself."

"No. I—I'm not talking about yourself. Others."

The lead prosecutor objected to the witness being asked to speculate on what other people knew and to report as hearsay. He was sustained. The defense counsel tried again:

"Isn't it generally true, sir, rumor goes around the jail among the jail mates—inmates?"

"I don't understand what you mean. The only persons in there was me and Jesse and a bunch of Mexicans."

Bozgoz grunted. There was a pause. He coughed. He sniffed. Danny Randolph filled the pause:

"And they didn't speak English. There wasn't nobody in there to talk to but me and Jesse to talk to each other."

It went on like that, with longer pauses between questions. After lunch, the judge sustained the prosecutor's objection to the defense's documenting Randolph's convictions. It had been effective testimony for the prosecution.

Danny Randolph was followed to the witness stand by Jesse's former "girlfriends" Diane and April. Diane testified to seeing Pratt with a welding rod on two occasions, one at his home in Kent. April said he brought a towel to her apartment in which one welding rod and two red knitting needles were wrapped. The women estimated that the objects were eight to ten inches in length and smaller in diameter than a pencil.

The women may have identified the medical examiner's "ice pick–like instrument" with which the victim had been stabbed.

THIRTY

Elizabeth Helle, mother of accused murderer Jesse Clarence Pratt, walked slowly to the witness stand Friday, then repeated to the jury what her son told her about the June 1986 death of Carrie Lynette Love.

—Lu Wolchin,
Klamath Falls Herald and News

Most of the next four days were taken up with the presentation of forensic evidence by criminalists Larry Dickenson and Mike Howard, augmented by additional testimony from Detective Ken Cooper, as well as by fingerprint expert Loren Laird. The criminalists described their detection of bloodstains in the sleeping bag, in the truck cab and sleeper, as well as the subsequent blood typing, DNA testing, and enzyme analysis of these and tissue samples collected during the autopsy.

Mike Howard explained how he was able to make sense out of the tangled gobs of hair vacuumed from the truck interior. The primary tool he used, he said, was a comparison microscope. It was really two microscopes similar to ones the jurors may have used in biology class, he explained. These are mounted side by side and joined by an optical bridge, so the left side of the image is what the left microscope sees while the right side of the image is what is under the other objective lens.

Surprisingly, he said, it is much easier to achieve a match with fibers than with hair. "Hair," Howard explained, "has a structure something like a pencil. It has a point and a center like the lead going down the middle of a pencil; it has a cortex like the wood; it has scales that can be compared to the paint. And it has a root.

"There are only two pigments that result in the many shades of hair," he elucidated. "One accounts for blond through red, the other brown to black. The great variety of hues we see are determined by how many of these pigment granules there are, how big they are, and how they are packed. The hair itself is naturally white—like mine is getting because the cells are not producing much pigment anymore.

"Because of the many possible variations in color, thickness, and structure, it is relatively easy to exclude hair in a sample as *not* coming from a given person. I could probably quickly eliminate ninety-five percent of the people in the courtroom as having hair that was *not* consistent with a given sample. But since one hair differs from another on the same head, a *positive* identification is not possible."

Fibers were different, he explained. With fibers, one *can* get a positive identification. After determining the polymer out of which the fiber is made (e.g., nylon, polyester, acrylic—or natural fibers like wool, cotton, or silk), there are many identifiable markers, some coming from characteristics of individual spinnerette orifices from which synthetic fibers are extruded. One can measure diameter, color, refractive index, surface characteristics (pits, cracks, streaks, cross-hatching), the kind and distribution of delusterant on the surface to kill shininess; and one can rotate the samples side by side under polarized light to bring out such subtle differences as how optical properties change with rotation.

Lieutenant Howard illustrated his testimony with a series of slides he had made through his comparison microscope, showing the jury why he had arrived at the conclusions he had drawn. There was no question in his mind that he had found cross contamination between the fibers found in the cab and sleeper, and those in Carrie's and Jesse Pratt's clothing with those collected from the sleeping bag and pillowcase that Bruce McDonald had found in the ditch.

"All of these items were once in contact in a common environment," the scientist declared. He had also concluded that the red polyester fibers under Carrie Love's fingernails were identical with those in Jesse Pratt's red T-shirt. Howard repeated his positive identification of the paper towels found in the ditch—out of which the infamous mask had been made. These also matched the opened roll of Bounty towels found in the truck, he said. They not only had the same embossing and decorative pattern, but both exhibited the identical manufacturing defect along one edge—the string of pinholes. This defect was *not* present in the roll that was still sealed in its plastic wrapper, nor was it present in green Bounty towels he later purchased at a grocery store in Bend.

For good measure, to confirm his conclusions,

Howard had done an X-ray fluorescence analysis to measure proportions of metallic element components in the paper (which, he explained, vary from batch to batch). And he did thin-layer chromatography on the green dye to make sure the samples matched chemically. Finally, he was even able to physically match some of the torn edges of the paper.

Enver Bozgoz conducted nearly all of the cross-questioning of these forensic experts. Many of his long, convoluted questions were so hypothetical and theoretical that the scientists asked that they be repeated. After hearing the court reporter read back her transcription, the witness explained several times that, because the question was based on an invalid premise, he couldn't answer it.

The cocounsel's obvious objective was to persuade the jury that the forensic work had been careless and incomplete because of the state's predilection for proving the guilt of its only suspect. Bozgoz's questions were often directed to the wrong witness. Serologist Dickenson, an expert in blood work, repeatedly denied he was qualified to answer questions in areas that were the specialty of criminalist Howard. Mike Howard denied any expertise in determining time of death, pointing out that this was the province of the medical examiner, Dr. Jamison.

Each witness was criticized for firstly, not having brought a thermometer to the crime scene to take the temperature of the body; secondly, for permitting the one brought by the police officers to be broken while it was measuring the temperature of the gravel (*after* the police had, in fact, already recorded the body temperature); and thirdly, for not having gone into the village of Chemult (population 250) to see if they could purchase a replacement for the special long-temperature-range clinical instruments designed to measure the core temperature of a body as it cools.

The interrogation went on for days, reminiscent of violin exercises by Charles Dancla that repeat the same simple theme over and over with endless minuscule variations.

One series of defense questions was devoted to examining Mike Howard's declaration that the Number 1 tire on the Number 5 axle was the only tire that "had a consistency with" the marks on Carrie Love's left arm. As with human hair, he said, he could not testify to a positive identification, but he believed he could rule out all the other tires on the eighteen-wheeler.

Bozgoz asked if it wasn't true that millions of tires had probably been made with the same tread pattern as the one exhibited on the Number 1–Number 5 tire. Howard acknowledged that might be true. Getting a little testy as the questioning ground on, he added that if Bozgoz brought a million of them into the courtroom, he would testify that the marks on Carrie Love's left arm were consistent with all of them.

Well, Bozgoz wanted to know, was the imprint a perfect match? How did the criminalist know it was exactly the same size and shape as the tire tread?

Recovering his patience, Howard pointed out that there was a tape measure in the picture of Carrie's arm that made it easy for him to enlarge it to life size so he could make that comparison.

Well, how close? Was it a perfect match?

It was *very* close, but the scrubbing impact of the side treatment of the tire against the flexible skin of the victim would naturally make a small difference in the pitch of the tread marks.

Would they be larger or smaller?

That depended on the dynamics of the impact and the stretching and recovery of the skin, Howard explained.

Would temperature make a difference?

Possibly.

Aha! Well, then: so wasn't it a bad thing that Howard had not brought a thermometer to the crime scene to take the temperature of the body, that he had permitted someone to step on the only one available, and that he hadn't gone into Chemult to try to buy another one?

It was the seventh time the cocounsel had played the same theme.

On Friday morning, March 22, Elizabeth Helle, Jesse Pratt's mother, ascended the five steps to the witness stand. She had been flown in from Kenai, Alaska, by the prosecution.

Mark Runnels asked her if she had visited her son in the Klamath County Jail. She had. Three times—the first time just before the first trial.

Had she asked him about the crime?

She had.

What had he said about it?

"He told me if she had fucked him the way he wanted her to fuck him, he would not have had to kill her. Because when he wanted a woman he got her."

It made the Sunday *Herald and News*, albeit in expurgated form.

THIRTY-ONE

"He draweth out the thread of his verbosity finer than the staple of his argument."
—William Shakespeare,
Love's Labor Lost

Elizabeth Helle's bombshell slowed down the trial for hours as the defense sought to contain the damage. In the conduct of his cross-examination, Kenneth Hadley would seek to destroy the credibility of the witness. To this end, over prosecution objections, the defense counsel managed to introduce a stack of documents that included Veterans Administration psychiatric records concerning Jesse Pratt's father. Much of this material was apparently brand-new to Helle, and Hadley would try to persuade the jury that the revelation of it upon her arrival in Klamath Falls had made Jesse Clarence Jr.'s mother very angry and that she had somehow turned this anger against her son, thus tainting her testimony.

Jesse Clarence Pratt Sr., according to these VA records, had left school at age fourteen after completing sixth grade. At fifteen, he had married a fourteen-year-old girl with whom he lived for ten years, fathering three children. Although the couple eventually divorced, they later remarried.

While still married to this wife, Jesse senior had married Elizabeth—shortly before going to Europe early in World War II. Elizabeth had later received a telegram informing her of his death. On the witness stand, she confirmed that she had been visited at the time by a sergeant who told her the dramatic details of her husband's dying on the battlefield in Germany.

But such was obviously not the case, since Jesse Pratt, Sr. later applied for Veterans Administration benefits and, in fact, had lived until 1979. VA analysts believed that, unknown to either of his wives, the elder Pratt probably switched dog tags with a dead soldier and deserted.

At the time, Elizabeth testified, the shock of learning that her husband had been killed in action had driven her into clinical depression. (The defense attempted to establish that this had caused her to develop a serious drinking problem while she was pregnant with Jesse junior, thus damaging the fetus.)

Believing she was a widow, Elizabeth later remarried. Meanwhile, according to the VA, Jesse senior had himself remarried in 1966 without getting a divorce from Elizabeth, making himself a double bigamist.

Claiming that her being made aware of these things and having them publicly disclosed had made her a hostile witness, Kenneth Hadley entered a motion to quash Elizabeth Helle's testimony. After lengthy arguments from both sides, Hadley's motion was denied.

* * *

While the above courtroom drama was unfolding, Peter McDonald was on American Airlines Flight 1139, en route to Portland—where he would pick up Alaskan Air 2111 into Klamath Falls. By the time Byron Chatfield and Bill Carroll got back to their rooms at the Klamath Falls Travelodge in late afternoon, McDonald had already checked in. He spent the next several hours briefing the pair on his findings, as summarized in the report he had sent them earlier. It had been nine months since McDonald had been in Klamath Falls to collect and analyze the tire footprint evidence in the case. Explaining how he had arrived at his conclusions helped refresh his memory and prepare both the prosecutor and himself for his testimony the next day.

Although Carroll took McDonald to a local restaurant for a snack before Pete went to bed (he had been up since 3:00 A.M. Pacific time), Chatfield skipped dinner to prepare for the court session in the morning. McDonald later recalled how hard Chatfield worked at his presentation, and not just that day.

"He would be at his desk when I left for my motel room after one of those sessions, and he would be at his desk in the morning when I went to breakfast. I don't know when he slept."

Because witnesses were sequestered, when he arrived at the courthouse the next morning, March 22, McDonald was not allowed into the courtroom until arguments over the admissibility of Elizabeth Helle's testimony were resolved. After Pete was permitted to enter and took the oath, Chatfield asked his witness to introduce himself to the jury and to outline his educational and professional qualifications. In a modest, low-key voice, McDonald described his 28-year career with Firestone, the last twelve as director of tire design. Prompted by Chatfield, he acknowledged that he had been awarded half a dozen patents.

McDonald described his present occupation as a consultant in tire footprint identification. He had given technical papers and seminars to such organizations as the American Academy of Forensic Scientists, the International Association of Investigators, the International Association of Forensic Scientists, and similar groups as far away as China. Holding up a copy of McDonald's book, *Tire Imprint Evidence,* Chatfield had him verify that he was its author.

Pete seemed a little embarrassed to admit that he had been profiled in such national magazines as *Time* and *People,* as well as in specialized publications like *Police Times* and *Law and Order.* But when Byron Chatfield invited him to explain the elements of tire footprint identification, McDonald became the affable instructor who had taught classes at the FBI Academy, and who had given seminars to police academies and law enforcement groups throughout the United States and Canada.

Invited by lead counsel Chatfield and with the court's permission, McDonald stepped down from the witness stand, and with the aid of a chart easel, the onetime architectural artist-illustrator gave the jury a felt-tip chalk talk. He began by drawing the cross section of a tire, explaining how the rubber top cap of a retread is vulcanized to a used tire carcass. Before he was finished, the jury also knew something about tread design. Pete also defined such elements as "pitch length," "groove width," "skid depth," "sipes," "transverse slots," and "noise treatment." Then, guided by further questions from Chatfield, he got into the specifics of the present case.

With the aid of life-size photographs, McDonald showed how the configuration of macula running diagonally across Carrie Love's chest was consistent with the tread of a Long Mile Highway Rib recap. He demonstrated how he had used his side-treatment rubbings of the Number 1–Number 5 tire on the trailer to identify it as a Goodyear Custom Cross Rib 11-22.5 "Hi-Miler" truck tire—and that his side treatment rubbings of the retread edge were clearly consistent with the marks on Carrie Love's arm. With the actual tire and wheel in the courtroom, he called attention to the succession of molded "round and square bars and pockets" on both the tire shoulder and on the victim's body. McDonald then pointed out to the jury that one of the bars was shorter than the others, probably caused by the splice in the recap tread stock, and he showed them this anomaly on both the tire and the victim's arm.

Chatfield invited his witness to demonstrate how the pattern on Carrie Love's left arm could have been made as it was squeezed by the sideward pressure of the Number 1–Number 5 tire on Pratt's rig.

McDonald took off his suit jacket and rolled up his shirtsleeve. Producing the Foamcore model he had sculpted from his own side-treatment rubbing of the tire in question, he coated the carved acetate surface with red stamp-pad ink. He then applied it to his left forearm, creating a red imprint of the shoulder of the tire.

With his left arm extended, displaying the bright red pattern, and carrying a life-size matching photo of Carrie Love's left arm in his other hand, Pete walked slowly down the length of the jury-box so that each juror could make a personal judgment.

Readily apparent in both imprints was the unmistakable signature of the short bar at the tread splice. It was a dramatic, positive identification. Almost as an anticlimax, the witness also pointed out the similarity of the tread pattern on the victim's chest with the imprint of the Number 1–Number 5 tire he had made on white cardboard on the floor of the Klamath Falls garage.

Finally, McDonald explained how, by means of the molded seven-digit identification number, **R XVN 034,** branded into the tire sidewall, he had tracked down the Seattle retreader, Puget Sound Tire Company—and how the company's operations manager, Rick Wooten, had sent him the tire's bill of sale to Northern Star. The Northern Star check in payment for the retread, dated June 4, 1986, was entered into evidence. The check was signed by Carrie L. Love.

It was now Enver Bozgoz's turn to try to undo the damage. Although it soon became apparent that he had studied McDonald's book, the technical deficit between the interrogator and the witness grew wider than at any time during the trial. The cocounsel asked for dimensions in millimeters, although the scale in the picture was calibrated in inches; he confused millimeters with centimeters; he confused tread width with tread depth—perhaps deliberately.

And when the witness testified to the amount of skid depth (depth of the tread groove) remaining, the lawyer argued that there were no "skid marks" at the crime scene.

Cocounsel Bozgoz asked to see "the three-by-five cards" the expert had prepared in studying the photographs, as specified in his book. McDonald gently explained that such a deck of reference cards was a suggestion he had put into his book for the forensic *photographer* so that the criminalist could keep track of his pictures. It was not something *he* did as the pictures' *analyst*.

"So," Bozgoz retorted accusingly, "you don't practice what you preach?"

"No," Pete said simply, "you don't understand."

Bozgoz wanted to know whether the wide Long Mile Highway Rib top cap that had left marks on the body could be vulcanized to the narrow 15-inch diameter tires of a Scout vehicle. The tire expert didn't see how it could.

The defense counsel continually tried to get the forensic scientist to agree to simplistic generalizations that would be useful to impeach his testimony. Leading back to the unknown body temperature of the victim, he asked McDonald to confirm "that temperature of skin is important factor in tire marks on flesh."

McDonald didn't agree.

Arguing with the witness, Bozgoz reminded him that objects expand when heated—offering him the example of putting a jar under a hot water faucet to expand the lid when it was difficult to get it off. More creatively, the nonscientist added his personal observation that "telephone wires are tight in winter but hang almost to the ground on hot summer day. If tire is warm, doesn't that make a difference?"

"I'm not aware of any," the witness responded. Bozgoz couldn't believe it and said so. So the witness added some new expert testimony the defense would probably rather not have had.

"Firestone Central Research did a series of studies of tire treads under a variety of dynamic conditions and found that the shape of tread elements did not change with either temperature or load."

It was getting late on Friday afternoon. The week had run out before the defense ran out of questions. When Bozgoz told the judge that he needed much more time for cross-examination, there was an audible groan in the courtroom. Judge Piper adjourned the court until Monday morning, warning the jury not to become contaminated by discussing the case with anyone, including one another.

By Monday morning, March 25, 1991 Enver Bozgoz had decided to create a demonstration of his own. Pete McDonald later recalled how it went:

"Mr. McDonald, you did this big demonstration in inking this piece of plastic and then putting it on your arm," Bozgoz said. "Would you mind if we did this again?"

"No," I said, "that would be all right."

"This time let's do it on your *right* arm," the lawyer suggested.

I said, "Well, it was on her left arm, but okay." So I took my jacket off and rolled up my right sleeve.

He said, "This time *I'll* do it on your arm." I agreed.

He then took my ink container and just slopped the ink all over the model, obviously intending to make this look as different as he could—including printing it on the wrong arm. And then he smashed it down on my arm so that ink splattered all around—and I was trying to avoid getting it all over my suit and shirt. Then he took the model off. And it looked essentially the same as my left arm, except that it had more red.

And so, without being asked, I got up and took that around to the jury, and that just made the point over again. It had just the opposite effect of what the defense counsel was intending.

Bozgoz dropped that line of questioning. Then he tried some other avenues. Obviously attempting to challenge my qualifications, he asked whether I had ever done any experiments in which I ran over bodies to determine what kind of marks were produced by different thicknesses of flesh. And the jury looked at each other and sort of laughed, as if to say "Who would expect a guy to run over bodies?"

I said that I had never done any testing in which I had run tires over bodies either at Firestone or more recently; however, I *had* worked on three other cases in which there were bloody imprints on bodies that I had used for tire identification.

Perhaps reacting to the jury's laughter, the counsel scolded the witness. Poking his forefinger into McDonald's face, he angrily shouted the question.

"You tellin' us, sir, then, even though you come up here, you qualify yourself as an expert, but you have not done those type experiments?"

I repeated that I had not.

Again, he dropped that line of interrogation. I think he was grasping at that point. He began questioning how this Number 1–Number 5 tire could

have run over the victim. And I thought he was
going to get into the question I had wrestled with—
about why was it the *only* tire. But instead, he said
he didn't think the jury had understood my testimony about how the tire could have scrubbed
along her arm after running over her head, and he
proposed that we demonstrate it.

"All right," I said, "how would you like to do that?"

With that, he's taking his coat off, and he pro-
ceeds to lie down on the floor in front of the jury
and says, "Let's say I'm the victim. How could this
tire have gone over me?"

"Well," I said, "you know, we have this tire right
here in the courtroom. And it's mounted on the
wheel. I could roll it over here and we could show
the jury just how it went over the body."

Well, of course, he didn't want a two-hundred-
pound tire and wheel assembly running over his
chest.

"No, that isn't necessary," he said. "Just *show* the
jury."

I looked around and wondered how I might
demonstrate anything without a tire. Then I guess
the devil in me came out and I said, "Well, we still
have some red ink here—and I could just mark that
across where the tire went."

He quickly got up off the floor. And with that, I
heard the jury laugh like I never heard a jury
laugh. It was sort of like, "You got 'em! After he put
all that ink on your arm and tried to mess you up."

After that incident, the defense's interrogation got
more than a little dirty. Bozgoz demanded to know
how much Pete McDonald was being paid for his
services and how much he had collected to date.

Including two trips to the West Coast and photo lab expenses, it had come to a substantial sum.

In his redirect examination, Byron Chatfield had established that a portion of McDonald's time and considerable out-of-pocket expense was due to requests that had been made by the defense. He did not embarrass the defense by revealing that Bozgoz had never reimbursed McDonald $1,608 for the crate of evidentiary materials he had asked him to send to the defense's expert witness in New York—including full-size prints of the 40-inch-diameter tire and the twelve-foot-long tire imprint made in the Klamath Falls garage.

Interestingly, although Professor Peter DeForest of New York's John Jay University received the materials and later called McDonald for clarification, the defense never asked its expert witness to testify.

After lunch on Monday, McDonald revealed that he had examined a photograph of the Scout vehicle with a magnifying glass during the lunch break. Sunlight on the right rear wheel had made it easy to study the tread, he said. And it was very different from the treads typically employed on large truck tires. The Scout tire had sporty white sidewalls with molded radial lines—a tire that was not at all consistent with the marks on Carrie Love's chest or the ones on her arm.

The defense then asked the expert about the left rear tire on the Scout, its left front tire, and its right front—all of which were obscured in the picture. Bozgoz abandoned his interrogation with a parting shot that was not a question:

"You don't practice what you preach!"

The state rested its case.

THIRTY-TWO

Asphyxiation did not contribute to death.
                                    —Dr. William Brady

It was now the defense's turn.

Kenneth Hadley rose at once to move for a judgment of acquittal on Count One, "based on the fact that there was no evidence showing attempted rape, nor therefore for the allegation of *aggravated* murder." The carefully chosen words suggested that the defense counsel may have been resigned to his client's probable conviction of the lesser charge of "intentional murder," and he appeared now to be merely trying to save Jesse Pratt's life.

As to Count Two, Hadley pointed out that "maiming" didn't seem to have a definition in Oregon law. But "torture" had been defined as having to be a "separate objective from killing the victim." To a nonlawyer it seemed a bizarre defense. The defense counsel went on to explain the legal subtleties of his reasoning.

"The only serious wounds were to the heart, and these were *not* separate from killing the victim." Her other wounds, he suggested, "would have healed, probably without scarring—if the person hadn't been killed."

As to Pratt's running over her body with a vehicle, Hadley cited the medical examiner's testimony that there appeared to be a "reasonable medical probability that the victim was dead by that time"—in which case, "this cannot be maiming at that point." Although these grim nuances were picky technicalities, they would be matters of life or death for Jesse Pratt.

Judge Piper told the lawyers that he would require twenty or thirty minutes to consider the defense motions.

When the judge returned, it was obvious that he had been keeping up with the details of the case. As to the motion for a directed verdict of acquittal on Count One, he pointed out that there was substantial evidence of intent to rape in the record. He therefore denied the defense's motion.

"On Count Two," he said, "the court has located the medical examiner's statement that puncture wounds to the heart and vena cava could have caused death in as little as five minutes, but it might have been half an hour or longer." The doctor's testimony had also contained the opinion that "asphyxiation could have caused death in half an hour to an hour." And although Dr. Jamison had said that the most likely medical probability was that Carrie Love was dead before the crushing injury to her head occurred, there nevertheless was "evidence of attempt to maim Carrie Love beyond causing her death in the course of conduct that followed."

The crushing injury itself, the judge ruled, showed that there had been *intent* to maim. Justifying his opinion, Judge Piper cited precedent in two Oregon cases. He therefore denied the motion for a directed verdict of acquittal on Count Two as well.

The jury was then invited in, and the defense began presenting its case. Its first defense witness was Charles Crawford, a local Klamath Falls tire dealer. Crawford's direct examination was conducted by Kenneth Hadley, who established that one, lots of Long Mile retreads were sold in the area, and two, these bands of premolded retread rubber could be put on many different sizes of tire, including those intended for commercial pickup trucks. *But*, the dealer added, the Long Mile tread was much more common on over-the-road trailers.

When Byron Chatfield rose to cross-question the witness, his manner was a lot like Hadley's. He just seemed to be asking a few friendly questions to clarify details of Crawford's direct testimony. But in the process he first established that the dealer had never seen such a recap on a small commercial vehicle; secondly, that it would be inappropriate for a four-wheel-drive (FWD) vehicle; thirdly, that he would not recommend that it be used on a Scout because it would be too slick for off-road operation.

In redirect examination, defense counsel Hadley persuaded the witness to speculate that a Scout owner in southern California might be able to get away with using such a smooth tread on a Scout that was driven primarily on the highway. In re-cross, Chatfield got Crawford to admit that he had never seen such a tire on a Scout—in all of his twenty-seven years of experience in tire sales.

Since Pete McDonald had already identified the sporty tread and sidewall of the right rear tire of the

Scout, much of the above seemed a pointless waste of time—unless other wheels on the FWD vehicle were equipped with totally different (and admittedly inappropriate) tires.

When Dorothy McDonald took the witness stand, it may have been Bozgoz's knowledge that she was a reluctant if not downright hostile defense witness that managed to get the lawyer off his game. He began by asking her if her husband was Richard McDonald.

"No," she corrected, "*Bruce* McDonald."

After establishing that she had worked at Manley's Tavern for eleven years, the defense lawyer asked her about its location.

"How far east [*sic*] Manley's Tavern from Highway 97?"

Dorothy McDonald hesitated a long moment before answering, apparently reluctant to correct the counsel again. Manley's Tavern is *west* of the Crescent Lake Junction of Highway 97 and Oregon 58.

"About fifteen miles," she finally answered.

It was not a welcome answer, since Pratt had claimed he dropped off Carrie Love within sight of Highway 97.

The witness was shown the purse that she and her husband had found in the pillowcase, and she was asked whether she had told a state police officer that she thought she had recognized it.

"No," she said. "I just told him I thought it looked familiar." Bozgoz gradually brought out Dorothy McDonald's earlier recollection that she thought she had seen such a purse in the hands of a young woman who laid it on the bar at Manley's Tavern on

Monday evening, June 16, 1986—and that the woman had been there with a trucker.

"Could you describe this couple?" the counsel asked.

"Not really." It was a curt response. "They were only there for five or ten minutes," she added. "They ordered a glass of water and a Pepsi, went to the bathroom, and left."

Had she seen a green truck-tractor in the parking lot?

"No." Then she amended her denial. "I don't remember. I don't usually go outside." Someone else might had told the officer about such a vehicle, she thought.

When Chatfield had his turn, Dorothy McDonald's hostility disappeared and her memory improved. The jury learned firstly that Dorothy McDonald could not identify the purse she and Bruce had found as being identical to the one she had seen at the bar; secondly, that it was daylight when the couple was in the tavern—probably not long after she came to work at 6:00 P.M.; and thirdly, even if she *had* seen a Kenworth, she couldn't possibly remember a specific truck in the parking lot on any given night because there were *usually* some trucks there.

Chatfield asked her about the woman with the purse. How old might she have been? The witness said the customer had been old enough that she didn't "card" her.

"I'd say she was at least 28," Dorothy added.

"Would you have characterized her as a 'teeny-bopper'?"

"No!" It was a modulated chuckle.

The prosecutor asked McDonald whether when she went through Carrie Love's purse that night she had recognized the picture in Carrie's ID photos as being the woman she had seen in the tavern the night before. She definitely had not.

Bozgoz stood up at the defense table.

"You see a lot of trucks going by Manley's Tavern on Highway 58, don't you?"

"No," Dorothy responded brightly, "Manley's Tavern doesn't have any windows."

"Okay, but you work by highway and you travel on the highway. Had there been lot of trucks go by there [*sic*]? You see trucks, don't you?"

McDonald admitted she saw trucks on the highway.

"And when you see one tire, you could not tell one tire from another, could you? And more tires are manufactured that look like that, right?"

Chatfield entered an objection. The question had nothing to do with the witness's previous testimony. Bozgoz reacted before the judge could rule.

"I withdraw the question. That's all I have, Your Honor." The cocounsel sat down.

When Trooper James Rector took the witness stand, he read from the report he had written at the time. It said Mrs. McDonald had told him about the green truck and her estimate of when the couple had arrived was "between 8:30 and 9:00 P.M."

Prosecutor Chatfield, during cross-examination, put a schedule into evidence showing that sunset had not occurred until after 9:00 P.M. on June 16, lending credence to Dorothy McDonald's claim that it was still daylight when the couple came in. (The travel/distance timeline constructed by Ken Cooper had previously fixed the time of Carrie Love's death as well after midnight.)

The first defense witness called on Tuesday morn-

ing, March 26,1991 was the former evidence officer
for the Klamath Falls State Police Post in 1986. The
trooper confirmed that the vaginal swabs taken at the
crime scene had not been refrigerated at the Klamath Falls Police Post. But this damaging admission
was largely neutralized when the defense's independent serologist testified that she had not been asked
by the defense to examine this evidence (in the first
trial) until the samples were more than six months
old—making her results inconclusive. Moreover,
when questioned by the prosecution, the technician
freely admitted that her tests on *fresh* samples of
spermatozoa were also frequently inconclusive.

Dr. William Brady, noted pathologist and former
state medical examiner, was to be the defense's star
witness.

After the doctor was sworn in, Kenneth Hadley
had him recite his impressive list of professional
credentials—which included his authorship of a
standard reference, his lectureships in teaching
hospitals, and the fact that since his retirement he
still performed about two hundred autopsies per
year as an independent consultant for prosecutors,
defense counsels, and lawyers involved in civil suits.

In the years since his testimony in the first trial,
Dr. Brady seemed to have mellowed—perhaps having learned more about the character of Jesse Pratt
in the interim. The pathologist had no hesitation
about confirming Dr. Jamison's conclusion as to
the primary cause of death as recorded on Carrie
Love's death certificate: "Stab wounds to the heart
and great vessels." And at first he seemed inclined
to agree with the next line on the document that asphyxiation was a contributing factor to her death.

In a rich baritone worthy of a film narrator, the doctor stated unequivocally, "There is strong evidence of asphyxiation. There is no question that, during her lifetime, her airway was partially obstructed—by an obstruction placed over the face." He cited such confirming indicators as pulmonary edema and foam in the victim's trachea, and he had seen photos of the tape marks on the victim's face.

But the medical expert did finally render the judgment the defense wanted the jury to hear. It was his opinion that Carrie Love probably would not have died from asphyxiation alone. Although he admitted that "she was undoubtedly asphyxiated over a considerable period of time, there was nothing in Dr. Jamison's report to support the position that asphyxiation played a part in *directly* causing Carrie Love's death."

Under Byron Chatfield's gentlemanly cross-examination, the doctor was invited to describe a victim's typical reaction to such deprivation of air.

Brady said it would be an "exceedingly unpleasant experience—frequently panic," inadvertently helping to establish that "torture" had occurred, since as defined in Hadley's argument for acquittal on Count Two, "torture, under Oregon law, has to be a separate objective from killing the victim."

Dr. Brady added that the balloonlike alveoli in the lungs had not, according to Dr. Jamison's report, been distended as described in textbook asphyxiation. Chatfield asked him about possible causes of deflation of these pouches after death when such classic asphyxiation had occurred. If, for example, a victim's chest was run over by a truck, would that deflate them?

"Oh, of course," the doctor conceded. Brady may not have known about the tire tread bruise across Carrie Love's chest.

During the afternoon session of the court, the doctor became more guarded. His criticism of Dr. Jamison's work hardened. The younger pathologist's analysis now seemed to have been somewhat incomplete. Kenneth Hadley's last question produced an abrupt reversal of his expert witness's earlier testimony.

"Asphyxiation did not contribute to death."

Witness Barry Matson had formerly sold parts at a California truck stop. He was a reluctant witness. Enver Bozgoz showed him an invoice and asked him to identify it. Matson said it looked like a receipt for a fuel tank cap. Bozgoz asked him if he had sold "this dizzle cap" to a trucker driving a Kenworth.

"This invoice doesn't have anything to do with me," Matson snapped.

Fumbling through his documents, the defense lawyer presented another.

"How about this?"

"It's *blank*. There's nothing on it!"

Bozgoz paused. It was a long, flustered pause. Well, had Matson sold a "dizzle cap" to a trucker driving a Kenworth?

"Sort of" was the answer. It seemed that a trucker had come in with a ball of rags stuffed into his fuel intake pipe. The rags were soaked with fuel and duct taped in place.

"The guy was all out of breath and wanted something done," the witness said. "There was fuel all

over." But Matson didn't have the cap size that fit
the fuel tanks on this older-model Kenworth. So, to
help the man out, he had built up a smaller cap
with strips of rubber tape and then wedged the cob-
bled stopper into the fuel pipe like a cork.

Matson said he gave the driver the name of a truck
stop in northern California where he might be able
to buy a cap that would fit—telling him that the rubber pieces he had stuck together might fall into the
tank when his improvised plug was pulled out.

"Do you remember what day it was?" Bozgoz asked.
"Nah."

Before the witness was excused, the prosecution made sure the jury understood that the
makeshift stopper the trucker had brought into
the truck stop was made of *rags* and duct tape, not
paper towels. And, contrary to Pratt's testimony
in the first trial, the plugged tank apparently had
fuel in it after all.

When Ken Cooper took the stand once again, he
was first criticized by Enver Bozgoz for not making
a plaster cast of a tire track found in the mud at the
south end of Milepost 206. Handing the detective
an enlarged photocopy of his own diagram, Bozgoz
asked him to point out where the tire mark had
been. He couldn't, Cooper explained, "because the
rut was so far away from where the body was found
that it was way off this chart."

The detective was berated by the cocounsel for
using a Polaroid camera at the crime scene to photograph the tire imprint on Carrie Love's arm
instead of a 35mm camera, and for not shopping in
the hamlet of Chemult to replace the special clinical thermometer that had been broken while

taking a reading in the gravel pile. It was getting to be a very familiar refrain.

Ken Cooper replied that core temperature of the body was irrelevant at that point because the body had apparently been buried in cold, moist gravel for some time.

"And would you tell the jury where did you get your medical education to make the decision?" Bozgoz demanded.

Actually, Cooper said, he had attended a number of homicide seminars over the years.

Well, had he read Dr. Brady's book?

The witness acknowledged that he had not. He was excused.

At this point, to the surprise of spectators in the courtroom, the defense suddenly rested its case. Jesse Pratt would not be called to the witness stand.

Judge Piper promptly adjourned the court and dismissed the jury for the day.

THIRTY-THREE

How forcible are the right words! But what doth arguing reprove?

—Job 6:25

When the jury members had filed into their seats the next morning, Wednesday, March 27 they were greeted briefly by the judge, who turned and addressed the court.

"Summation of counsel!" Judge Piper ordered, his deep voice echoing in the lofty courtroom. He uttered his instruction with what sounded like relief, if not a celebration of the milestone. The guilt phase of Jesse Pratt's second trial was, at last, drawing to a close.

Byron Chatfield rose from the prosecution table and walked across the courtroom to the jury box. His tone held little promise of the drama to follow. He began by stating what seemed obvious: the jurors should base their decision on the evidence that had been presented, adding that all of the exhibits that had been hastily passed among them during the trial would be available to them in the jury room to examine at their leisure.

He reminded the members of the jury that he

had posed two questions at the beginning of the trial—questions that they would now have to decide. First, "did the defendant *intend* to commit rape; and in the course of and furtherance of that, did he personally and intentionally kill Carrie Love?" Second, "did the defendant intentionally kill Carrie Love in the course of *intentionally maiming* her?"

The prosecutor defined the elements that had to be proved in order to constitute aggravated felony murder. He explained that it was not necessary to prove that sexual intercourse had occurred, but only that a "substantial step toward overcoming forced resistance [to rape]; forceful compulsion" had to be shown. In this regard, he reminded the jury that "Carrie Love had her hands bound behind her back," and that "she had been personally and intentionally choked in the furtherance of the defendant's objective to commit rape."

Having put those words in the jurors' minds, he repeated the essence of Count One: "Did he attempt to commit rape, and while doing that, in the course of and furtherance of that, did he personally and intentionally kill Carrie Love?"

Chatfield then turned to Count Two: "Did the defendant not only intentionally cause the death of Carrie Love, but did he cause her death in the course of intentionally maiming her?"

The prosecutor then read from the law, defining maiming as "inflicting injuries that cripple or mutilate in any way, seriously wound, disable, or deprive the victim of the use of any limb or body member, or rendering the victim lame or defective in bodily vigor." His voice dropped to an apologetic

whisper as he explained the nuance of the prosecution's having to show that "death occurred *during
the course of* intentional maiming, not *as a result of*
intentional maiming."

As if providing an illustration of what was required to meet the definition, he reminded the
jury of the locations of each of Carrie Love's stab
wounds.

"During the course of intentional maiming, she
died. She was stabbed in the heart. Death occurred
during the course of intentional maiming."

He spoke slowly and deliberately, his voice now
beginning to rise in volume. He seemed genuinely
consumed with outrage as he angrily declared, "He
maimed her and he intended to do it!"

As he spoke, Byron Chatfield walked slowly back
and forth in front of the jury box, reciting the ugly
examples that obviously upset him, his eyes burn-
ing his personal conviction into those of each juror
who met his gaze. At the defense table, Enver Bozgoz scribbled furiously on a yellow legal pad.

Pausing, calming down a bit, the prosecutor began
reviewing the chronology of the case as presented by
the prosecution's witnesses, beginning with Bruce
McDonald. He spoke of Pratt's plans for the Los Angeles trip and that Mona Bennett was originally to
have been the one to go on that fateful journey, even
though she had been employed at Northern Star for
only three days, until her inability to find a baby-sitter
resulted in Carrie Love's taking her place. When he
got to the testimony of Connie McClintock, he reminded the jury about the roll of silver duct tape she
said she had been kicking around on the floor of the
cab of the Kenworth before Jesse Pratt and Carrie

Love left Seattle—and that this roll of tape was missing when the truck was searched in Phoenix.

Then he got into the "string of lies" Jesse Pratt had fabricated in attempting to construct an alibi—lies he had told to Mona Bennett about dropping Carrie Love off at My Place Tavern before the police had even discovered the body. "It was a lie he had repeated to the police in Phoenix before, much later, changing his story." And, the prosecutor reminded them, Pratt had told Mona he was calling from California when his phone bill showed he was calling from Klamath Falls, Oregon. He had even asked Mona "whether Carrie's things had been found along Highway 97"—before Mona knew about Carrie's death.

"Why is he lying?" Chatfield asked, his voice rising in a crescendo once again. "Because he killed her!"

During the silence that followed, the noise created by defense cocounsel Bozgoz angrily ripping yellow sheets off his legal pad could be heard throughout the courtroom.

The state's lead counsel now reviewed the forensic analyses presented by Lieutenant Mike Howard—particularly his matching the manufacturing defect on the Bounty paper towels in the truck cab with those found in the ditch along Highway 97. Chatfield reminded the jury of Peter McDonald's testimony and how it had proved that it was the Number 1 tire on the Number 5 axle of Jesse Pratt's trailer rig that ran over Carrie Love.

Finally, his voice becoming barely audible, Chatfield told the jury he believed they would find that all this evidence proved beyond any reasonable doubt that Jesse Pratt had personally and inten-

tionally maimed and killed Carrie Love in furtherance of his intention to commit rape.

His summation had taken about an hour.

Enver Bozgoz delivered the defense's summation.
It was full of patriotism and American values—values
he treasured, he said, since emigrating from Russia.
He told the jury how he learned to read English by
studying comic books, later graduating to Big Little
Books, and then to other literature before daring to
go to high school.

He read much of the Declaration of Independence to the jury and parts of the United States
Constitution. He pointed out a major omission in the
first draft of the latter document—a flaw that was ultimately rectified by the passage of the Bill of Rights.

But the assistant defense counsel's first words
contained a harbinger of the low road to follow:

"Your Honor, counsel, ladies and gentlemen of
the jury, this is a case about the unsolved murder of
Carrie Love—and a $10,000 'job' that was done on
the Founding Fathers in here. Why?" This $10,000
figure would turn up many times in the cocounsel's
closing argument.

"Mr. Chatfield spoke to you for an hour and a
half," Bozgoz continued. "He needed that time to
try to convince you they had done job they were
supposed to do. They tell you they proved guilt of
Mr. Pratt beyond any *reasonable doubt*."

He would repeat those last two words scores of
times in the next few minutes as he launched into his
American history lesson and his reverence for the
Bill of Rights—and how different he found the

American tradition from conditions in his native Russia. He told the jury how pleased he was that the state of Oregon had adopted the same standards for individual rights in its constitution. He focused on the U.S. Constitution's Sixth Amendment, which provides for "a defendant's right to be judged in a public trial by an impartial jury in the town in which the event occurred."

"But Mr. Chatfield gave you a snow job," Bozgoz declared.

He told the jury what the judge would tell them about their responsibility to evaluate the evidence presented by each witness. Then, taking off the gloves, he began his effort to tear down the credibility of his personal nemesis Peter McDonald. (The cocounsel had obviously not forgiven the forensic scientist for the humiliation to which he had been subjected.)

"I'll show you how phony that $10,000 expert was." (The recurring figure was apparently the counsel's estimate of McDonald's bill for his time and expenses.) Bozgoz cleared his throat with a wet, modulated cough that bespoke his disgust. "And why he came here and how they practiced in Mr. Chatfield's hotel room—for $10,000 the public and citizens and taxpayers of this county paid. I'll take off my jacket after while and demonstrate.

"That 28 years of work in office." His voice dripped with derision. "Ohio. They brought on us that man has six patents. What that have to do with this case? Just seriously, what has that to do with this case?" He was getting very loud. "That man has six patents!

"It's a principle about prime rate, too. And greed! The judge will tell you in evaluating each witness's testimony—the measure and quality of a witness's testimony—evidence of the bias or interest of a witness. Evidence of a witness's *greed*."

He quoted the judge's instruction that "'if a witness lies under oath in some part of his or her testimony, the witness is likely to lie in other parts of his or her testimony. Therefore, if you find that a witness has lied at some point, then you may distrust the rest of the witness's testimony.'

"He lied! He got caught with his pants down in the wrong place by Mr. Chatfield. He wish now that Mr. McDonald had not been called!"

When Bozgoz revealed what he claimed was a lie, his explanation was difficult to follow. It had to do with McDonald's measuring a dimension on a photograph as ten millimeters when the value, according to Bozgoz, should have been fifteen millimeters.

"He had to go along with Mr. Cooper!" Bozgoz thundered. "What I call a $10,000 fraud."

McDonald had to lie, Jesse Pratt's lawyer explained, because Cooper was not qualified to evaluate tires. So, he reminded the jury, he had given Mr. McDonald a quarter and a nickel, and asked him to make an impression with the nickel the size of the quarter—and the witness admitted he couldn't do it.

Dropping his aggressive tone, Bozgoz confessed that "Mr. Hadley told me I was too rough on Mr. McDonald." If some members of the jury felt that way, he apologized to them (although, it was apparent, not to Mr. McDonald).

"I could have been rougher," he declared. "I had a flashback. I thought I was back in Russia."

Having apologized to the jury, Bozgoz tossed out a final dig.

"Would you buy a used car from Mr. McDonald?"

Shifting gears, the assistant defense counsel asked a different question—and then answered it.

"Who is Mr. Pratt? You know what we heard from a black guy, Mr. Slack: 'He's the nicest, kindest guy I ever met.'"

It seemed an odd endorsement for the counsel to have chosen.

Bozgoz now launched into the second movement of his summation. His theme was that the police never followed up on any clues that might have led the investigation away from Jesse Pratt. He began by quoting what he said was a passage from Dr. Brady's book:

"'Assumption is the mother of all screwups.'"

The cocounsel's litany of police neglect included a criticism of criminalist Mike Howard's work—at first attempting to say something nice about him.

"Mr. Howard. I like him. He's nice guy. He's scientist. But why didn't he find out who had sex with Carrie Love?

"Carrie Love rode in truck. Why did he spend two days proving that fuzz balls were same. But there were other fuzz balls they did not identify. Why didn't Officer Howard tell you? He didn't because he didn't want to. Why is it that they want to convict Mr. Pratt on speculation? Because they hadn't done their job!"

Bozgoz ridiculed the testimony of Diane and April about Pratt carrying knitting needles. Perhaps, he suggested, Pratt had bought them for some girlfriend or for a grandchild. As to Carrie

Love's body being nude, he told the jury that lots of people sleep in the nude.

"The officers have an unsolved case," he declared. "I'm asking these questions. I want Mr. Chatfield to answer them for me when I finish:

"Why didn't they check those bloodstain traces they saw in Luminol fluorescence for blood type? Why didn't they run tests on duct tape? Why didn't they go to stores in Seattle to see if they could find Bounty paper towels with pinholes in paper?

"They only looked someplace where they weren't going to find it. Why? Ask Mr. Chatfield.

"Did they compare dust under Mr. Pratt's fingernails with dust in gravel pile? No! Why not—with all this money blowing around from the state of Oregon hiring $10,000 experts? Why didn't they run a test?"

Bozgoz told the jury he was ordering twelve thermometers out of his own pocket, and he was going to contribute them to Oregon State Police posts because they apparently don't have enough money to buy them on their own. He planned to give several to Dr. Jamison, he said. He suggested once again that the Klamath Falls Police Post could buy a used refrigerator for ten dollars at a flea market to properly store vaginal swabs.

At times, Bozgoz made up quotes that appeared nowhere in court testimony. He criticized the fingerprint work of Lieutenant Howard—who, he apparently forgot, did not do fingerprint work. Howard, he said, had failed to check unidentified fingerprints after the state later acquired its computer program.

"Why didn't they run 'em? Because Detective

Cooper told him, 'Don't run 'em. This way we can always blame it on Mr. Pratt.'"

As he neared the end of his summation, Enver Bozgoz appealed to the consciences of the jurors. He told them that after the case was over, they would be watching the waves come into the Pacific Ocean shore, or they would be driving down the highway and they would worry.

"'Where is Mr. Pratt now? Did I do justice?' He is innocent until proved beyond a reasonable doubt guilty. Hold the state of Oregon to that! You promised you would require them to prove beyond a reasonable doubt. You have taken oath. Neither Ken Hadley or Jesse Pratt can look into your heart. But when you go home tonight, you can. In the morning, you will come in and say we find Jesse Pratt 'not guilty' because state of Oregon did not prove beyond reasonable doubt. Jesse Pratt does not have to prove his innocence. The accuser has to prove beyond a reasonable doubt."

Pratt's cocounsel now prepared the jury for the demonstration he had promised.

"Some of you think I may have overstepped my bounds when I jumped all over Mr. McDonald, and I apologize if you think so. I want to show you."

Bozgoz took off his coat, rolled up his shirtsleeves, and picked up McDonald's Foamcore model of the shoulder portion of the Number 1–Number 5 tire.

"See the way Mr. McDonald did," he explained. "This is plastic, and you can't make plastic wet. So, he left area which is not proper detail. And when he put this, you see, he put black paper in back so you don't see there's no ink on it.

"And that's the reason what I did. When I saw that I took it, I put the ink on it and slapped on his arm."

He pressed it on his own forearm. "And that was pure red. And you see, for example, *this* area. There's no ink on it. You see how white that area is?

"That's the purpose of that. He practiced this fraud and he showed the fraud to Mr. Chatfield in his hotel room. Mr. Chatfield let him testify to that effect, because these guys—these boys from big town—they come into this little town and they look at us. Say, 'Hey, we get all this. We'll put one on them.' That's what they do. That's the purpose of that black paper, so you would not see.

"Now you take back on Friday, when Mr. McDonald came up in here. And how self-assured he was. Boy! He was talking and he was drawing diagrams. All that. But when I caught him on this thing, you remember. You think back. He wished he wasn't in courtroom.

"Then I guarantee you one thing. He had the most terrible weekend that he ever experienced. He was worried that he might run into me in a restaurant or in a bar. But I wasn't there. I didn't want to see that guy."

With that, Bozgoz asked the judge's permission to be excused. He already had his client's permission, he said. He was going on vacation and didn't want to miss his plane. He would not be present to hear Byron Chatfield's response to his questions.

After a brief recess, Judge Piper called on Kenneth Hadley. The judge seemed surprised that the lead counsel had nothing to say. Enver Bozgoz, Hadley said, had spoken for the defense.

Byron Chatfield took the floor for his rebuttal.

He told the court that he was surprised Mr. Bozgoz made no comment at all about the lies the *defendant* had told.

"Instead, 'The police didn't do this. The serologist didn't do that.'

"There is no evidence of attempted rape? Was she nude? Was she bound up for no reason at all? Did Mr. Slack know what he was doing when he opted out when Pratt asked him to participate in a bondage threesome?

"'Many people sleep naked,' the defense said. How many people sleep naked with their hands tied behind their back and a mask taped to their face!

"Mr. Bozgoz spoke of individual rights," he said. "Carrie Love had some rights, too. But her rights are now terminated.

"I don't need to say we proved this beyond reasonable doubt. The evidence speaks for itself. Just use your own reason and common sense. You don't owe me anything. You don't owe Mr. Hadley or Mr. Bozgoz anything. Evaluate. Use your common sense."

Judge Piper told the members of the jury to bring a toothbrush, a razor, or whatever else they might need when they returned in the morning, prepared to spend a sequestered night if their deliberations carried over to the next day.

THIRTY-FOUR

Everything has an ending: there will be
An ending one sad day for you and me. . . .
— Katharine Tynan Hinkson (1861–1931),
  Irish author, "Everything Has an Ending"

Asked later about his reaction to the assistant defense counsel's allegations, Peter McDonald seemed remarkably sanguine. He explained that he had learned to accept the fact that "some lawyers feel obligated to adopt such tactics." He cited an experience he had after testifying in a trial in Pennsylvania.

"After the courtroom had emptied out, the defense attorney came over to me and said, 'I'm sorry to have had to put you through all this. But that's my job.'"

Asked about the "black paper" on the Foamcore about which Enver Bozgoz had made such an issue, McDonald said there hadn't been any paper of any color on his plastic model. It was made of white Styrofoam and transparent acetate. But one possibility had occurred to him, he said.

"I painted the white Foamcore black in order to make the model look more like a tire. And, since the acetate was clear, you could see the black through it, and the assembly looked more like part of the side treatment of a black tire. So maybe it was the layer of black paint he was talking about."

And yes, of course, McDonald had shown the demonstration to Byron Chatfield at the Travelodge.

"It is standard procedure to communicate the detail you'll be presenting in your testimony to the lawyer who will be questioning you. How else is he going to know what to ask?

"But, interestingly, when I showed him the model, Chatfield said he thought Bozgoz would object to my using it because I hadn't disclosed it in the material I had sent to the defense. I hadn't thought up the template experiment until the trial was scheduled. But we decided to try it anyway, and we were surprised when he not only didn't object, but he actually used my model to repeat the demonstration himself. I don't think it helped his case."

Judge Piper's instructions to the jury on Thursday morning (March 28) were lengthy. After giving them all the standard directives and cautions, he read the charges against the defendant. They sounded a lot like the words Byron Chatfield had implanted in the minds of the jurors during his summation:

"The defendant," Judge Piper said, "is charged with the offense of aggravated murder as follows: Aggravated Murder Count One: The said Jesse C. Pratt, on or about the seventeenth day of June 1986, in the county of Klamath and state of Oregon . . . did unlawfully and intentionally attempt to commit the crime of rape in the first degree; and in the course of and in furtherance of said crime which the defendant was attempting to commit, the said defendant personally and intentionally caused the death of another human being, to wit, Carrie Lynette Love . . . by asphyxiating her and stabbing her in the heart.

"Aggravated Murder Count Two: Further, for, and as a part of the same action . . . he, the said Jesse C. Pratt, on or about the seventeenth day of June 1986, in the county of Klamath and state of Oregon . . . did unlawfully and intentionally cause the death of another human being, to wit, Carrie Lynette Love, by stabbing her, asphyxiating her, and driving over her head with a motor vehicle in the course of maiming of Carrie Lynette Love, contrary to the statutes . . . and the peace and dignity of the state of Oregon."

Judge Piper went on to define maiming, using essentially the same words Byron Chatfield had used. He told the jury that the defendant had entered a plea of not guilty to the two felony murder counts. Then, asking the two alternate jurors to remain behind, and after appointing two jury bailiffs, Mary Horton and court reporter Carol O'Brion, the judge sent the jury off to begin its deliberations.

In less than an hour, he received a note from the jury: "Why is this the second trial? Would you give us an exact reason?"

Addressing the lawyers for both sides, the judge told them he planned to tell the jury that it was not material to this trial to know the answer to their question. They should make their decision based on the evidence.

"Anybody have a problem with that?" he asked.

Kenneth Hadley had some reservations that were put on the record. Judge Piper asked the bailiffs to bring the jury back in to answer its question. The jury members got a second chance to stretch their legs when they were summoned back into the courtroom at 6:00 P.M. Judge Piper asked the group if they were close enough to a verdict to decide to return after dinner, or whether the court should make arrangements for a motel for them. After a brief discussion among themselves, the weary jury opted to have dinner and retire for the night.

Shortly before ten o'clock on Good Friday morning, March 29, presiding juror Daniel King rapped on the inside of the door to the jury room as he had been instructed to do when the jury had reached a verdict.

Jury bailiffs Horton and O'Brion both responded. They told the jurors it would take a little while to locate the trial lawyers and assemble others so the court could hear their verdict. Carol O'Brion immediately notified Judge Piper. She and Mary Horton began calling others in the courthouse who had an interest in the trial. It would have been difficult to find anyone in the building who didn't.

Carol called the county jail, where Jesse Pratt began changing out of his prison garb to be led unshackled into the courtroom in civilian clothes. He would wear his inevitable beige corduroy blazer.

Sheriff's deputies and other courthouse employees began streaming into the courtroom, alerting newspaper reporters and others who were chatting in the hallway. They reacted at once, quickly filing inside. Within minutes, the corridor was empty and the spectators' gallery was full. The bailiff called the court to order as Judge Piper took his seat on the bench.

"Members of the jury, have you reached a verdict in this case?"

Receiving an affirmative answer, the judge asked for the two documents the jury had prepared. He read them to the court:

"In the Circuit Court of the State of Oregon for the *County of Klamath, State of Oregon,* plaintiff, versus *Jesse Clarence Pratt,* defendant: We, the jury, being duly impaneled and sworn in the above entitled court and cause, do find the defendant on the charge of aggravated felony murder, Count One, guilty of the crime of aggravated felony murder, all of our number concurring."

Jesse Pratt sat calmly at the defense table. He didn't appear to have heard the verdict. The judge read aloud the date and signature on the document. He then turned to the second page.

"Another form bearing the same title: We the jury, being duly impaneled and sworn in the above entitled court and cause, do find the defendant on the charge of aggravated murder, maiming, Count Two, guilty of the crime of aggravated murder, maiming, all of our number concurring."

Although Jesse Pratt's face was now clean shaven and perhaps easier to read for this trial, it exhibited no visible reaction.

The judge verified the unanimity of the verdicts with two separate jury poll ballots. He then told the jury that it would be necessary for them to reassemble in a few days for the penalty phase of the trial, so it was extremely important for them to prevent themselves from being contaminated by any unauthorized information about the case. They were not to talk about the case to the press, to members of their families, or to anyone else. They were not even to read the afternoon newspaper accounts of their own verdict.

The jury was excused until Wednesday, April 3, 1991, when the penalty phase of the trial would begin.

THIRTY-FIVE

*I do not feel guilty the way I raised my son. I raised
him to the best of my ability, and he had everything
a child needed. He had a home; he had food; he
had clothes; he had bicycles; he had everything.*
                                        —Elizabeth Helle

In Jesse Pratt's first trial, the penalty phase had
taken only a few hours. This time it would take
eleven days.

When court reconvened on April 3, Enver Bozgoz, who had now returned to the proceedings,
introduced a series of motions in limine, aimed at
excluding a number of prosecution witnesses. His
objection to most of this testimony was that he believed the offenses Jesse Pratt had committed in the
past were not sufficiently violent. Repeated harassing, or obscene telephone calls, for example, could
not be construed as crimes of violence. Further,
some of the black witnesses might testify that "Jesse
Pratt preferred Negro woman" [*sic*] and "since
there was no Negro woman on jury, this could be
prejudicial."

The defense's motions were denied.

In his opening statement, Byron Chatfield told the

jury they would have four decisions to make this time: One, was the conduct of the defendant committed deliberately? Two, was his conduct appropriate to the "provocation," if any? Three, would the defendant constitute a threat to society in the future? Four, should the defendant receive a death sentence, a life sentence without possibility of parole, or a life sentence with the possibility of parole?

They would be hearing a great deal about the defendant's character and background, Chatfield said, from the time he was a young person to the present. Was there anything there that might suggest that he deserved a sentence less than death? This would be their decision. They would be hearing, he added, from former girlfriends, former wives, other inmates who had served time with him, and others; they also would be given information about the defendant's prior convictions.

Kenneth Hadley delivered the opening statement for the defense. His tone was subdued as he pointed out that Jesse Pratt was not a serial killer; instead, he was a troubled person who had probably inherited psychological problems from his father. He did the best he could with what he had—which wasn't a great deal. His IQ of 70.5 in grade school was in the borderline retarded range. It had recently been measured at 77. The jury would hear from psychologists who would testify that he had suffered brain damage as a child. His mother had said he was a fine young man until, somewhere along the line, he went astray. Discounting Elizabeth Helle's testimony for the prosecution, he cast aspersions on what he claimed was her drinking problem—especially while she was pregnant with Jesse Pratt.

As the prosecution launched its case seeking the death penalty, there followed a procession of former girlfriends, ex-wives, and the now-grown children of some of these women, all of whom testified to Jesse Pratt's cruelty, his sudden rages, which frequently culminated in violent physical abuse, and a variety of outrages committed by the defendant. In agreeing to testify, each had been promised that her present address would not be disclosed.

Jesse Pratt had married his first wife when she was seventeen—after getting her pregnant when she was only sixteen. She left him eight times. "I always thought the next time he beat me I was gonna die," she said. Yet she was charmed by Jesse into coming back every time until her final exit—after which she filed for divorce.

Pratt often took rejection and abandonment by these women as a gross personal insult. He would repeatedly call them in the middle of the night, stalk them, disable their cars, and occasionally try to run them off the road with his truck or his Cadillac. He actually crashed one of his vehicles into the rear end of one of their cars. Several former wives and girlfriends had obtained restraining orders to keep Pratt away from them, but he paid little attention to these court orders.

Having promised one new wife that he would take her to his home in Alaska after they were married, the two of them—together with the woman's four children by a previous marriage—moved into a temporarily unoccupied mobile home in Anchorage that was actually owned by one of Pratt's former girlfriends. When the former girlfriend returned to her property, Pratt refused to let her in, threatening her life if she complained.

After things turned inevitably sour with this wife, Pratt took her to the hospital in Anchorage with a fork stuck in her shoulder. While she walked into the emergency room on her own, Pratt held her children hostage in his truck—lest she tell the doctors the truth about the "accident."

Of all of Jesse Pratt's abused wives, the most pathetic was unquestionably Nancy, whom he married in 1977, and whose permanently scarred upper lip bore its own testimony to the defendant's cruelty to women. Not long after they were married, he told her that she could add to their joint income (she was already working for Allstate Insurance at the time) by working truck stops as a prostitute on weekends. When she refused, he beat her up.

Later, when Pratt's friend Leroy Lantz, a small-time crook and professional pimp, came to visit the pair in Seattle, Jesse forced her to have sex with Leroy. Pratt later sold her to Lantz for $1,000 and Leroy put her to work as a prostitute in Sacramento.

Kenneth Hadley and Enver Bozgoz alternated during cross-examination of these unfortunate women, most of whom had by now remarried and were managing to live reasonably normal lives—at least until they were persuaded to submit to the trauma of testifying in this second trial.

Hadley was a gentleman as usual. Even Ernie Bozgoz, as he introduced himself, was remarkably subdued. He was even polite—for a while, at least. But soon he began to criticize the witnesses for going back to Jesse Pratt after their separations and for not insisting that "he see a shrink."

One woman, it developed, *had* extracted a promise from Jesse that he would seek counseling before she agreed to return to him. But he never did. Bozgoz then asked why she didn't insist he see a psychiatrist *before* she came back.

"Because I didn't think of it," she said simply.

"Then why didn't *you* go to a shrink yourself to find out why you kept going back to him?" Bozgoz wanted to know. The woman bristled.

"Because I was only seventeen or eighteen at the time, and I was trying to make my marriage work," she shot back.

"So then why didn't your parents insist you see a shrink? Why didn't your best friend insist?"

It went on like that with most of the women. Since it was unlikely that the defense cocounsel was helping his client's cause, the prosecution refrained from objecting to his line of questioning.

Career felon David Whaley, who had spent thirteen of his forty years in assorted prisons, but who was on parole at the moment, was the first of a number of convict witnesses who had done time with Jesse Pratt. Called by the prosecution, Whaley would testify about the abduction of Thelma Adams, for which he and Jesse Pratt had both served time at Walla Walla. It was during their earlier stay in the Rio Consumnes Correctional Center in California that both had met Leroy Lantz. It was, in fact, Leroy Lantz who had told Whaley about Jesse Pratt's offer of $3,000 "to beat up some guy."

Whaley was very up front about the details of the armed invasion of the Barnes Trucking Company offices, matter-of-factly confessing his own involvement in the crime.

Scarcely touching that part of Whaley's testimony when it was the defense's turn, Kenneth Hadley attempted, in his seemingly unassuming way, to solicit an expert opinion from a habitual inmate to establish that Jesse Pratt would not constitute a threat if sentenced to life in prison. It provided a little desperately needed comic relief.

"Are penitentiaries able to handle most prisoners, one way or another?" The question sounded casual.

"No," Whaley responded.

"Well, people are watched pretty carefully, aren't they?"

"Not really, no."

"But if you do something wrong, you get in trouble, don't you?"

"Well, only if you get caught."

"What's it like to be in prison?"

"Well, it's like your home. You have to stay there, and you have to deal with it. If you can't deal with it, you don't belong there, and you better not do no more crimes."

In redirect, Byron Chatfield elicited Whaley's opinion that prisoners are not prevented from doing violence to one another and there are plenty of potential weapons: razor blades, forks, even sharpened spoons.

Encouraged to elaborate, Whaley provided a little insight into the deadly seriousness of prison business. It seemed there had been a group of convicts at Walla Walla who were plotting to kill Jesse Pratt "because of his mouth."

"But because they knew I was his crime partner, they come to see me. I told them if they hurt a hair on Jesse Pratt's head, I would kill them because that man owes me money [the $3,000 he had been promised for his help in the Adams abduction] and he's gonna pay me."

Thelma Adams took the witness stand to relate the details of her Tukwila, Washington, kidnapping in 1980 and her subsequent rape by David Whaley and Jesse Pratt in the Country Squire Motel in Eugene, Oregon. The courage and resourcefulness she had displayed on that occasion reemerged during Enver Bozgoz's cross-examination.

The assistant defense counsel skirted any discussion of her actual kidnapping and rape until several hours into his interrogation—except to imply that the abduction had really been her fault because she had refused to talk to Jesse Pratt after leaving him. Instead, the counsel focused his attention on her relationship with the defendant while she was living with him.

He suggested that Jesse must have loved her because he gave her a white fur coat for which he had paid $3,600. (This was news to her, she said.) And the reason Pratt had gotten angry when she used a serrated knife to cut his cheese was because he was afraid she would cut herself, and was concerned for her well-being. (Thelma was skeptical of the counsel's analysis and said so.)

Bozgoz asked endless questions about the honesty of *her* feelings for Jesse Pratt. He berated her for staying with him, for acceding to his sexual demands after deciding she no longer loved him, for not leaving him sooner, and especially for accepting his airline ticket to return to him from Missouri, where she had fled after leaving him the first time. It was therefore obvious, he said, that she loved him.

"Love had nothing to do with it," Thelma told him. Rather, when Jesse was trying to persuade her to return, he told her about his having "blown away" someone in Alaska, and he had implied the same thing could happen to her. Wounded, the interrogator attempted to ridicule the witness.

"You were afraid he would blow you away by telephone from Seattle, Washington?"

"No," she responded calmly, "I was not afraid he would blow me away through the telephone from Seattle."

Several witnesses who had been Jesse Pratt's fellow inmates in the Klamath County Jail followed Thelma Adams. They told stories about how Pratt threw his weight around, especially with younger prisoners. He had threatened to stab two of the witnesses with a sharpened pencil. To intimidate them, he was quoted as saying he "had killed one bitch" and told about "gettin' adrenaline rushes when he was battlin' her with the ice pick."

In his cross-examination, Bozgoz called the witness a "snitch and a prostitute who was testifying for money. For the price of a lunch, you betray your friends."

"They wasn't my friends," the man protested. "They was drug dealers and murderers in there. Let's get somethin' straight here. I *volunteered* to come up here to testify against this man because I think people's lives may be at stake in the society.

Could be my life; could be my kid's; could be somebody else's life."

When one convict revealed that Pratt bragged about "even having been on Death Row," those last two words nearly derailed the trial. Kenneth Hadley again moved for a mistrial. Alternatively, if this motion was denied, he moved for a directed verdict of life in prison. If the trial continued, he asked the judge to instruct the prosecution to warn every witness to avoid any such reference.

It was a request to which Byron Chatfield immediately agreed, but the judge said he would take the defense motions under advisement. He permitted the trial to continue, however, for the balance of the afternoon.

Diane, one of the girls who had testified about Jesse Pratt's knitting needles and welding rods during the guilt phase of the trial returned to the witness stand in midafternoon. This time she told the jury what these objects were used for. She also wanted to make it clear that she had turned her own life around since the days when she had resorted to prostitution to feed her drug habit.

When Enver Bozgoz attempted to excoriate and discredit her after she admitted to such a past, she bristled. Sitting straight up on the witness stand, she proudly told him she had been sober for nine months and was currently going to school to acquire word-processing skills so she could get a job.

During this second trial, Bozgoz didn't bother her, she later explained. It was the defendant's presence that intimidated her. Deliberately.

"During my entire testimony, he played games," she said. "At first, he wouldn't look at me. When he did, he was just so *cocky*—as if he were laughing, right after I had said something.

"But sometimes he just glared. It was kind of spooky. The looks he gave me were like the way he looked when he knew he was hurting me and enjoying it. He really threatened me. It was as if he were saying, 'I will hurt you again some day.'

"Then all of a sudden, he smiles at me. Then it was like, 'Ha, ha, I got you!'"

When court was adjourned for the weekend, Hadley's motion for a mistrial hung over the case.

The lawyers for both sides were sitting on the edges of their chairs when court reconvened on Monday morning April 8, 1991. Having reviewed the cases cited by both sides, and having studied several more he had researched on his own, Judge Piper announced his decision.

It was the defense that had precipitated the "Death Row" remark, he said. Moreover, the prosecution had not capitalized on the unfortunate disclosure. Although he did not suggest that the defense had deliberately provoked the remark to cause a mistrial, it was the result of the defense's aggressive cross-questioning of a witness who, with three felony convictions on his record, might not be expected to follow the rules.

Further, since the jury knew the defendant was on trial for aggravated murder, of which they had already convicted him, and since the remark was isolated and made in passing, it had not been so damaging in the penalty phase of the trial as to constitute grounds for a mistrial.

Judge Piper then denied each of the defense's motions. The trial would not have to start over from the beginning. The jury was invited back into the courtroom.

A number of witnesses were called to the stand to address the question of whether the defendant would constitute a threat to society in the future. They included Mel McClintock, Pratt's former friend and longtime business associate, who related how Pratt had offered to have his thirteen-year-old stepdaughter killed so she could not be a witness against McClintock in the statutory rape case for which he was now serving time.

It took about ten minutes for the prosecution to put that much on the record. The witness's cross-examination ground on for hours, during which McClintock fiercely denied the defense's allegation that he was testifying as part of a deal to have his sentence reduced. He readily admitted and deeply regretted his crime, he said. He had undergone counseling, and he was trying to make amends as best he could. He fully realized that in agreeing to testify he had put his own life in danger—not that he would be killed by Pratt himself, but he believed he risked death at the hands of other convicts, since he had broken the prison code.

Jesse Pratt's half sisters, Judy and Cecilia, testified that they believed their brother would have them killed if he knew where they lived. Judy told the court that after her brother's previous imprisonment, she had invited him to come live with her and her children in Las Vegas. Clarence thought that was a wonderful opportunity, she said. He would run a string of prostitutes out of her home. When she refused, he began threatening her.

Jesse Pratt's mother, Elizabeth Helle, was the last witness for the prosecution. During her testimony, she cleared up the details of the complex family relationship in which the defendant grew up. Helle had been married to five husbands. She divorced only one, who was a notorious womanizer. The other four died—one of cancer, one of another illness, one in an auto accident, and one (who could not adjust to civilian life after retiring from the military) was a suicide.

Jesse got along well with all of his stepfathers, she said. There was never any physical or sexual abuse of the boy by any of them. She denied that he ever had a head injury (or ever went to a hospital), or that he ever had a paper route—countering an unsubstantiated defense claim that Pratt had sustained a head injury while delivering newspapers. Pratt dropped out of high school in tenth grade, she said, and did not graduate. His personality changed from that of a loving, compassionate boy to a threatening bully at the age of eighteen or nineteen, after he left home to live on his own. During that period, he would come to see her occasionally and demand large sums of money: "Or I'll have you killed, and I'll have your daughters killed."

Much of Bozgoz's cross-examination consisted of bawling out the witness for having conceived and raised a son who got into so much trouble. He also challenged the genuineness of her fear of him. Jesse Pratt had, after all, been out of Walla Walla prison for nearly a year before he got into trouble again. "He never tried to kill you, did he?"

Cocounsel Bozgoz pointed out that Elizabeth had to admit she was still alive.

"But I lived in fear all those years," she shot back.

"Ma'am, you might be living in fear because you feel guilty the way you raised your son. Isn't that right?"

"No, that is not right!" Elizabeth's voice was an angry shout that echoed in the courtroom. "I do not feel guilty the way I raised my son. I raised him to the best of my ability, and he had everything a child needed. He had a home; he had food; he had clothes; he had bicycles; he had everything."

"And the best of your ability was that half time you were so drunk that you end up in the hospital." It was an accusation, not a question.

"That is not true! When I went to the hospital, he was not even living at home with me."

Bozgoz cleared his throat. He noisily turned pages. So, Elizabeth filled the silence.

"He didn't even know I'd been in the hospital for four or five months—if not longer."

There was more page turning by the interrogator. A longer pause ensued. The counsel changed the subject.

"You and Cecilia, you always told that you were scared he gonna get outta jail, he gonna come and kill you. How many times any person ever attempt to hurt you in any way?"

"Nobody has, but you live in fear that they might."

"All right, you—you live in a fear that they might. Is that because, ma'am, that every once in a while you get drunk?"

"I haven't been drunk in seventeen years," she countered. She was very angry.

Once again, the prosecution did not object to the line of questioning because, as Byron Chatfield later conceded, one, Mrs. Helle was doing all right on her own, and two, Mr. Bozgoz was digging his own—or, more accurately, his *client's*—grave.

"You have a guilty feeling," Bozgoz declared, summarizing for the jury what he hoped his interrogation had shown. "That's all I have. I be in your bad books, just like Cecilia."

This time Chatfield did interrupt with an objection. Cocounsel Bozgoz cleared his throat again and sat down.

"The prosecution rests," Mr. Chatfield announced.

THIRTY-SIX

I had no idea Jesse could speak without profanity.
—Probation Officer Earl Runestadt

Before the defense began calling its witnesses, Kenneth Hadley introduced three more motions, all of them having the objective of preventing the death penalty question from even being submitted to the jury.

Grounds for the first motion were that the prosecution had presented insufficient evidence. It was denied. The second motion called the court's attention to the fact that one potential witness requested by the defense could not be found by the state. Judge Donald Piper ruled that the state had made every reasonable effort to locate the requested witness, and he turned down that one as well. As to Hadley's third motion, alleging that this second trial constituted "double jeopardy," the judge decided to reserve judgment until he could study the cases cited by the defense counsel. By the next morning, having done his homework, Judge Piper was in a position to deny the remaining defense motion.

In support of its effort to prevent Jesse Pratt from being executed, the defense would call no less than twelve character witnesses—six of whom had been flown in from Alaska at state expense. The first four were personnel associated with the Klamath County Jail. They included two guards, a security sergeant, and a nurse who visited the inmates. Each was asked the critical question of whether it was likely that Pratt would constitute a danger to others in a prison situation. Their endorsements were luke-warm at best.

The defense had also imported two inmates from the Oregon State Penitentiary in Salem. One testi-fied that Pratt always kept his cell and immediate area clean, and he never saw him get into a fight. The other refused to answer any questions unless his lawyer was present. He was returned to Salem without testifying.

Two former employers and the widow of a third, all of whom knew Jesse Pratt in Alaska during the early 1970s, testified that when in their employ the man was a hard worker (as a tire changer) and didn't get into trouble. They knew nothing about his personal life—and, interestingly, knew nothing about the current case. All agreed that "he had a big mouth."

Another witness from Alaska was the Reverend Robert Ray. In a rich Southern accent, he testified that he had seen Jesse Pratt at his Anchorage church every Sunday morning from 1972 to 1976, "except when it was raining." And he "never saw one day of anger in him." In fact, "my wife and two daughters were crazy about him."

Explaining that the purpose of this part of the defendant's trial was to decide whether or not he

should get the death penalty, Kenneth Hadley
asked the minister if he had an opinion.

He did: "The business I'm in, whether it's a jury
or what, I don't personally feel no person have no
right to sit up and make no decision on whether a
man is to die or not." He had felt that way, he said,
even when his own daughter had been murdered
by her boyfriend.

Enver Bozgoz then introduced Jesse Pratt's former
parole officer in Anchorage. Earl Runestadt had
known Jesse Pratt from 1971 until Runestadt had retired in 1981. In a meek voice, the man described his
former charge as "rough cut, quite profane—(whenever he came down the hall to my office he called me
an 'ugly SOB')—he was warm in his own way, but not
an individual of great intellect.

"But we had a good rapport," he added. As Jesse's
probation officer he "tried to be a 'good listener.'"

The aging witness seemed to be doing his best
to be supportive of his former client. But Enver
Bozgoz's questions were not as succinct as those of
his cocounsel, Kenneth Hadley, and the interrogation became somewhat murky.

"Mr. Runestadt," Bozgoz began, "it appears that, as
you said, you were straight with him and he was
straight with you. And we have had a few witnesses in
here testifies before you from Alaska. And there were
these former employers and also family that he lived
with. During the period of time that he lived there
with a Negro family, and he apparently really respected them. Can you tell us from your knowledge
of Jesse and your knowin' two of his wives at least that
he threatened and was abusive to woman, or that his
girlfriend? Can you tell why one moment Jesse is so

nice, respects especially black people, he does not use a profanity, but, on the other hand, when he yells—with you, I mean joking manner, I suppose, use a profanity—and he threatened—ah—harm to there to his wife. In other words, two different individuals. So do you have a opinion why?"

"It's kinda hard to reconcile," the witness replied after a pause. "I would imagine—I'm not a psychologist, but I would imagine . . ."

Byron Chatfield objected to the witness testifying as to what he would "imagine." It would be all right to ask him for his *opinion*, the prosecutor suggested.

"To answer the question . . . ," the witness began. Then he changed his mind. "I really don't think I should."

"Well, let me put it this way," Bozgoz offered. "The people that come from Alaska down here—and, of course, the life in Alaska must be different than the life outside of state of Alaska. But these individuals that came from Alaska down here and they think very highly of him, whether the white, his former employer, or the Negro family that he lived with. And you being a probation officer, you have dealt with numerous individuals on probation, you have handled cases of all kinds, I presume, and different races, and different men or woman. Based upon your education in college that you majored and minored, and also based on your experience as a probation officer dealing with the public, can you give us opinion—or whether he object to word 'imagine'—you can use your opinion, you're entitled to it—and tell us why he is this individual, as he indicates, he had a home life less to be desired, and why he's so many people come up and speak so highly of him, and then, as you said, you help one of his wives to leave Alaska because he threatened her?"

A long pause ensued. Finally, the witness spoke.

"I—I—I'm not real sure that I can understand the question, or that I can answer it very well." He paused, struggling. "You want to know why—how— to see if I can reconcile why so many from Alaska have spoken about—some quite favorably—and yet he's had these difficulties with women?"

"Yes," the defense cocounsel said, quickly adding, "white woman but not colored woman, but a white woman," thus clarifying his question.

"Well," the former probation officer offered, "his relationship with his own mother was—was not good."

Bozgoz asked the witness why sometimes Jesse Pratt had a foul mouth and sometimes he was careful about his language.

"I had no idea Jesse could speak without profanity."

It broke up the courtroom.

When it was time for cross-examination, Byron Chatfield had the witness confirm page after page of the "chronological notes" he had made during the years when he was the defendant's probation officer. First, the prosecutor had him read the string of felonies Pratt had committed by the time Runestadt met him. The crimes included robbery, burglary, assault, theft of a U.S. government check, theft of a truck and trailer, threatening a motorist with a gun (while on probation when he was forbidden to own a gun), and other crimes of violence. The prosecutor had the witness acknowledge that some of this violence was against men—thus attacking the witness's claim that Pratt got along well with men and had problems only with women.

Chatfield called Runestadt's attention to his own write-up of how he and another probation officer had helped one of Jesse Pratt's wives escape further violence. They had boxed up her belongings and driven her to the Anchorage airport so she could get away, not because her husband had "threatened her," as the witness had stated in his direct testimony, but because he had *beaten* her five times—once when she was six months pregnant.

Runestadt did seem to remember that. His voice was disintegrating.

Had the probation officer recorded in his report that he had told Pratt that "beating a woman was not acceptable, and is unforgivable"?

"That's what it says," the witness admitted. It was a hoarse, barely audible whisper.

Had he told the defense's investigator, Sylvia Mathews, that Pratt had threatened to kill both of his sisters?

By this time, Runestadt didn't seem to remember what he had told anybody. Mercifully, after about ten minutes of cross-examination, Byron Chatfield told the court he had no more questions.

It was Enver Bozgoz's final turn for redirect. Instead, he offered a personal assessment.

"Let's get one thing clear. We been beatin' a dead horse for some time." Judge Piper let him get away with it.

Ending the day, Michelle Quinn, who operated a foster home for troubled children in Klamath Falls, testified that some of her charges were victims of fetal alcohol syndrome and had a resulting attention deficit disorder; others had been victims of sexual abuse. Although it depended on the child, neither group did as well in school on the average as children without these handicaps, she said.

Her testimony would provide ammunition for the defense's summations. So would the expert testimony of the two psychological consultants hired by the defense at state expense.

The first of these was Dr. Faulder Colby, the neuropsychologist who had evaluated Jesse Pratt after giving him a battery of mental tests. Kenneth Hadley devoted some time to establishing Dr. Colby's educational and professional background, which included a Master of Arts in divinity before he settled on psychology as a career.

Perhaps influenced by Pete McDonald's chalk talk, the defense invited the psychologist to come down the steps to a chart easel and give the jury some background about neuropsychology. It turned out to be a very long but rather interesting lecture, taking up half the morning. He drew a picture of the brain, then attached it to a spinal cord. He sketched a neuron with many "wires" attached. He explained what an axon was. He drew each of the brain's major components, explaining the function of the left and right temporal lobes, the parietal lobe, the prefrontal motor cortex, and particularly the frontal lobe, "which puts a cap on basic emotions."

Expanding on this element, Dr. Colby explained that "a child doesn't have a fully developed frontal lobe, so he can't think things through like an adult. When the frontal lobe is damaged, its logical reasoning power and governing ability over basic emotions become inhibited. When alcohol, for example, shuts down the functioning of the frontal lobe in an adult, the person might make the mistake of taking on a whole bunch of policemen, even though it is obvious to others that he has no hope of prevailing."

As the lecturer tore off each completed page from the large chart pad, it was submitted by the defense to be marked as a court exhibit.

Although it was clear where his testimony would be going, it literally took all day to get it on the record. In great detail, the doctor described the minutiae of the tests he had given Jesse Pratt. These were designed to measure basic intelligence, memory, attention, concentration, motivation, perceptual ability, motor function, and a variety of other factors. But he wasn't able to complete the series because Jesse Pratt got angry in the middle of the last test. He had torn off the blindfold he was wearing during a motor memory exercise involving objects of various shapes and refused to continue.

It had been a test designed to identify subjects who have sustained a head injury. The test measured mistakes. A higher score indicated more mistakes. Subjects who have never had such an injury invariably have a score of less than 34, he said. Pratt's score was 62. The unexpected determination did not alter the expert's opinion about his subject's probable brain damage, because, in order to have his computer calculate a score, he had entered all the remaining task results as if Pratt had done a perfect job of correctly placing the objects in the proper sockets. Highlights of Dr. Colby's conclusions included:

- The defendant reads at less than a third-grade level.

- 99.2 percent of the population reads better than Jesse Pratt.
- His IQ was now probably in the high 70s; 80 is below average; below 70 is retarded. Pratt had scored 70.5 in tenth grade.
- Even though he had told his half sisters that he "knew how to handle psychologists," the consultant didn't think he was faking.

Turning to issues that were critical to the penalty phase of the trial, Dr. Colby believed that his subject probably was incapable of functioning well in society, but he might do well in a prison environment, "as long as the rules are very clear." But, he cautioned, he couldn't say for sure.

Kenneth Hadley asked the psychologist why the defendant never picked fights with men. Dr. Colby couldn't tell from his limited tests. He did not suggest what seemed obvious to some of the spectators in the courtroom: Jesse Pratt was a coward.

The psychologist was convinced that his subject had a "very fuzzy, spotty memory for his childhood." Pratt thought that he might have been raised in an orphanage, since he had vague memories of women dressed in black, and Colby thought these could have been nuns in a Catholic orphanage.

Dr. Colby could not conclude with certainty that the defendant had sustained a head injury. All he could say for sure about his subject was that "he didn't come in with much, and he lost a lot." He did agree that Pratt would be less likely to be dangerous in a prison setting. And with time he might be easier to get along with since, as people age, they calm down.

Hadley pressed his luck. Although he may be a danger to society now, the defense counsel ventured, perhaps in twenty or thirty years Jesse Pratt might no longer be dangerous in the outside world?

"I would not be willing to predict that," Dr. Colby said. During cross-examination, he clarified his position.

"There is no evidence in the literature to suggest that he is likely to become a 'sweet old man.'"

Chatfield asked the witness a number of questions about his October 1990 report. The prosecutor began reading selected excerpts. He read them slowly and carefully, with voice inflections that interpreted the phrases he found meaningful for the jury:

"'Mr. Pratt will likely do all right in situations which are highly structured, undemanding, and conforming to *his* preconceived notions about the natural order of things. In his case, that may mean a predominantly male-dominant society. A prison environment is one such situation. So it is not surprising, therefore, that Mr. Pratt has done quite well in prison settings.'

"You mention that in your report?"

"That's what it says," Dr. Colby confirmed.

"And then it goes on," Chatfield continued, "'However, in an open setting, or in a nonconfined situation, he can be expected to be much more volatile. In such settings, when things are going the way *he* wants them to, or *expects* them to, he may do all right. However, in situations where conflicts might ensue, such as when women, whom he appears to consider subservient, give him a difficult time, he may easily lose control and behave quite irrationally.'"

"Yes," the author agreed.

"You included that as one of your findings?"

"Yes."

"When you say, 'behave quite irrationally,' are you really talking about violent, assaultive conduct—some response on his part which could include that?"

"Certainly with his history—and I would predict that is more likely than not in the future."

The prosecutor paused to let that sink in before he asked his next question.

"Dr. Colby, I'm sure you're aware there are women in the correctional facilities that work in there. If a woman were in that position and basically bossed the defendant around, giving him orders, is this the sort of situation wherein the defendant could act violent, or there could be some kind of irrational behavior on his part?"

"That's a possibility."

Another pregnant pause.

"You're aware of homosexuality occurring in a penitentiary?"

"Yes."

"And if, in fact, he has had an overattachment with a homosexual, including transvestites, with whom in the past he's had contact, and if, in fact, in a prison setting, there became that sort of an attachment, then could he act out violently if this particular person was taken away from him, separated from him?"

"Following your line of reasoning, that's possible."

There was a longer pause this time while the prosecutor gave the jury time to think over what they had heard.

"And based on what you know, will you agree that one of the major reasons for fights and violence in prisons include homosexual love triangles?"

"That's certainly true."

It was almost half a minute before Chatfield spoke again.

"You go on in your report—and you've done this in regard to 'Findings and Conclusions' that you've made, on page ten:

"'First, it is unlikely that he is a safe person if left to his own devices. He can be predicted with some confidence to be violent and assaultive in the wrong situations.'

"You mention that in your report?"

"Yes."

"And when you say that—as you mentioned before—that he can be predicted with some confidence to be violent and assaultive in the wrong situations—you are saying more likely than not? Would that be correct?"

"More likely than not," the doctor agreed.

Chatfield read the final paragraph in Dr. Colby's report.

"'It should constitute a serious error in judgment for various review bodies to assume that since he behaves so well in a closed and supervised setting, he will be all right outside. Mr. Pratt's history strongly argues in favor of being kept under tight and rigidly supervised control for the remainder of his life.'

"Since we are talking about an 'organic problem,'" the prosecutor asked, "is the defendant unlikely to learn from past mistakes?"

"He's *not* going to change is my prediction. . . . The

problem is that with a damaged brain he has an inability to learn. He can no more learn to have an undamaged frontal lobe than you can learn to not have a broken foot when your foot is broken. I have no reason to assume that his assaultive behavior as it has been displayed in the past is going to change in the future. I have no reason to assume that."

Pratt's "bicycle accident," if it ever happened, was turning out to be more of a liability than an excuse.

Chatfield asked about the possible use of antipsychotic drugs to reduce violent, assaultive behavior. Although Dr. Colby was not a psychiatric physician, he was familiar with the results of such experiments. The bottom line was that such drugs often have such devastating side effects that it is unethical to prescribe them for nonpsychotic subjects without their permission, and such cooperation on the part of Jesse Pratt seemed unlikely.

Dr. Colby's testimony had taken the entire day. In producing this expert witness, the defense may have given the prosecution more points than it had racked up for its client.

THIRTY-SEVEN

Sweet Analytics, 'tis thou hast ravished me.1594
    —Christopher Marlowe (1564–93),
                   Doctor Faustus

On Friday morning, April 12, 1991 the jury would meet another psychologist.

Introducing himself as Dr. Ralph C. Underwager, "director of the Institute for Psychological Therapy" in Northview, Minnesota, he was, he said, a licensed consulting psychologist as well as a clinical psychologist. He and his wife, who was also a psychologist, had written several books, including *Child Sexual Abuse, The Real World of Child Interrogation,* and *Solomon's Dilemna: False Allegations of Sexual Abuse in Custody Battles.* Underwager listed cities all over the world in which he had lectured. He had been a professional expert witness in a number of child abuse trials, he added.

The psychologist had met the defendant a month before the trial began. Although there had been nothing in Jesse Pratt's previous record suggesting that he had suffered sexual abuse as a child, after they read Dr. Colby's report of October 1990, Pratt's lawyers had invited Dr. Underwager into the case.

Interrogated by Enver Bozgoz, Dr. Underwager devoted the entire morning to the effects of sexual abuse on male children. Typically, the psychologist said, boys subjected to such mistreatment tend to develop a distorted view of sexuality and become very confused about their own sexual identity. Since the defendant displayed such a profile, Underwager had concluded that he must have been sexually abused.

Bozgoz asked his witness to explain what tests he had run to be sure that Jesse Pratt was not faking.

The therapist hadn't run any, but he was convinced of his diagnosis because of the amazingly detailed descriptions Pratt had provided—even relating one of his traumatic experiences to current events at the time. The assertion seemed in conflict with Dr. Colby's testimony about Jesse Pratt's "vague, spotty memory of his childhood."

The expert's testimony included a seemingly irrelevant excursion into the rather different effects of sexual abuse on female children. His lecture then drifted into a description of "acts of worship practiced for thousands of years by the world's earliest religions," during which, he said, "entire villages congregated in fields for communal orgies between everybody and everything—sex between males, females, goats, sheep, or anything else," in order to insure an abundant crop from these fields at harvest time. He told the jury that infants of both sexes learn in the first three months of their lives that stimulation of genital tissue is pleasant, adding that children can be influenced by their emotional environment while still in the womb.

The defense cocounsel asked for Underwager's

professional opinion of why Jesse Pratt, in the now-famous ménage à trois, began the event by inserting a knitting needle or welding rod into his penis, then switched to having sex with Diane, interrupting that dalliance for sex with transvestite Sunshine before returning to his own urethral insertions. Why it was necessary for the jury to have this information was unclear. And the psychologist's answer wasn't very illuminating.

"It was very primitive. It felt good."

When Bozgoz returned to the primary issue to be decided in this penalty phase of the trial, Dr. Underwager stated that he sincerely believed that Jesse Pratt would not be dangerous in a tightly controlled prison situation, where the rules were very clear, and that Pratt could, with competent psychotherapy, overcome the many psychological problems with which he had been saddled for forty years. If he did not think so, the doctor said, he wouldn't be in the profession he was in. It might have been a good place for Bozgoz to quit.

"What is the effect of the death penalty on human beings?" the defense cocounsel now asked.

Byron Chatfield objected to the question and the jury was sent out of the courtroom, but the witness remained. Interpreting Bozgoz's question to be an exploration of the death penalty as a deterrent, the prosecutor stated that the question was irrelevant. Whether the Oregon law was good law or bad law, it was the law, he said.

Bozgoz, however, said that wasn't what he had in mind. Judge Piper permitted him to question his witness, still out of the jury's hearing, but the defense lawyer's question now changed.

"What is the effect of the death penalty on human behavior?" It produced a detailed answer.

"The death penalty certainly deters the behavior of the person that is put to death," the witness said, adding, "It is my conviction as a theologian that the state has the right to take the life of a person. [Although Dr. Colby had indicated that he had a degree in divinity, this was Underwager's first reference to *his* expertise in this field.]

"I am not opposed to the death penalty in principle." As to whether the death penalty was a deterrent, he said that depended. The literature showed that it was not a deterrent in the United States because our society is not sufficiently Draconian, but in a society where justice is swift and harsh, the record showed that it *was* a deterrent to violent crime.

Bozgoz attempted a retrograde maneuver.

"I withdraw the question since Mr. Chatfield objects to it." The withdrawn question would, of course, remain in the transcript, but the jury would not discuss it.

Byron Chatfield began his cross-examination by verifying that cocounsel Bozgoz had called Dr. Underwager only a month before the trial. He asked about the psychologist's research in preparation for his testimony. The only documents the expert witness had reviewed, he revealed, were Dr. Colby's report, a report from the Veterans Administration about Jesse Pratt's father, and the state police interviews with April, Diane, and Sunshine.

Because of the impressive variety of sexual abuse Pratt had cataloged for Dr. Colby (alleged anal rape by two sequential stepfathers, a similar act committed by an anonymous male "dark-haired" friend of his mother's, and later molestation by a female friend of his mother), Chatfield asked Dr. Underwager whether he had "just accepted the defendant's claims at face value."

"No, of course not." It was a petulant answer. But the witness was forced to admit he had made no effort to corroborate the defendant's claims. Nevertheless, he argued, utilizing sophisticated verification techniques pioneered by the Germans (e.g., the very nature of the language Pratt had used, especially his injection of unrelated peripheral material like 1954 current events in his life) he was convinced that Pratt was speaking the truth. Besides, Pratt had *wept* when he told him about it.

"So," Chatfield observed, "everything you have concluded is based on the premise that he was sexually abused?"

"Yes, I *believe* it," the witness confirmed.

"And if it didn't occur, then what does that do to your evaluation?"

There was a long pause. The hitherto resonant lecture voice of the psychologist suddenly became softer—even a little meek.

"If it did not occur, then I made a mistake."

Chatfield began exploring the psychologist's acceptance of other statements Pratt had made to him. What, for example, had the interviewer learned about the kidnapping and rape for which the defendant had served time? "The situation," as he understood it, was a "business dispute between Pratt and another trucking firm, in which he had taken someone away from their office because he didn't like the way they were treating her."

The psychologist volunteered Jesse Pratt's own assessment of his relationships with women. "They are just fine, he said repeatedly, until it became sexual. Then *he* changed, fearing they would try to dominate him." The relationship then disintegrated into a "fight," which Underwager understood to mean a *verbal* exchange—an argument. He seemed to know nothing about Pratt's record of repeatedly beating his wives and girlfriends.

As to the events that resulted in the current trial, the defendant had told him that Carrie Love had been an occasional sex partner after she seduced him once "by appearing nude in the sleeping compartment of the truck he had bought her."

What was the doctor's understanding of the events that led up to Carrie Love's fatal journey?

"He asserted that he had dropped her off after a dispute over money," the witness said. "He thinks what happened then is that, after he left her off, she called the other girl who worked in the office—who then called another man, who picked her up and subsequently murdered her. Since everyone knew he used a special route, that was the reason the body was left on that route."

Asked whether he had applied the same kind of analysis toward verifying the truth of this account that he had applied in the defendant's allegation of sexual abuse, the doctor said he had not.

Had he done *anything* to verify the accuracy of what he had been told?

"No," the witness declared indignantly, his voice breaking. "As I said, that part of this situation, I did not see then, nor do I see it now, as *my* responsibility. That's not the task that I was asked to be involved in." His tone was getting professionally stuffy.

"Isn't it important to you to determine the accuracy of the information that you provide?"

"No!" It was almost a falsetto this time. "No, that has nothing to do with—ah—ah, the basic responsibilities I have," he added, his voice now dropping half an octave. "I am not a judge; I am not a prosecutor; I am not a law enforcement officer. I am a psychologist—a healer. My basic function is, hopefully, to heal."

"You're a healer?"

"I would like to think that, yes."

Chatfield returned to the subject of possible risks to others that Pratt might pose if he was sentenced to life in prison. Dr. Underwager revealed, "He would be no more dangerous than the usual prison inmate," adding, however, "By definition, people who are in prison are more dangerous than people who are not in prison."

Referring to the remarks in Underwager's report about the defendant's confinement in the Walla Walla prison, the prosecutor addressed the paragraph that said Pratt had masturbated to fantasies of a prison nurse he had met there. The prosecutor may have been intending to explore whether Pratt had confessed to fantasies about imposing physical abuse, but all he asked initially was whether the defendant's fantasies had been about sexual activity with the woman.

"Oh, no!" The witness's tone bespoke his disappointment at such a crass misinterpretation of his client's romantic fantasies: "It was about reaching out for, and getting, some sense of intimacy that he never got. What we're talking about is the development of a loving, full, intimate relationship that is composed of shared time, shared experience, shared values. And tenderness, and gentleness, and hope, and visions, and wants, and longing, and pain, and terrors." His voice was rising with the passion of his conviction.

"All those things that are a part of what it means to be *one* with another person. That kind of love and closeness and hope—of two lives meshed and fused and molded together. Then sexual experience becomes much more than just genital stimulation. Then the joining of bodies becomes one flesh, oneness, and fullness, and togetherness, and peace, and love. That was what Mr. Pratt was reaching for."

It was beautiful, almost poetic prose worthy of a first-class romantic novel. It would have worked as a sermon in an R-rated marriage ceremony designed to inspire eternal faithfulness. But it didn't sound anything like Jesse Pratt—except, perhaps, to demonstrate the defendant's manipulative charm.

Following the afternoon break, Byron Chatfield's questions got tougher. While in his earlier lecturing mode, Underwager had said he had recognized many indications of sexual abuse in Pratt's personality profile, at which point, for emphasis, he had said, "a, b, c, d, e, f, g, h, i, j, k, l, m, n, and so on."

The prosecutor now asked him to enumerate and explain these references. At first, the witness could come up with only three: inability to have intimate relationships, anger and rage, and memory problems.

"Lots of people have those," the prosecutor suggested.

Well, there was also sexual compulsiveness, homosexuality, and anxiety about his manhood. Chatfield reminded the witness that he had characterized Jesse Pratt in his report as having "good social intelligence, an ability to focus his intention and plan ahead."

The prosecutor asked if chronic *lying* was not, in fact, an indication of a sociopathic disorder—lying to cover unsavory conduct, lacking remorse, continuing to commit antisocial acts, criminal or whatever. Didn't these constitute part of the profile of what Underwager's profession called a "sadistic personality disorder"?

Chatfield cited the rest of what his investigation had revealed about Pratt's profile: "Physical cruelty to achieve dominance over others, humiliating or demeaning others, pleasure in psychological or physical abuse of others, fascination with weapons, violence, torture, cruel and demeaning behavior beginning in childhood."

Underwager would have none of it. Jesse Pratt could not possibly derive pleasure from hurting others because he was *masochistic*, not sadistic. He enjoyed being hurt *himself.* The psychologist's tone was getting pompous again.

What about Diane's description of Pratt's obvious pleasure in his hurting her when he was having intercourse with her?

"I don't know whether he was hurting her or not," Underwager protested. Besides, he said, lots of men get inadvertently carried away during sex.

What about Pratt's fascination with bondage, and Sunshine's refusing to submit to it himself, or to participate in a threesome during which Pratt wanted him to help tie up a female prostitute?

Well, the witness didn't think the transvestite was a very reliable witness.

Getting personal, Chatfield now asked the doctor about other trials in which he had testified on behalf of people accused of child molestation. Had more than one judge disqualified him—and barred his testimony?

"No," he answered—quietly adding, "not disqualified."

Well, had they barred his testimony?

The answer was yes—six or seven times!

Was at least one of these because Underwager's theories were not generally accepted in the psychological community?

"Yes," the witness conceded, "but the judge was *wrong*." The way he said it sounded like a complacent shrug.

As it turned out, Dr. Underwager's testimony had most recently been barred in a trial in Klamath Falls. It was at that trial that Enver Bozgoz had met the psychologist while defending a man who was accused of molesting his own daughter.

THIRTY-EIGHT

For the day of the Lord is near in the valley of decision.

—Joel 4:14

It was 1:30 in the afternoon before Byron Chatfield was able to begin his summation for the state. He reminded the jury that this had been a very long trial. Two months had elapsed since February 12 when jury selection began. Now, he told the twelve men and women, having found the defendant guilty in the first phase of the trial, it was their responsibility to decide the punishment to be imposed.

"As a jury, you have an awesome responsibility in a case like this. You have an obligation to decide the case based on the evidence presented. It is not a pleasant duty."

He reminded them that they would have four decisions to make: First, whether the conduct of the defendant was committed deliberately; second, was the conduct appropriate to the "provocation," if any; third, would the defendant constitute a threat to society in the future; and fourth, should the defendant receive a death sentence, a life sentence without possibility of parole, or a life sentence with the possibility of parole?

As to the critical fourth question, he told the jury, "We don't have a burden of proof if the answer to the first three is 'yes'—unless you find evidence that dictates a verdict of less than death. Evidence must be uncovered that justifies something other than death."

Chatfield went on to suggest that they would not find any in either the character or the background of the defendant, or in the details of how he committed the crime of which he had been convicted.

"He tortured her, he tied her up, he put a mask on her, he repeatedly stabbed her, and he ran over her." His voice dropped to a whisper as he said it.

The prosecutor reviewed the testimony of the witnesses the court had heard since the trial itself began on March 13. A theme running through his entire summation was "the defendant's unpredictable internal alarm system." No one else could hear it, he said, "but when it rang, he flew into a rage and attacked those around him." The prosecutor reviewed the testimony of Pratt's ex-wives and girlfriends, some of these women still bearing the physical scars that were the result of his abuse as they appeared on the witness stand. One, he reminded them, had been beaten when she was six months pregnant.

The most damning excerpts came from the defense's own expert witness, psychologist Faulder Colby. He recalled some of them for the jury:

"'In situations where conflicts might ensue, he may easily lose control and behave quite irrationally.' I read that statement to Dr. Colby from his report. And I asked him, when you say 'behave quite irrationally,' are we talking about violence and assaultive conduct of the defendant in his behavior? And his answer was yes.

"Is there anyone more dangerous than that? Someone who has no remorse for what he does? He explodes! Even *he* doesn't know when that internal alarm system is going to go off. He's a walking time bomb. If he isn't getting what he wants, if he isn't satisfied, he reacts; and he reacts violently—as his victims have told you."

Exemplifying Pratt's irresponsibility, Chatfield reminded the jury of the defendant's story that he had dropped off Carrie Love on Highway 97 after a dispute over money (having abandoned his earlier alibi about dropping her off at My Place Tavern). He assumed that she made a telephone call and then someone else must have picked her up and murdered her, for which he assumed no responsibility and obviously felt no remorse. "Except, of course, that wasn't what happened. He killed her himself—and even for *that* he felt no remorse.

"We're talking about whether the defendant constitutes a danger to any part of society," the counsel said. In this regard, he told them, they could examine his FBI rap sheet in the jury room. Chatfield ran down the list of felonies of which Pratt had been convicted in his adult criminal career, adding that the questionable practice of expunging juvenile records omitted the crimes he had committed as a minor.

The prosecutor returned to Dr. Colby's report and the testimony of the defense's expert witness.

"'Mr. Pratt will likely do **all r**ight in highly structured and undemanding situations which conform to his previously conceived notions about the natural order of things; however, he is apt to lose control in conflicted situations.' And when I asked him, 'More likely than not?' He responded, 'More likely than not.' His report went on:

"'The implications of these findings are significant. It is unlikely that he is a safe person if left to his own devices. He can be predicted to be violent and assaultive in the wrong situations. Mr. Pratt's history strongly argues in favor of being kept under tight and rigidly supervised control for the remainder of his life.'"

The prosecutor compared the work of Dr. Colby with that of Dr. Underwager. He was less than complimentary about the latter psychologist. But even Underwager had found it difficult to claim that Jesse Pratt was not dangerous, the counsel pointed out:

"'He has a lack of good judgment when frustrated. Therefore, he may have an impulsive and explosive reaction when under stress.'" The prosecutor reminded the jury that he had the witness acknowledge that his statement meant "violent and assaultive behavior."

That the deputy attorney general's summation was more than the performance of a skilled prolocutor became obvious during a subsequent interview. Chatfield was convinced of the need to put an end to the possibility of further violence from this egocentric predator—even though the prosecutor's personal feelings about the right of the state to impose the death penalty seemed not to be significantly different from those expressed during the trial by the Reverend Robert Ray.

Chatfield got genuinely angry and very loud

when he spoke of Jesse Pratt's consistent history of criminal behavior—and when he ridiculed what had seemed to be the slipshod professional performance of Dr. Underwager. But when he got down to the vital decision the jury was about to make, his voice once again grew soft and intimate as he spoke to each juror, one to one.

"The defendant has hurt people—for his own pleasure. He killed Carrie Love for his own satisfaction. He's a predator to women, weaker people, younger people. Whether we're talking about people on the street, whether we are talking about other inmates, whether we are talking about corrections officers, men or women—they all have a right to be defended against his behavior, his threats, his assaultive conduct.

"The defendant has worked his way up to this point with no feelings, no remorse, no warning, and he reacts to that victim who is closest. His internal alarm system continues to ring. Only we don't hear it."

Chatfield's voice became barely audible. For the somber jurors and the rapt audience in the theater that was the court, he might have been speaking on a darkened stage, illuminated by a single, muted blue spotlight.

"Who's next? That's going to be a decision that you are going to make. Thank you for your attention." The blue spot irised out.

No stranger to the courtroom as theater, Enver Bozgoz attempted to inject comic relief. He told a joke.

"Members of the jury, last week during the lunch-time, I think it was Friday, I was asked a question. The question was, what is a difference between a dead skunk that crosses a highway or a lawyer that jaywalks the Main Street to get a cup of coffee?

"I didn't know the answer. So they told me what the answer was: There's one hundred skid marks on a highway before the vehicle hits a skunk. But there's no skid marks on a highway for motorists to hit a lawyer."

The joke bombed. There wasn't a smile in the courtroom.

"Now, listening here, it makes sense. Why? We have a situation right now. Mr. Chatfield says, 'Kill Jesse Pratt!' And I could see that I have to plug my ears because at times the lawyer screams so hard that it hurts my ears. Maybe I'm too old, and that's the reason."

The position that defense cocounsel Bozgoz would try to advance was that the prosecution wanted to kill a handicapped man because of his handicap. For the rest of the day, he would argue that the unfortunate defendant was being discriminated against because he suffered brain damage from a bicycle accident as a child, was the victim of repeated sexual abuse, and was handicapped because his mother drank during her pregnancy with him.

Bozgoz began by reminding the jury of Michelle Quinn's dedication to the dysfunctional children in her foster home. Then he wandered off into what seemed to be a tirade against racism.

"Never mind sex abuse. Twenty years ago, we didn't have a name for alcohol fetal syndrome. We couldn't treat these kids. What Mr. Chatfield suggests—what Hitler did during the World War II. He would eliminate all the Jews because he didn't like a Jew. But Mr. Chatfield doesn't have the guts to say, 'Let's kill 'em all. Sexually abused kids, alcohol fetal syndrome kids. Let's kill 'em all.' He does not want to say that. But that's what he's asking you to do. He's asking you to condemn a man that society didn't know what was the problem."

The assistant defense counsel turned away and walked back to the defense table. He returned with a beer bottle, brandishing it in front of the jury.

"This is a bottle of beer. What does a bottle of beer have? 'Government Warning: Surgeon General warns woman should not drink alcoholic beverage during pregnancy.' That label came out probably within the last two years.

"If anybody was warned before 1960 and had some sexual abuse, according to Mr. Chatfield, he doesn't deserve to live."

The speaker returned to World War II and Nazi Germany. Hitler, he said, killed individuals—not because they were Jews, but because "they were of Jewish *race*. But, on the other hand, let's look at the United States of America! After Pearl Harbor, what did we do with Japanese who were born here, who were citizens of the United States? We interned them. Why? They were of Japanese race.

"Mr. Chatfield started—said, 'You have to decide the punishment. You twelve have to do it.' Twelve jurors have to decide. Jesse Pratt lives or he dies. If he dies, he has to die for something he never asked. He has to die because he was born. He has to die because his mother never took care of him. She lied and cheated on his father while his father was in World War Two fighting Germans. Four months after he went to war, she sent him Dear John letter. She didn't give a damn if he died during war."

For the next thirty-five minutes, Bozgoz tried Jesse Pratt's mother in absentia. He condemned her for failing to give her son "when he was nineteen or twenty, the name, address, and telephone number of his father"—rejecting her insistence that she didn't know her husband was still alive after she was notified of his death in combat (having signed over his $10,000 in GI insurance money to her father-in-law, who, Elizabeth decided, was more needy than she was).

Referring to the four questions the prosecution had told the jury they would have to decide, Bozgoz paraphrased what he said would be the judge's instructions:

"In answer of these four questions, you are considered any mitigating circumstances received in evidence, including but not limited to defendant's age, and the extent and severity of the defendant's prior criminal conduct, and the extent of mental emotional pressure on the week the defendant was acting on the time the murder was committed."

Bozgoz described his jail interview with Jesse Pratt, during which the defendant revealed that he had suffered sexual abuse as a child.

"During his entire life, Jesse Pratt was embarrassed by that. So he never said anything about it to anyone." On the subject of Pratt's prior criminal conduct, the defense cocounsel retried the kidnapping and rape of Thelma Adams, taking the position that the lovesick Jesse was just trying to straighten

ings out between Thelma and himself. Other
ings his client had done really weren't that bad:

"Mr. Chatfield says he's a dangerous man because
hen his wife gave the keys to her apartment, he
ok a television set. He's a dangerous man and li-
ble to commit a crime of violence because he
rge a check or stole a television. He's a dangerous
an, deserves to be killed because he failed to pay
trailer bill. Or, he's a dangerous man because he
sed Diane's loan for a truck and brought another
oman back. He's a dangerous man because he
lked his half sister into puttin' up part of the
oney for the truck. Let's kill 'em.

"He was gonna throw a hot grease on one-a his
ives, but he didn't. He's chasing her, shootin'
is mouth. Let's kill 'em. He's a dangerous man
ecause he brags continuously. He's a dangerous
an because he has sexual fantasies—an interest
prostitution. An' he says he's closest to Devil.
e's a dangerous man because he told Sandra
chmidt [one of Pratt's girlfriends] 'pull the cur-
in' in a house.

"He gave his mother, Elizabeth Helle, six hundred
ollars. He spend money like there was no end to it.
hat's why we should kill 'em because he's a dan-
erous man. He gave six hundred dollars to his
other when her husband died. He came home,
oncerned about his mother. Let's kill 'em because
e was concerned about his mother. He asked his
other, 'You need any money, your husband died?'
e gave her six hundred dollars. Let's kill 'em."

Perhaps remembering an earlier omission, the
ounsel felt his client should get credit for failing to

pursue and intimidate one of the wives who divorced him. Instead, he gave her new husband a job.

Bozgoz returned to the four questions to be answered, all of which, he emphasized, must be unanimously answered yes by the jurors in order to secure the death penalty for the defendant.

"If any one of you believes there are mitigating circumstances [that] exist and they did not overcome that beyond a reasonable doubt, and you feel that Jesse Pratt was a victim of the circumstances, a victim of ignorance of the people back in '40s, he was a victim of his own mother, then you have to stand up and tell Mr. Chatfield that you have the courage to say no. If you answer one or more of the questions 'no,' the law requires the penalty shall be life imprisonment without possibility of parole."

But Pratt's cocounsel was still holding out the hope of eventual parole. He spoke of the defendant's life sentence resulting in a minimum of thirty years (which, however, would require a favorable vote by ten of the twelve jurors).

Bozgoz envisioned the rosy picture of Jesse Pratt spending those thirty years undergoing the psychotherapy recommended by Dr. Underwager, seeing the beckoning "light at the end of the thirty-year tunnel," looking forward to being released at the age of seventy-six, *cured* of the mental handicap he had suffered all his life because of neglect and cruelty.

Those terrible sexual indignities "made him think this would make him a homosexual." It was a terrible stigma to have other males think one was gay. He read from a professional psychiatric paper that attributed "post-traumatic stress disorder" and "chronic unhappiness" to such experiences. He told the jury that his client had the mentality of a ten-year-old boy in the body of a forty-six-year-old man. Once again, he appealed for just one juror to say "no."

Bozgoz lamented the fact that there had been no nurturing foster homes like the one Michelle Quinn operated when Jesse Pratt was younger, "because she wasn't born yet." As he neared the end of his summation, the counsel's rhetoric once again became shrill.

"Jesse's rotten. Kill 'em! Get rid of him! Not a human being. Never will amount because we don't want [to] give him any psychotherapy while he is in penitentiary. We don't want to do that. It's easier to kill than help this human being to be a human being." He muttered something inaudible about Hitler and genocide.

"I don't want to talk anymore," the cocounsel announced. He thanked the jury for paying attention for two months. He was confident, he said, that one of them would say no.

He paused. Before retiring, Enver Bozgoz decided he had one more thing to say. He repeated his vision of Jesse Pratt emerging "on the other end of the tunnel" three decades hence, a happy, well-adjusted, seventy-six-year-old, cured of the tragic handicaps that had hobbled his life—and grateful to the jurors who had spared his life.

"Out there," he promised, "you know what you see? Kenworth truck that once won't break down. Thank you."

Some of the jurors exchanged glances. One shrugged.

* * *

By the following morning, with the permission of the court and the prosecution, defense counsel Kenneth Hadley had decided to add his own summation. When he spoke, he sounded upset. If Bozgoz had hurt the defendant's case, Hadley seemed determined to put that right.

Before turning the proceedings back to the prosecution, he said, he wanted to add a few remarks. He wished to address the principal issues the jury would confront when it repaired for its deliberations. His manner was subdued. His tone was sincere.

The counsel spoke of Dr. Colby. He reminded the jury what the psychologist had said about the defendant: "The simplest explanation is he didn't come in with much, and he lost a lot somehow. We don't know exactly why."

Hadley admitted that the defense could not prove factually that Jesse Pratt had been sexually abused, but when two respected professionals come to the same conclusion, each citing the three common personality traits of such males, "which three things fit Jesse Pratt like a glove," one had to give their opinions some credence, he believed.

There were two other points he wanted to address, he said. The state had emphasized the defendant's abuse of his wives and girlfriends. Far from minimizing these, Hadley reminded the jury of his own opening remarks: "The way he treated them is sad, and there is no justification for that—except for the explanation of the doctors. This relationship dysfunction. Certainly it's there and we can't dispute that."

But, as to what they were deciding today, "the truth is when you made the guilty decision two or three weeks ago, the decision was made that Mr. Pratt is not going to be back into those types of relationships anymore. Sometimes I think we're forgetting what we're here for. Mr. Pratt is going to die in prison almost certainly, either by lethal injection or by natural death. If he gets the 'true life'—life without possibility of parole—he comes out only when he's dead. He's not going to be out in relationships with women again."

Hadley suggested that even a thirty-year minimum was a very long time, "and at that point, it is just *eligibility* for parole." If the jury was worried about it, "you have the power to say that he's not coming out of that prison alive, purely and simply.

"So we feel that all those conversations and all the argument about his ex-wives and girlfriends—while it's true, and something we wish wasn't true—it really isn't relevant to the question of whether he's going to be dangerous, committing criminal acts of violence in the society that he's going to be in—which is a penitentiary situation."

In such an environment, it was unlikely that a convict would be *permitted* to be dangerous. In such a society, "as tough as prison-type folk are," he believed it was unlikely that he would be a danger to *those* people. The jury had met some of them here in this courtroom, he reminded them.

"Prisons are constructed to handle people who are a heck of a lot more dangerous than Mr. Pratt. It seems to me if we were standing here and he'd never been in prison, and I could ask you, 'Would you like to see him go to prison for a year and see how he would do before you decide to silence him with a lethal injection?' that you'd be interested in that kind of test. In this case, you *have* the test."

In the jury room, he told them, they could review the records of the four years Pratt had spent in custody. He had never struck a guard, either female or male, and was close to being a model inmate. With the man's ten-year-old mentality, when guards told him he couldn't make other inmates take off their shoes before walking across the floor he had waxed, he went to his cell and pouted for two days and refused to talk to anybody. This was less than a dangerous reaction, he felt. The defense counsel reminded the jury that several witnesses had said, "He'll make it in prison."

Hadley reviewed the traumatic experiences in Pratt's home life that were undisputed: the drunken homecomings of Cecil Stacey (one of Pratt's stepfathers) during which the boy tried to intervene to prevent the man from abusing his mother; the suicide of one stepfather and the death of yet another in a car accident; the fact that his sisters disappeared from the family—all this impacting on a child with brain damage and a marginal IQ.

Hadley then apologized for something he had said in his opening statement.

"I said that Jesse Pratt 'was not a serial killer.' I got to thinking later, did I really say 'just committed one murder,' because I sure didn't mean to say that. It's a tragedy what happened here." What he was trying to do, the counsel said, was to differentiate between a compulsive reactor like Jesse Pratt and a serial killer who stalks people with the intention of murdering them.

He hoped that even though the jurors had found Pratt guilty of aggravated murder, "I've got to believe, and I hope you agree, that he didn't leave Seattle with the intention of killing Carrie Love." Hadley offered no excuses for what Pratt did, he said, but "it wasn't planned like a Bundy or someone, just preying on people." It had happened for the reasons the doctors had described—personality factors that were beyond his control.

"We talked a lot yesterday—said a lot. We feel a lot on our shoulders, Mr. Bozgoz and me, the officers, others. We all worked pretty hard and we want to give you everything we can."

It sounded like an apology for his cocounsel's performance.

"We want to say everything that needs to be said—and we don't want to go on to the point of saying too much. So I'm going to make it [as] short as I promised you I would.

"You're going to have to make a decision you probably hoped you'd never have to make. And I think I mentioned to some of you during jury selection what the foreman of a jury in Vancouver, Washington, said after the trial was all over. He said he was personally against the death penalty because of what it put the jury through. I recognize you have a pretty tough job. We hope we've done ours the best we can.

"The burden of Jesse Pratt's life will pass from our shoulders to yours at this point. We hope that you, or at least one of you, will agree that enough killings have taken place. To kill another person is not going to bring Carrie Love back. It doesn't make our society a better place. And we ask you to say no to that. The bottom line is that Mr. Pratt is not dangerous in the prison situation where he is going. And we ask you to look at the fourth question of mitigation and realize that he didn't have total control. His brakes simply don't work unless he's in a controlled situation, which is where he is going. Answer no to that question. Thank you."

Spectators in the courtroom felt Jesse Pratt had gotten a fair shake after all—perhaps more than was his due. Interestingly, Jesse Pratt had told Dr. Colby that he liked Bozgoz, but he didn't care for Hadley.

Byron Chatfield rose to speak to the jury for the last time.

"There are several things that I need to respond to, because in a few minutes you are going to have an awesome responsibility."

It was the prosecution's position, he said, that Jesse Pratt's very existence constituted a threat to society. As to his conduct in prison, he reminded the jury that there had been a plot by other inmates to kill him while he was in Walla Walla.

The prosecutor reminded the jurors that they could not speculate. Their decision must be based on the evidence presented. Pratt's associates Leroy Lantz and David Whaley "were still out there." Both had demonstrated their willingness to do a job for Pratt and collect on the debt later.

As to the traumatic events in Pratt's childhood: "How many people come before a court like this one who have had tragic lives? But they don't kill people—kidnap people."

The defense had taken the position that the defendant was not a plotter but "simply overreacts and

loses control and then commits acts he later regrets."
But the jury had heard evidence of deliberate, carefully planned acts carried out over a long period of time—including the kidnapping of Thelma Adams. The killing of Carrie Love was such an act, he declared.

"That was not merely lashing out and reacting. Carrie Love was nude. Her hands were taped. That mask was put on her face—layered. Remember the paper towels and tape? Stab wounds? And where are those stab wounds? Right down her spine; in front, they were around the heart."

Noisily clearing his throat, Enver Bozgoz interrupted.

"Your Honor, I'm going to object. Improper redirect."

After hearing his own summation of the day before, some thought it a measure of the defense cocounsel's temerity.

"Overruled," Judge Piper announced dryly. "ORC 58 B-4."

"Carrie Love wasn't as fortunate as Thelma Adams," Chatfield continued. "She couldn't slip a note to somebody in a rest room."

The defendant *wasn't* sexually involved with Carrie Love, the prosecutor reminded them. "He acted out a fantasy about Carrie Love." Evidence had been presented, he reminded the jury, that Pratt had told others about *planning* such a move on her.

Reading Pratt's rap sheet, he pointed out the escalation of violence in his crimes since 1968. It was, he said, an escalation that culminated in the death of Carrie Love. "Can anybody be more dangerous than that?"

Chatfield reminded the jury that Dr. Underwager had admitted that Pratt's personality fit the profile of a sadist, who enjoys hurting others. Yet, "Underwager wants to *cure* him and turn him loose!"

But, the counsel cautioned, revenge has no place in the courtroom. Their decision must be based on the law. And it had to be based on the evidence presented. Forgiveness had been mentioned, he said. And he agreed we must forgive the defendant.

"But along with forgiveness comes accountability, and the consequences for acts that cannot be taken back. The time for this accountability is now. It's going to be your responsibility to do that. It's distasteful, but it's a responsibility you have.

"It's unfortunate that it's come down to this. It's unfortunate because we're talking about life and death. And in this case, it's death.

"It's a tragedy. We all have responsibility. And now it's yours."

Once again, the blue spot irised out.

THIRTY-NINE

I would say that during the rest of my career, I probably will not see Mr. Pratt executed. If he is ever executed, I would be really surprised. I believe he will probably die in prison.
— Criminal Investigator Bill Carroll

The Wednesday, April 17, 1991, edition of the *Klamath Falls Herald and News* carried the story on its front page:

PRATT RECEIVES DEATH SENTENCE
FOR 1986 MURDER OF CARRIE LOVE

Death by lethal injection was the sentence pronounced this morning upon Jesse Clarence Pratt, convicted for the second time in the 1986 killing of then 20-year-old Carrie Lynette Love.

An air of anticipation filled the courtroom of Circuit Court Judge Donald A. W. Piper as courthouse staff, police officers, spectators and attorneys awaited the jury's verdict.

In its verdict, read aloud by Piper, the jury unanimously answered yes to each of the four questions submitted to determine Pratt's sentence, concluding with "Should the defendant, Jesse Clarence Pratt, receive a death sentence?"

There was no change in Pratt's demeanor or expression as he heard the death penalty pronounced.

"The jury substantiated what we have known all along, and made its determination based on the evidence," said Mark Runnels, the Klamath County deputy district attorney who prosecuted the case with Byron Chatfield of the State Attorney General's office. "It was a long trial with a lot of evidence, testimony, and emotion," he said, "and I'm very glad it's over."

Before sentence was formally pronounced, the victim's mother, Connie Love, read in a tearful and quavering voice a statement to the court describing her pain and guilt for "not being there the one time I was needed most" by her daughter.

Byron Chatfield had asked the judge's permission for Connie Love to address the court. Although the jury had been dismissed by the time Carrie's mother spoke, the courtroom remained jammed with spectators. Jesse Pratt had not yet been sentenced. Connie Love stood before the bar near the prosecution's table.

"We are here today because Carrie is not," she began. "Carrie cannot cry out for justice." When the defendant looked up briefly and their eyes met, Connie stared him down. There was a long silence. Although Jesse Pratt had shown no emotion during the trial, he now looked away uncomfortably.

Connie returned her attention to Judge Piper. She

spoke for about five minutes. "If Carrie were here, I believe she would ask, 'Why, Jesse? Why? I trusted you.'" Connie returned to her seat in the gallery. She would later write a poem about the experience.

Judge Piper spoke.

"Jesse Clarence Pratt, is there any reason why the court should not pass sentence at this time?"

"No." It was a sullen answer. It was the first word the defendant had uttered in court during the entire trial.

"Is there any statement you'd care to make in your own behalf?"

"No." Although he kept a straight face, Pratt's voice was noticeably tighter this time and a full tone higher—almost breaking.

Judge Piper peered at the defendant over the top of his black horn-rims.

"Jesse Clarence Pratt, it is the judgment of the court that you're convicted of two counts of aggravated murder. By reason of the law, the evidence, and the verdict of the jury in this case, it's the judgment of the court that you be, and hereby are, sentenced to death by lethal injection. In furtherance of that, it's the order of this court that the sheriff of Klamath County shall deliver you to the superintendent of the Oregon State Penitentiary at Salem, Oregon, within twenty days of this date, pending determination of the automatic and direct review by the supreme court.

"The defendant is remanded to the custody of the officers."

Court was abruptly adjourned.

EPILOGUE

"It is the sincere hope of this office and the citizens of Klamath County that we have heard the last of Jesse Pratt." District Attorney Ed Caleb's statement appeared in the April 18 issue of the *Klamath Falls Herald and News.*

It would not be the end of the legal process, however. On May 3, Judge Piper's court was reconvened to hear the defense's motion for a new trial. The motion was offered by Enver Bozgoz.

"This is a routine matter that defense attorneys file in major cases," Caleb explained to the press. "We would expect that the judge will deny the motion and they'll go on with the appeal."

Bozgoz's motion was based on two allegations: (1) the note the jury had sent out during their deliberations at the end of the guilt phase (asking why this was the *second* trial) constituted misconduct by the jury and was prejudicial; (2) Judge Piper's speaking of the "preponderance of the evidence" in his instructions, instead of insisting upon proof beyond any conceivable "reasonable doubt," was judicial error.

But, as Ed Caleb had predicted, after studying the

precedent cited by both sides, Judge Piper issued a ruling on May 8, 1991, denying the defense's motion.

Preparing the "automatic" appeal to the Oregon Supreme Court would take much longer. The new document was put together in Salem with the aid of material provided by Pratt's trial lawyers.

Hadley and Bozgoz had prepared a list of no less than twenty "errors" they had identified during the guilt and penalty phases of the second trial.

Two of these had to do with comments made by alternate jurors. One was a reaction, heard only by a bailiff, to seeing photos of Carrie Love's autopsy: "Nobody deserves that kind of treatment." The other was an astute if improper question by an alternate: "What happened to Carrie Love's suitcase?"

Since the first comment was heard by none of the jurors, and since the second, a matter unresolved by testimony, "did not introduce any extraneous information," Judge Piper had previously denied motions for a mistrial on each when they were brought up during the trial.

There were rehashes of other previous complaints. But the primary issue raised in the defense's appeal had to do with Jesse Pratt's initial indictment after he was first arrested five years earlier. The plea began:

"Article VII, Section 5(2) of the Oregon Constitution mandates that seven grand jurors hear and consider all of the evidence presented before a valid indictment can be found."

In 1992, in a "postconviction relief case," a defendant by the name of Goodwin had had his indictment dismissed by a lower court of appeals when it was found that a grand jury of less than seven members had indicted him. But the Oregon

Supreme Court had never reviewed the matter. So the rape-murder of Carrie Love by Jessie Pratt became a test case, since, on one of the many days the seven-member Pratt grand jury had met, only six members had been present on July 1, 1986.

With the backlog facing Oregon's high court and the attention this test case would require, it could be years before a ruling on the matter would be handed down. After that, if the state's supreme court upheld Pratt's conviction, his case could ultimately be appealed to the United States Supreme Court—all at taxpayer expense, since Jesse Pratt was classified as an indigent defendant. To date, the cost of Jesse Pratt's two trials had been estimated at $500,000.

On June 17, 1993, on the seventh anniversary of the day when Carrie Love was murdered on June 17, 1986, the Oregon Supreme Court announced its ruling on the appeal of Jesse Pratt's conviction for aggravated murder: "The judgment and conviction and sentence of death are confirmed. We think such a challenge now comes much too late."

Five months later, on November 30, 1993, the United States Supreme Court refused to review the case, thus authorizing the prosecution to seek a death warrant. But the defense still had the option to file a "motion for postconviction relief," which it did.

While the process inched along, Jesse Clarence Pratt has continued to be a guest of the state. Within days of his sentencing by Judge Piper, Jesse Clarence Pratt, ID# 7146442, once again occupied one of the nine cells on death row at the Oregon State Penitentiary in Salem.

Inside their cells, inmates cannot see one another. The steel cubicles are on one side of a long, bare corridor with ports on the opposite wall through which the cells can be watched from a parallel corridor without entering death row. At each end of the stark, brightly lit inner corridor, a small, octagonal steel table is bolted to the polished floor. Each table is surrounded by four metal stools welded to a common base plate. This facility became Jesse Pratt's home while the automatic appeals of his death sentence slowly percolated through the system.

As of this book's completion, it is where he still is. Nine years after the Oregon Supreme Court's decision, eleven years after Pratt's sentencing, and sixteen years after the murder of Carrie Love, Jesse Clarence Pratt is alive and well, living in the Intensive Management ("Supermax") Unit of the Oregon State Prison in Salem.

Eventually, according to Oregon Statute 137.463 (if the prisoner has not died of natural causes in the meantime), a "warrant shall appoint a day on which the judgment is to be executed, and shall authorize and command the superintendent to execute the judgment of the court."

Then, as prescribed in related Statute 137.473, "the punishment of death shall be inflicted by the intravenous administration of a lethal quantity of ultra-short-acting barbiturate in combination with a chemical paralytic agent until the defendant is dead."

The statute further provides that, at the request of the defendant, "the superintendent of the prison shall allow no more than two clergymen" and "no more than five friends or relatives" to be present. Such a delegation would seem unlikely in Jesse Pratt's case.

When the directives of these statutes have been carried out, the bizarre life of Jesse Clarence Pratt, unmourned, will have irised out.

But Byron Chatfield thinks it is unlikely that Pratt will ever be executed. His prosecutor believes that Jesse Pratt will probably live out the rest of his life in prison—defying the decision of the jury and the judgment of the court.

Chatfield's assistant prosecutor, Klamath County deputy district attorney Mark Runnels, has a different perspective on the case—and on the nation's justice system:

"If Jesse Pratt had served out his sentence at Walla Walla, Carrie Love would be alive today."

ACKNOWLEDGEMENTS

I first heard about this case when Pete McDonald and I had lunch a few days after he returned from Klamath Falls. His testimony had been crucial in nailing down Jesse Pratt's conviction. Author of the standard reference *Tire Imprint Evidence*, Pete's expertise as a forensic scientist is also documented in court records all over the world. He has been my collaborator on this work for nine years. Although Pete provided the initial motivation for the book and subsequently recorded about a dozen tape cassettes for me, I am also indebted to every one of the principals in this story for the details that appear in this documentary.

The courageous Connie Love, who lent me photographs of her daughter—and even some of Jesse Pratt—also showed me the awards she has received for organizing Spokane's Violent Crime Victims Support Group, which has grown to more than three hundred members. Connie still keeps in touch with Bruce and Dorothy McDonald, at whose "Town House" in the woods on Crescent Creek the couple told me about driving down Oregon 97 that fateful morning in June 1986, when they made the discovery that precipitated seven years of police investigation and prosecutorial efforts to bring a rapist-murderer to justice.

I could not have written this book without the personal narrative provided by Oregon State Police detective Ken Cooper, case agent and lead investigator, who recorded hours of material for me at his home. One of the last times I spoke to him after the second trial, Ken had been finding more time to devote to his moose antler sculptures than he wished. He was waiting for an assignment.

"This is the hardest part of my job," he said. "When a guy has a job like mine, his life takes on meaning when he gets a call at three o'clock in the morning. He knows it's bad and he knows they need him. The adrenaline starts pumping, and by the time he's dressed and out of the house, he's ready to go. He doesn't even need a cup of coffee."

Not long after that, it was difficult to contact Cooper except on weekends. He was out of town almost continuously, once again putting together the all-white pieces of yet another puzzle—hoping he would soon get to turn it over and see the picture.

In two lengthy conference calls, criminalist Mike Howard of the Oregon State Crime Laboratory gave Pete McDonald and me a course in hair, fiber, and paper identification, in addition to providing new forensic details in this case—years later—all from memory. Meanwhile, the multifaceted McDonald has created a series of oil paintings and sculptures based on tire forensic cases in which he has participated, including this one. His art show has toured universities, police academies, and museums, and it now hangs in a vaulted lobby of the

University of Akron—which, coincidentally, offers a curriculum in criminal justice.

At the Klamath County Courthouse, I appreciated the help of Melina Johnson and Charlene Divine of District Attorney Ed Caleb's office. And it was through the courtesy and generosity of Circuit Judge Roxanne Osborne (lead counsel for the prosecution in Pratt's first trial) and her judicial assistant, Carol O'Brion (court reporter in the first trial), that I not only had access to court transcripts of the first trial, in which Osborne had successfully achieved a conviction, but I was permitted to listen to audio recordings of the entire second trial.

Not long afterward, on September 20, 1993, the Klamath County Courthouse, scene of both trials, was heavily damaged by an earthquake measuring 5.0 on the Richter scale, making the building unsafe to enter. While county officials pondered over whether the Greek Revival structure could be saved, a second earthquake struck three months later, forcing the decision that the building would now have to be demolished—as would many others in the town. These events were covered, of course, by the *Klamath Falls Herald and News*—to which I am indebted for the photo of Jesse Pratt and his two counsels at the end of the second trial, as well as for permission to publish the newspaper's copyrighted stories.

I am especially grateful for the time Oregon deputy attorney general Byron Chatfield and his criminal investigator Bill Carroll devoted to my education while I was in Salem, and on the telephone thereafter. It was Bill Carroll who put me in touch with Diane, Pratt's onetime girlfriend, who was, by then, building a new life for herself, and who was kind enough to meet with me in her Seattle home. She regards both Ken Cooper and Bill Carroll as "big brothers."

They are all heroes in this story.

And, finally, I must express my gratitude to Hudson, Ohio, librarian Ron Antonucci, who edits *The Ohio Writer*, to Paul Bauer, self-confessed true crime junkie and proprietor of Archer's Book Shop in Kent (which specializes in true crime and baseball), and to Jillanne Kimble of EditLane.com, all of whom read drafts of the manuscript—contributing excellent editorial suggestions and leaving their fingerprints all over the resulting book.